BLOOD
AND
VOICE

BLOOD
AND
VOICE

NAVAJO WOMEN
CEREMONIAL PRACTITIONERS

Maureen Trudelle Schwarz

LINGUISTIC AND CULTURAL CONSULTANT, Mae Ann Bekis
FIELDWORK ASSISTANT, Amelda Sandoval Shay

THE UNIVERSITY OF ARIZONA PRESS
TUCSON

The University of Arizona Press
© 2003 The Arizona Board of Regents
First printing
All rights reserved
♾ This book is printed on acid-free, archival-quality paper.
Manufactured in the United States of America
08 07 06 05 04 03   6 5 4 3 2 1

Library of Congress Cataloging-in-Publication Data

Schwarz, Maureen Trudelle, 1952–
Blood and voice : Navajo women ceremonial practitioners / Maureen
Trudelle Schwarz ; linguistic and cultural consultant, Mae Ann Bekis ;
fieldwork assistant, Amelda Sandoval Shay.
   p. cm.
Includes bibliographical references and index.
ISBN 0-8165-2300-2 (alk. paper) — ISBN 0-8165-2301-0 (pbk. : alk. paper)
1. Navajo Indians—Medicine. 2. Navajo women—Biography. 3. Indian
women healers—Southwest, New—Biography. I. Title.
E99.N3 S357 2003
610′.89′972—dc21
2002152761

British Library Cataloguing-in-Publication Data
A catalogue record for this book is available from the British Library.

Publication of this book is made possible in part by the proceeds of a permanent
endowment created with the assistance of a Challenge Grant from the National
Endowment for the Humanities, a federal agency.

This book is dedicated to

past, present, and future Asdzą́ą́ Hataałii

who dedicate themselves to following the Holy People

in order to assist fellow Navajo in need.

There are Holy People everywhere. They are probably right here with us now. That is how we heal, they hear the songs and they heal the patient. They are always with us. When you are talking to me, they can hear what we are saying right now. They are probably wondering, "Why are these women asking all of these questions? Are they becoming medicine persons?" [Laughter]

—Mary Ben Jones Whitney, Tohatchi, New Mexico

CONTENTS

ACKNOWLEDGMENTS

The research upon which this book is based was made possible by the generous support of many individuals and institutions. First and foremost, I wish to thank the Navajo people with whom I consulted and collaborated: *ahéhee'* to each of you. Your kindness and patience are immeasurable. You have given the ultimate gift—knowledge. In addition to those whose voices are foregrounded in this work, I wish to thank the many Navajo men and women and their families who offered warmth, friendship, and hospitality during my visits to the Navajo reservation.

The clarity of Navajo exegeses essential to this book depends on careful translation of Navajo accounts. This was accomplished with the assistance of several people over the years. I wish to thank Percy Deal for accompanying me to the home of Eunice Manson and translating her narrative. I also want to thank Dr. Wesley Thomas of Indiana University for assistance with translations of several interviews. In addition, two of my Navajo colleagues must be singled out for special thanks regarding this project: Mae Ann Bekis and Amelda Sandoval Shay.

While one could argue that all ethnographic research is collaborative in one sense or another, something special occurred between Mae Ann Bekis and I, which can only be described as a spark that ignited into true intellectual collaboration. I met Mae Ann Bekis of Tó'tsoh, Arizona, in 1992. Over the years, I consulted her on a variety of topics. When I told her about my interest in researching Navajo Asdzą́ą́ Hataałii she took a profound interest in the project. At every step of the way, Mae Ann Bekis served as a sounding board, discussing ideas and findings. Throughout the years, she kept an ear open for information about women singers in communities across the vast Navajo reservation and told me about them as she learned of them. She assisted me in finding a Navajo woman willing to travel with me as translator and research assistant. Moreover, she spent part of the summer of 2001 at my home in Syracuse, New York, painstakingly verifying and clarifying translation of over twenty interviews conducted with women who are monolingual Navajo speakers. Her contribution has been of inestimable value.

Amelda Sandoval Shay accompanied me for days on end during the summers of 1998 and 2000 as we searched for women singers on often-sketchy information. Once a woman singer was found, Amelda Sandoval Shay did her level best to explain the purpose of my project, describe the nature and scope of questions to be asked, and assuage concerns. She patiently translated all of my questions, no matter how difficult or seemingly absurd, and the interviewee's answers. Her assistance was invaluable to this project.

I am grateful to the following organizations for much-needed financial support for my research on Navajo women singers: the Andrew W. Mellon Foundation (1998–99); Maxwell School of Citizenship and Public Affairs Dean's Office, Syracuse University (1999–2002); and the Appleby Mosher Research Fund (2001). Gratitude is also owed to the following for support of my previous research upon which this study is based: the Costume Society of America for a Stella Blum Research Grant (1990--91), the Whatcom County Museum for a Jacobs Research Fund Grant (1992), the Arizona Humanities Council for a Study Grant (1992), the National Science Foundation for a Summer Fieldwork Training Grant (1992), the University of Washington for funds from a Royalty Research Grant (1993), an award from the Institute for Ethnic Studies in the United States (1993), a W. W. Stout Fellowship (1994), and an award from the Graduate School Research Fund (1995).

Special thanks are owed as well to Christine Szuter and the caring staff at the University of Arizona Press, who gave this project their expert attention at every stage of production. Rose Byrne is also due thanks for her meticulous copyediting and indexing, which improved the accessibility of the text.

Last, but certainly not least, I wish to thank my family—Greg, Ragen, and Ryan Schwarz—whose generosity and humor has been boundless—without their love there would be no book. *Ahéhee' shiyázhí* to each of you.

BLOOD
AND
VOICE

CHAPTER I

THE STUDY OF
NAVAJO FEMALE
CEREMONIAL
PRACTITIONERS

MS I heard that there was a woman that did the Ant Way out towards Many Farms, but she's gone now. Did you know of her?

AED Yeah. I think.

ABD Yeah, she's gone.

AED Yeah, she's, she's gone.

MS What was her name?

AED I don't know, I, I just know her as a . . .

MS What did you know her as?

ABD All, I know, Asdzą́ą́ Hataałii.

MS Singing Woman?

AED Singing Woman.

ABD Mm-hmm. (Interview with Agnes Begay Dennison and Alfred E. Dennison)[1]

LD The world of the Navajo ceremonies was dominated by men.

MS Right.

LD It was completely dominated by men until, well my grandfather told me. He was the one that told me, he said, "My mother," he said, "she has the name of Hataałii, they called her Asdzą́ą́ Hataałii because, because she is a woman, but then she is a singer too, a chanter" . . . And she was the one that, she was the one that was the sister to the chief. His name was Greyeyes? Out of the Lukachukai area. That's what, he was the chief, he was the one that ah, he was the one that had the most knowledge in this ceremony and he was the one that taught most of the people who went throughout the reservation. They would come to his residence and he would teach them or else counsel them in a certain way to do a ceremony then. . . . This was back in the 1800s. . . . She was the one that, she was the one that, the herbs, she was the herbalist.

MS Oh, she was an herbalist?

LD She was an herbalist *and* she was a chanter. And she's the one that, she was the one that introduced a certain herb, a certain herb, and that, well she was the one that went and got the complete knowledge of a certain herb that would cure a lot of the real hard cases like cancer, the heart failure, and then also kidney failure, and a lot of female problems, you know, genital problems whatever, you know, and sexually transmitted diseases. (Interview with Deswood)[2]

Blood and voice are the key symbols designating the shift from child to adult in the Navajo world—marked by the onset of menstruation in females and the deepening of the voice in males.[3] These entities mark antithetical powers, which are nurtured, manipulated, and controlled during the life cycle of all Navajo persons within a larger complex of activities and restrictions. The powers manifest in blood and voice are not limited to Nihookáá Dine'é, or "Earth Surface People" (as the Navajo identify themselves), rather, these contrasting yet complementary powers are forms of the forces which control all reproduction and growth (come to life in blood) and that which can be used to restore order when needed (manifest in voice). Following puberty, young men and women are carefully trained in regard to personal responsibilities over the powers manifest in blood and voice. This guidance is vital because inappropriate acts on the part of ancestors to the Nihookáá Dine'é rendered certain types of blood dangerous to health and well-being, since these kinds of blood are considered to be concrete manifestations of libidinous desires and sexual activities gone awry. Thus, if these types of blood are inappropriately combined with voice, the force that makes each effective is neutralized, or at the very least, disrupted.

For males, change in the voice and development of underarm, pubic, and facial hair mark the onset of sexual maturity. Traditionally, this change triggered the Kinaaldá, "puberty ceremony" (Schwarz 1997:155–172, 229), and training in the control of voice and blood in the contexts of hunting and warfare (Hill 1936). Likewise, for females, the onset of first menstruation triggered performance of the Kinaaldá (Schwarz 1997:173–229) and afterwards teachings about sexual activity and reproductive capacity, as well as training in the proper control of menstrual blood (interviews with Charley; Dooley, 1992a; Kee, 1992a).

The power manifest in the flow of voice conveys tremendous force when used to tell the numerous stories making up Navajo oral tradition or when it appears in the form of song or prayer during ceremonies. Voice can be used to heal or protect, because it is associated with the powers of protection and restoration of order.[4] The various expressions of voice—speech, song, or prayer—are simultaneously embodiments of an individual's thoughts and mediums for calling the power of the Diyin Dine'é, "Holy People."

Various forms of temporal and physical boundaries were developed or are routinely created in the Navajo world to contain and control the powers in blood and voice. Control and containment are evident on the personal level by rules governing the activities of women while menstruating and men while hunting, on the social level by rules disallowing improper sexual relations, and on the cosmic level by strict rules governing the containment and control of songs and prayers, or oratories; stories of Navajo origin are seasonally restricted to the winter months and the voice of a singer engaged in healing must be contained within a controlled setting—a sanctified hooghan, "traditional Navajo earthen floor home."[5]

Navajo consider the fundamentals of human nature and the forces of the universe to be in delicate balance. Illness in the Navajo world represents imbalance amongst these elements brought on by breach of taboo, witchcraft, or unfortunate contact, such as the witnessing of a fatal automobile accident. Religious practitioners restore a patient's balance within her or his physical and social context by means of the power of the supernaturals called to the ceremony by the singer's voice in the form of songs and prayers in combination with ritually prescribed behaviors. Length of ceremonies varies from a few hours to nine nights. Financial cost correlates with the length of the ceremony because the patient's family and extended kin must hire a singer and feed numerous people, the singer and his or her assistants, as well as relatives and other guests in attendance.

All of this becomes truly interesting when we consider that, despite the fact that as Charlotte Frisbie pointed out, "[f]or almost a century there has been an implicit, if not explicit, assumption that women are not ceremonial practitioners" (1989:27), Navajo women can and do successfully fill this role. It is significant that women such as the woman from Many Farms, Arizona, mentioned by Agnes Begay Dennison, and Louella Deswood's great-grandmother were referred to as Asdzą́ą́ Hataałii, or "Singing Woman or Women," because while the term nahałáii, or "practitioner," is applied to singers, curers, prayer-makers, diagnosticians, and witches, "in short, to anyone who attempts to influence the course of events by ceremonial means" (Kluckhohn and Wyman 1940:15), the term hataałii indicates exceptional knowledge of ceremonial matters. Washington Matthews notes "the man who knows only how to conduct one of the minor ceremonies is not called hatali" (1902:4). Rather, the term hataałii is reserved for those who know "at least one complete chant" whereas "a curer's repertoire may be confined to a part of a single ceremonial or may include portions of as many as twelve ceremonials" (Kluckhohn and Wyman 1940:15). While several published accounts mention women ceremonial practitioners, other researchers have noted the complete lack of any female ceremonial practitioners in the communities in which they have worked.

For example, after conducting research on Navajo women's ceremonial knowledge in the Ramah area, Clyde Kluckhohn concluded that "there are no women singers and curers" in the region (1938:91), Kluckhohn and Leland Wyman report that during the late 1930s no women singers were found in the Pinedale-Coolidge-Smith Lake or the Ramah regions (1940:15), and Alexander and Dorothea Leighton note that "Many women are diagnosticians but they rarely become singers" (1944:29). Writing in the mid 1940s, Kluckhohn and Dorothea Leighton note, "Of all adult Navajo men past the age of thirty-five today, probably one out of every five or six can do divination or conduct Blessing Way, a chant, or some other rite. Many women are diviners, too, and a few women know other rites" (1974 [1946]:225). On the basis of his 1972 fieldwork in the area, James Chisholm pointed out that "[w]omen can become singers after menopause, but there are no female singers at Navajo Mountain" (1975:86). And Eric Henderson found no evidence of any women ceremonial practitioners in the Kaibeto Plateau region (1982:166).[6]

In contradistinction, writing in the early 1900s, the Franciscan Fathers noted, "As a rule women do not perform as chanters, though some are known to have done so. Many women are well versed in the medicinal flora of the country and are often consulted" (1910:382). In the late 1930s, Franc Newcomb and Gladys Reichard stated:

> The Chanters we worked with are men, but we do not mean to imply that women are barred from religious practise [sic]. If they were we might not have been allowed to participate as we have unless some special dispensation had been made. Nowadays women Chanters are few, formerly there were more, but probably never many compared to the number of men who chanted. One who was held in the greatest respect practised [sic] the Shooting Chant and died only a few years ago. At the present time Blue Eyes [sic] Sister is considered the greatest authority on this chant although she has not sung it for many years, perhaps never did (1937:14).

Berard Haile made passing reference to female singers in his study of the Enemy Way (1938:12); Kluckhohn and Wyman stated that "[w]omen practitioners are found among the Navajo, although female singers are rare" (1940:15). Reichard claimed that women were allowed to be ceremonial practitioners, even for such powerful ceremonies as the Night Way (1950:172). Two of the twenty-one singers interviewed by Chien Ch'iao in 1965 were women. The first, from Tsaile, Arizona, practiced Blessing Way and Flint Way Life Way, the second from Naschitti, New Mexico, practiced Eagle Catching Way and Blessing Way (1971:75). Ruth Roessel provides a preliminary overview on the lives of Navajo medicine women, including information on one woman who conducted the Evil Way and Lightning Way and another who conducted the Night Way (1981:121–122). In the early 1980s, David Aberle noted that "sometimes postmenopausal women" became practitioners (1982:227) and that some postmenopausal women were apprenticing through the then-current Navajo Healing Arts Training Program at Rough Rock Demonstration School (1982:228). James Faris acknowledges the existence of women ceremonial practitioners and documents information on several female apprentices of the Night Way (1990:92–94). His research on three women purported to be Night Way specialists revealed, however, that "such women never assumed principal responsibility for complete Nightways and had no Nightway medicine bundles and mask sets that belonged specifically to them," thus he concludes that they were not in fact full practitioners of this ceremonial (1990:99). And, Mary Shepardson notes, "Medicine men dominate the ritual Sings. However, women also can learn to be Singers and lead in ceremonies, regularly after menopause. They play important roles in the whole curing process. Diviners such as Hand Tremblers, mostly women, diagnose a disease and suggest the proper ceremony to be performed. Some women are herbalists who collect medicinal plants" (1995:171). Frisbie and Eddie Tso's report on the Office of Native Healing Sciences's registry of Navajo ceremonial practitioners found that of the 1,029 documented practitioners, 221, slightly over 21 percent, were women. While most women were identified as diviners or herbalists, this study clearly demonstrates that female practitioners of Blessing Way and curing ceremonials are practicing in communities throughout the Navajo reservation (Frisbie and Tso 1993:79–80).

Having met two female ceremonial practitioners while conducting research on other topics and having heard about other women singers, I decided to undertake a project focused on the life-courses of Navajo women who have apprenticed to become Asdzą́ą́ Hataałii or are practicing ceremonial practitioners. Aware of my interest, various Navajo acquaintances began accumulating information on women practitioners, and during the summers of 1998 and 2000 I traveled to communities across the reservation in search of Navajo women ceremonial practitioners. With the invaluable assistance of Amelda Sandoval Shay of Lukachukai, Arizona, Mae Ann Bekis of Tó'tsoh, Arizona, and Percy Deal of Hard Rocks, Arizona, I located, met, and interviewed twenty-three women (seventeen practitioners, five apprentices, and one widow of a singer).[7] In addition, over the course of our research we met seven other women practitioners and another apprentice who preferred not to be interviewed, learned of fourteen other women practitioners with whom we were unable to connect, and documented the existence of several deceased women singers.

No attempt was made to document details of particular ceremonies. Towards this same end, information about ceremonies is limited throughout the text to only that deemed absolutely necessary to maintenance of narrative clarity and no additional readings are suggested for gaining further information on any mentioned ceremonies. Rather, focus centers on how the reproductive life-course of Navajo women—menstruation, sexual activity, and pregnancy—influenced their apprenticeships and practices.

Initially I pondered whether or not women taking on this role were shifting genders; that is, if *singer* was a gender. Based on Navajo exegesis, I concluded that it is not. The practitioners that I interviewed are first and foremost women. As mothers and grandmothers they fulfill the culturally sanctioned role for women: nurturer. While there has not been a tremendous amount written on Navajo ceremonial practitioners of any gender, earlier works on men (Chisholm 1975; Griffen 1992; Henderson 1982; Mitchell 1978; Sandner 1979), on a *nádleehé* (Newcomb 1964), and on men and women practitioners (Ch'iao 1971), respectively, provide a solid core.[8] Information garnered from these sources is used throughout this work for comparative purposes to determine differences and similarities between the apprenticeship, initiation, and practice of men and women who become singers in the Navajo world.

Beyond contributing to anthropological insights on female healers cross-culturally (Bynum, Harrell, and Richman 1986; McClain 1989; Perrone, Stockel, and Krueger 1989), our understandings of the powers ascribed to women in Native North American societies (Klein and Ackerman 1995), and offering new perspective on practices that fall under the anthropological rubric of "menstrual restrictions" (Buckley and Gottlieb 1988), this study may prove useful to members of the Navajo Nation who are faced with a severe shortage of ceremonial practitioners. The training of more women might be a viable solution for this crisis. It is my hope that the disclosure of how women navigate cultural beliefs and practices to become singers will help to eliminate barriers that inhibit more women from filling the role of ceremonial practitioner in the Navajo world. Multiple strands of cultural theory inform this analysis, including contemporary perspectives on what are commonly called "menstrual taboos" and gender performativity theory.

Performativity theory arises from and extends the anti-structuralist—but often neo-structuralist—critiques made under the rubric of practice anthropology (Bourdieu 1977; de Certeau 1984; Ortner 1984; Sahlins 1976). Moving beyond the inherent limitations of practice theory with its overemphasis on habitus as a set of "structuring structures" (Bourdieu 1977, 1990), performativity theory offers the opportunity to explore and account for the nuanced permutations of personhood outside the norms or ideals enshrined in "cultural traditions"; essentially, it gets at the in-between aspects of life that do not fit such a neat picture. At its core, gender performativity theory is concerned with non-normative practice and its origin (Morris 1995:573). Because it "addresses itself to the lacuna in structuralist explanation, namely the problems of individual agency, historical change, and plurality within systems" (Morris 1995:571), performativity theory is the ideal base for an analysis of the life-courses of Navajo women who strive to become ceremonial practitioners.

In part derived from John Langshaw Austin's seminal analysis, the theory of gender performativity as Judith Butler has articulated it offers a particularly apt starting point for developing a theoretical means for illuminating the emergent personhood of women who take on a role largely viewed as appropriate only for men, that of singer. Austin distinguishes between constatives and performatives. The former being statements that describe some state of affairs, the latter being utterances that accomplish, in their very enunciation, an action that generates effects (Parker and Sedgwick 1995:3). Drawing on Austin's notion of the performative as "the act of enunciation that brings into being the object it names, Butler argues that gender is not a fact or an essence, but a set of acts that produce the effect or appearance of a coherent substance" (Morris 1995:572–573). Austin's distinction between illocutionary and perlocutionary acts of speech, that is, between "actions that are performed by virtue of words, and those that are performed as a consequence of words" (Butler 1995:197) is important here, for performatives are "not a description of some action, inner or outer, prior or posterior, occurring *elsewhere* than in the utterance itself. . . . [T]he action in question lies in the act of uttering those words in those circumstances" (Gould 1995:20).

The constitutive power granted language in performativity theory closely parallels Navajo views on the power of language and voice. In terms of Navajo personhood, the voice is considered part of the *niłch'i,* or "wind," that is, one's inner being (interviews with Bekis, 1995; Walters, 1995a).[9] The wind, which gives life to every Nihookáá Dine'é as it enters the body at birth, also gives the child the capacity to think, speak, and move. As poet Luci Tapahonso notes in the following passage, speech is sacred in the Navajo world: "We believe that the wind comes in at the top of your head when your hair begins to grow, and every time you speak, it is the wind that speaks. So speech is sacred, and you are very careful about how you say things. The Navajo language has no cuss words and no profanity." (Tapahonso as quoted in Baldinger 1992:35)

Voice, in the form of language, played a vital role in the creation of the Navajo universe. By some accounts, "the Navajo world was actually created or organized by means of language. The form of the world was first conceived in thought, and then this form was projected onto primordial unordered substance through the compulsive power of speech and song" (Witherspoon 1977:47). And, as Sunny Dooley of Vanderwagen, New Mexico, points out, this power prevails in the contemporary world:

In Navajo, when you say it it will happen. That's why they tell you, you shouldn't talk nonsense, you shouldn't just blah blah blah, you know. You just can't be talking any old way. . . . You can't be saying things any old way, meaning negatively, you know. . . . Like on television, you know, you hear people tell each other off, you know, and they don't think anything whatsoever about the power of their words. You know, and maybe English is not that powerful. I don't know. But it goes all the ways back to the fact that in Navajo, you can't swear. You can't say the 'D' word, you can't say the 'F' word, you can't say the 'S' word. We don't have those words in my language. . . . We believe that when we say it, when it comes out of our mouths, it is like little, little bubbles, you know, that put into motion all kinds of events. And that's why it's vitally important in Navajo to be well spoken, to be speaking well all the time. (Interview with Dooley, 1992b)[10]

Today the natural order of the Navajo world is reaffirmed on a daily basis through utterances of song and prayer, and restored whenever it becomes disrupted through the compulsive power of song and prayer carried on the singer's voice in all ceremonial contexts. Reiterative and citational practice is also fundamental to Butler's understanding of gender performativity.

Butler's theory, which defines gender as the effect of discourse, is concerned "with the productive force rather than the meaning of discourse and by its privileging of ambiguity and indeterminacy" (Morris 1995:567). Butler reiterates Candace West and Donald Zimmerman's claim that gender is not something that you possess (as a raw essence or quality) but rather that it is something that one does (1987). But she argues that although gender is a set of acts, it derives its force from the fact that acts are mistaken for essence and they eventually are believed to be mandatory (Morris 1995:573).

Butler argues that the success of a performative is dependent on the action echoing prior actions and the accumulation of a "force of authority through the repetition or citation of a prior and authoritative set of practices" (Butler 1995: 205). That is, unlike in Austin's now classic example of a performative, the "I do" uttered in the course of the matrimonial ceremony (1962:5), in the case of gender, Butler has found that "performativity must be understood not as a singular or deliberate 'act,' but, rather as the reiterative and citational practice by which discourse produces the effects that it names" (1995:2).

In like fashion, being a singer in the Navajo world is not something that one possesses but rather it is something that one does through nuanced actions and speech acts. On one level, becoming a ceremonial practitioner is performative in so far as it is based on the utterance of songs and prayers in a carefully prescribed manner and order. "Following" is the term the Navajo women singers and apprentices with whom I consulted used to refer to the lengthy process of apprenticeship wherein an individual attends ceremonies being performed by a particular singer who subsequently becomes a mentor. Gradually, apprentices do more and more of the acts integral to ceremonial practice. Consequently a woman is "doing" ceremonial practice during her tenure as an apprentice, yet she is not formally recognized as a practitioner until her new social role is "called into being" through a deliberate performative speech act in the context of an initiation ceremony, which is overseen by the man under whom she apprenticed. Some Navajo women practitioners also use the term "following" when referring to practice; in this case they consider themselves to be following the ceremony (interview with Mace) or the Holy People (interview with Nez).

The life-courses of Navajo women who strive to become ceremonial practitioners are illuminated through analysis of a shift in emphasis from performance to performativity that coincides with shifts in emphases from "doing" to "saying" to "witnessing" at critical stages in the process of becoming a singer. Tension exists between doing, saying, and hearing, or witnessing. Doing is dominant during the apprenticeship phase, saying is dominant during the initiation phase, and witnessing is most vital during the practitioner phase. On the surface, the quintessential performative moment in the life-course of a Navajo woman becoming a singer occurs during her initiation ceremony when her mentor says, "it is yours," or "you can perform this ceremony now." But, as pointed out by Andrew Parker and Eve Sedgwick, performativity also involves an element of witnessing. The witness permits, ratifies, and recruits the legitimacy of a speech act (Parker and Sedgwick 1995:11). In the case of Navajo women becoming ceremonial practitioners, the Holy People are the witnesses.

As Butler found with her study of the performative aspects of gender (Butler 1988:526), an account of the apprenticeship and practice of Navajo women singers as ritualized, public performance must be combined with an analysis of the sanctions and taboos under which that performance may or may not occur within the public sphere free of negative consequences. This contextualization links multiple strands of Navajo cultural thought because the boundaries created to contain and control the power embodied in blood and voice must be articulated before the ways in which women navigate them during apprenticeship and practice can be understood. Conflicts derive from two primary areas: prohibitions surrounding contact between certain types of menstrual blood or sexuality, and ceremonial contexts and guidelines in oral history regarding gender roles.

To garner an understanding of gender roles as well as how blood and voice came to have their current significance, pertinent portions of the Navajo origin story have been analyzed through consultation with Navajo experts. Key episodes in this narrative sequence reveal that sexual attraction was intentionally created by the

Holy People as a means of ensuring the continuation of life in the Navajo universe (Goddard 1933:138–139; Zolbrod 1984:53). Yet, during the "separation of the sexes," a pivotal event documented in Navajo oral history, the potentially dangerous powers of sexual attraction were unleashed in an uncontrolled setting (Fishler 1953:26; Haile 1981a:23, 25–27; Matthews 1994 [1897]:72; O'Bryan 1956:7–8; Stephen 1930:98–99; Yazzie 1971:30; Zolbrod 1984:62–63). Subsequent sexual aberrations on the part of men and women led to the birth of child-eating monsters that threatened the very survival of the Navajo ancestors (Fishler 1953:38–39; Haile 1938:77–79; Witherspoon 1987:15). These experiences rendered some types of blood dangerous—that shed during the butchering of game animals (interviews with Billie; Harrison; Kee 1992a; Walters, 1995a) and that shed by women after their second menstrual cycle.

Classic anthropological frames for consideration of menstruation have been the narrow confines of taboo, pollution, and the oppression of women (Meigs 1990:181). Cross-cultural investigations of menstrual taboos have tended to focus narrowly on limitations surrounding exposure to menstrual substances and to highlight the limitations placed on women's activities to the exclusion of other explanations for menstrual prohibitions and restrictions (Douglas 1966; Durkheim 1897; Stephens 1962; Weideger 1977; Young and Bacdayan 1965). The study of so-called menstrual restrictions gained new impetus with the publication of the provocative essays in *Blood Magic* (Buckley and Gottlieb 1988).[11]

In their call for a more finely drawn analysis of menstrual rules and "taboos," Thomas Buckley and Alma Gottlieb (1988:3–50) suggest, following Mary Douglas's revised position (1972), that it is most productive to see menstrual blood as powerful rather than as dangerous. They urge researchers to consider the positive as well as the negative effects of menstrual restrictions and, in cases where menstrual blood is considered dangerous, to consider *who* is endangered by it; that is, what categories of people are culturally defined as vulnerable to menstrual blood—men, women, or children. Thus, menstrual blood's potential negative or positive aspects and characteristics or its multivalence in the realms of cultural conceptions of the nature of life, death, and sacredness remain to be explored in each case study.

After the "separation," the decision was made to delegate political and ceremonial power to men (Shepardson 1995:172–176; interview with Walters, 1995a) and control over the domestic realm to women. This established acceptable gender roles. Thus, the voices of orators and ceremonial practitioners came to embody the power needed to maintain social order and to restore health. From the perspective of many Navajo women with whom I consulted, women have stepped forward since these roles were established to fill a gap left by men. An anonymous woman from Sanostee, New Mexico, recalls a comment made by her father before his death: "I see most women today in this generation that are working, putting food on the table, the men are just lazy, sitting at home. You hardly see men in the ceremonials no more. There's more ladies that are coming in. When you go to a ceremonial there's more ladies that are there. They're getting, the men are um, I guess you could say lazy." (Interview with anonymous woman, 2000)[12]

Mary Ben Jones Whitney of Tohatchi, New Mexico, concurs:

> Well, today there are not that many that are doing the ceremonies. Medicine people are scarce. And the few medicine men that we do have, they ask for lots of money. I think that this is why women are taking it up. I don't want to belong to what they are saying [referring to the Navajo Medicine Men Association], and I don't want to belong to what they are doing at the college. Somebody came to see me from there, they wanted me to come to the college and do some talking, and some singing, "We want you to teach some kids over there." I said, "No. They can follow me, that is the correct way to learn. I can show them how things are done, I can sing, I can pray, and that way they can learn the songs and prayers." (Interview with Whitney)[13]

Navajo women who choose to pursue careers as ceremonial practitioners face complex challenges. The involvement of women with this side of life takes place within limitations surrounding their reproductive capacities as well as those of their spouses. Rules prohibiting menstruating women from ceremonial contexts delimit a woman's apprenticeship and practice. An individual woman cannot completely control the periodicity of her menstrual flow, the flow can occur throughout the year, yet this flow dictates access to ceremonies, and it must be mediated to protect others. Thus, her opportunities for acquiring ceremonial knowledge and skills or practicing as a singer are limited during her childbearing years. Strict sexual continence rules for ceremonial practitioners can cause strain in marital relationships. Furthermore, Navajo oral history dictates that men are to be the leaders in charge of all ceremonial and political matters. Motivated to carry on time-honored traditions, women navigate the social and personal issues raised by these multiple challenges to aid fellow Navajo in times of need.

CHAPTER II

"IT IS A GIFT . . .
FROM THE
HOLY PEOPLE"

HW During the separation of the sexes the women did real bad so it was said that a woman would not become a leader.

MS But I heard that the men did pretty bad then, too. I mean—

HW And so—

MS Wait. What do you mean by during the separation of the sexes the women did badly? I thought the men did just as badly, that is why they all decided to reunite.

HW No, no!

MS No?

HW The women, they were not experienced leaders, they were not experienced hunters, they neglected the fields and so they were starving at the end of four years. So from then on they said, "A woman will not become a leader in the future. If we ever made a woman leader, chaos would reign!" So, this was accepted, culturally.

MS But women have so much control over daily life. I mean they are the ones—

HW No. But the women are in control of the household, the children, the fields, the livestock. See?

MS Yeah.

HW By the matrilineal society.

MS Uh-huh.

HW The men have leadership in ceremonies.

MS Right.

HW OK, so they are equally balanced. In traditional Navajo society, the roles and responsibilities of the man and the woman were equal. . . . It's all part of the natural order, you know, the role of each.

MS That is what I want to know more about.

HW In each of these.

MS So, the natural order—

HW Yeah.

MS and the role of men and women?

HW Yes.

MS Men would control the ceremonies?

HW Yes. The leadership.

MS So, then how come now they'll let women—

HW [Chuckles] Because we don't know any better now, we're getting away from that. (Interview with Walters, 1993)[1]

MS Some say that according to the oral histories, the diné bahane', men were to be in charge of the political and ceremonial realms. Ask her whether she feels that that is true?

AS According to the Navajo creation stories, according to the Holy People, men are the only ones talked about and are the only ones thought to be responsible for everything, like things in Window Rock [headquarters of the Navajo Nation Government] and ceremonial matters. What do you think about men being in control of all these entities?

JM I just think they are leaders. I think it is the woman who is in control, because she is the main one responsible for reproduction. She is the only one who places children on this earth. All of it was not assigned solely or totally to men, but equally distributed to women, too. From the time we started, from the underworlds, it was first mentioned that women cannot be leaders and that a woman could never become a ceremonial practitioner, it was said. That is how the stories were told. When the people arrived here in this world and from that time to today, women are the only leaders and women are the only real ceremonial practitioners. Men have taken a step back. (Interview with Mace)[2]

The Navajo individuals with whom I consulted about the establishment of gender roles, determining who would lead in ceremonial and political affairs, repeatedly made implicit or explicit reference to various elements and versions of oral tradition, which relates their origin as successive emergence upward through a series of subterranean worlds. The powers of sexual desire played a profound role in each of the underworlds through which Navajo ancestors traversed upwards to the present world.

Columns of gases or clouds stood at each of the cardinal points in the First World. In the eastern quadrant, where the white column and the black column met and engaged, as if in sexual intercourse, Áłtsé Hastiin, "First Man," was formed—with him a perfect ear of white corn was formed. On the western side of the First World appeared the yellow column, and next to it appeared the blue column. Where they came together, Áłtsé Asdzą́ą́, "First Woman," was formed—with her a perfect ear of yellow corn was formed (Yazzie 1971:9). These are the primordial beings that directed generative processes in this and subsequent worlds (O'Bryan 1956:1; Yazzie 1971:9). First Man had a fire of crystal and First Woman had a fire of turquoise. They were attracted to each other, and the powers of regeneration were set into motion.

In the last underworld, the first male and female beings with humanlike form were created (Zolbrod 1984:50–51). They lived as man and wife and had five sets of twins. The first twins were neither entirely male nor entirely female; they were nádleehé. The other sets of twins each consisted of an entirely male person and an entirely female person who initially lived as husband and wife. After a time they ended these incestuous marriages and married Mirage People (Zolbrod 1984:51–53) or other Diyin Dine'é. First Woman grew concerned as these marriages dissolved easily. Seeing the need for enduring marriages to guarantee the continuation of life, she developed a plan to strengthen the bond between men and women (Zolbrod 1984:53). Having resolved to be the leader in such matters, she created genitals and sexual desire to enable men and women to attract each other for a lifetime.

> She planned that it would be hard for men and women, once attached, to separate again. She decided that both men and women should have medicine to attract each other. Then she made a penis of turquoise. She rubbed loose cuticle from the man's breast. This she mixed with yucca fruit. She made a clitoris of red shell and put it inside the vagina. She rubbed loose cuticle from the woman's breast and mixed it with yucca fruit. She put that inside the turquoise penis. She combined herbs with waters of various kinds which should be for producing pregnancy. She placed the vagina on the ground and beside it the penis. Then she blew medicine from her mouth on them. That is why when people marry nowadays the woman sits on the left.
>
> "Now you think," she said to the penis. It did so and its mind

extended across Mesa Verde. When the woman's organ thought its mind went nearly half way across and returned to her hips. That is why her longing does not extend to great distance.

"Let them shout," she said. The penis shouted very loud, but the vagina had a weak voice. "Let them have intercourse and try shouting again," she said. When they tried again penis could not shout loud, but vagina had a good voice. The penis had lost its voice. (Goddard 1933:138–139)

With these actions, First Woman unleashed into the Navajo universe previously unknown powers of sexual desire, and these powers proved to be a double-edged sword, for they ultimately led to serious problems. With the use of these organs, First Man, First Woman, and their progeny flourished until lust led to conflict.

Navajo people routinely refer to these vivid narratives, which collectively make up their oral history, as a charter for life. Over four hundred composite accounts of the Navajo origin story have been transcribed by generations of outside researchers (Fishler 1953; Goddard 1933; Haile 1981b; Matthews 1994 [1897]; O'Bryan 1956; Stephen 1930), as well as by the Navajo tribe itself (Yazzie 1971). Statements suggesting ontological status are potentially misleading, however: an integral core of common elements permeates all recorded versions, but the accounts vary widely in detail.

Story differences reflect personal factors such as the narrator's stage of life, clan affiliations, or the level of ceremonial or other specialized knowledge acquired through life experience or occupational training. In addition to information shared with me by Harry Walters, of Cove, Arizona, Juanita Mace, of Torreon, New Mexico, and twenty-some other female consultants, I rely largely on the versions transcribed by Stanley Fishler (1953), Pliny Goddard (1933), Aileen O'Bryan (1956), Berard Haile (1981a, 1981b, and in Wyman 1970), Washington Matthews (1994 [1897] and Zolbrod 1984), Alexander Stephen (1930), and Ethelou Yazzie (1971) for my connective narrative, because they contain the most complete accounts of the events pertinent to this discussion. With the exception of the version edited by Yazzie (1971), these published accounts are limited by the fact that they were each collected from male consultants, the majority of whom had specialized training. My analysis, therefore, breaks new ground by bringing Navajo women's voices to discussions of oral history.

Close attention to exactly how these oral narratives are used to understand contemporary life provides insights into individual agency, historical change, and plurality of accounts. For example, men and women focused on different episodes when responding to specific questions about the role of women in ceremonial matters. Harry Walters's account epitomizes the views of men as they are represented in published versions. These accounts rather consistently hark back to the time before, during, and after the event he referred to as the separation of the sexes, especially to statements made directly after the reunion of men and women.

THE SEPARATION

> Women were not treated as equal. This is what the separation was all about. The adultery that was mentioned in there, you know, it is just "the straw that broke the camel's back." But, the women when they attained agriculture, the things began to change. Agriculture was beginning to be ahh, began to be a larger part of, you know, of the society. And then agriculture was given to the women to maintain.[3] And then so, the women began demanding equal, equality. The men refused. And then the women told the men, they said, "We don't need you anyway. We can live without you." And they lived separate. And what happened was, it was terrible. They found out they cannot live apart, that the man needs something that only a woman can provide and the woman the same. And they compromised. They were just going to sweep that under the rug again but this time they did a great wrong. They had abused themselves, you know, they did immoral acts. That is a crime against Nature, the "natural order" and as a result the monsters came. (Interview with Walters, 1995b)

The various published versions of the incidents leading up to the separation are replete with divergent explanations regarding the exact events that precipitated it. By some accounts, the men believed that they alone were sustaining life (Matthews 1994 [1897]:71–72; Zolbrod 1984:58–60) while others maintain that the women felt that they were doing most of the work necessary for life (Fishler 1953:25; Haile 1981b:13–14; O'Bryan 1956:6; Stephen 1930:97–98; interview with Walters, 1995b; Zolbrod 1984:59). According to Juanita Mace, "The women were saying that 'We are the ones who created life.' They were saying to the men that, that 'You men are living and alive simply because of the existence of women.' This disagreement initiated the start of the separation. The men said, 'Since you say that you can live and exist by yourselves, why not live by yourselves. We will move to this side and see.' The separation took place. This unsettled the living conditions of the time" (interview with Mace).

Regardless of the specific details, all published descriptions concur that the men and women disagreed about important aspects of their joint lives and general consensus exists that the powers of sexual attraction, in one form or another, played a fundamental role in the initial dispute which took place between First

Man and First Woman. Most accounts claim First Man was angered by adulterous acts on the part of First Woman (Goddard 1933:128–129; Haile 1981b:13–14; O'Bryan 1956:6–7; Yazzie 1971:28). Other tellings attribute the conflict that ultimately led to the separation to an off-hand comment made by First Woman after she finished eating a meal of a "fine, fleshy" deer procured by First Man, who was a renowned hunter (Matthews 1994 [1897]:218, n.32). Once her appetite was satiated, Áłtsé Asdzą́ą́ wiped her "greasy hands," "belched deeply," and had the following to say:

> *"Thank you* shijóózh *my vagina," she said.*
> *"Thank you for that delicious dinner."*
> *To which* Áłtsé hastiin *the First Man replied this way:*
> *"Why do you say that?" he replied.*
> *"Why not thank me?*
> *"Was it not I who killed the deer whose flesh you have just feasted on?*
> *"Was it not I who carried it here for you to eat?*
> *"Was it not I who skinned it?*
> *"Who made it ready for you to boil?*
> *"Is* nijóózh *your vagina the great hunter, that you should thank it and not me?"*
> *To which* Áłtsé asdzą́ą́ *offered this answer:*
> *"As a matter of fact, she is," offered she.*
> *"In a manner of speaking it is* jóósh *the vagina who hunts.*
> *"Were it not for her you would not have carried it here.*
> *"You would not have skinned it.*
> *"You lazy men would do nothing around here were it not for* jóósh.
> *"In truth,* jóósh *the vagina does all the work around here." (Zolbrod 1984:58–59)*

This said, First Man called all the men together to discuss the issues raised by the exchange. It soon became clear that each gender felt that theirs was making the more significant contribution to communal life, and that each group wanted to prove its independence and superiority by demonstrating that it could live without the other. First Man called Nádleehé to him and asked if the grinding stones, *ádístsiin,* "a set of stirring sticks," and grass brush—the implements of woman's work—were hers. Nádleehé answered in the affirmative (O'Bryan 1956:7).

Satisfied that Nádleehé would be able to complete all tasks usually done by women, First Man directed the men to build rafts and load them with all of the male children, Nádleehé, and their material possessions. This done, they traveled to the opposite side of a major river where they could live, with the assistance of Nádleehé, away from the women.

The men and women lived apart for four years. First Man returned to the women's side from time to time in the first year to take away male children as they were born (Fishler 1953:26). Since they remained on the side of the river where the agricultural fields were already prepared, the women initially fared better at procuring food from crops than the men did. But year by year, as the men continued to hunt and, under the guidance of Nádleehé, became increasingly adept at farming, their subsistence base exceeded that of the women (Fishler 1953:26; Goddard 1933:129; Haile 1981b:22–23; Matthews 1994 [1897]:72; O'Bryan 1956:7–8; Stephen 1930:98–99; Zolbrod 1984:61–67). The women, who grew weak with hunger, were soon "dying for want of everything" (Haile 1981b:25), including the companionship of their spouses. For, during this time, the sexual desires created by First Woman became ever stronger.

The women are said to have laughed and taunted the men with their powers of sexual attraction (Haile 1981b:23; Matthews 1994 [1897]:72; O'Bryan 1956:7; Stephen 1930:98; Yazzie 1971:30; Zolbrod 1984:62). In an effort to entice them to return, the women went to the shore where they lifted their dresses, turned their backs to the men, and bent forward. Exposing their genitals in full view of the men on the other side of the river, the women called out "First Ma-a-n! Do you see this, perhaps?" (Haile 1981b:23). "Don't you see what you are missing?" (Zolbrod 1984:62). Or, "How would you like to have some?" (Stephen 1930:98). With such activities rampant, loneliness and yearning for former spouses increased amongst the women and men on both sides of the river, leading members of both genders to seek pleasure by new means.

The few men who stayed behind with the women—Blue Fox, Yellow Fox, and Badger—went to extremes in their efforts to satisfy the passions of the women. "Yellow Fox and Blue Fox licked the women's hind ends to satisfy them. All three [Yellow Fox, Blue Fox, and Badger] put their hands and other parts into the menstrual blood of the women and that is why they have black mouths, hands and bodies" (Fishler 1953:26).

Ultimately, it seems that their efforts had the opposite of the intended effect—increasing the desires of the women, rather than quenching their passions.

> *Badger (of the north) wanted to copulate with the women but he had a bad penis, crooked like a hook. The first one he tried was Joshdel-hashi, then all the others. It made them crazy and they went wild with desire to copulate continually. Some of them took a corn cob wrapped with any soft substance and continually performed the sexual act*

artificially. Some tried to swim the river to get to their men but were
drowned. Some died crazy with wild desire. This and lack of food
caused the death of most of the women. (Stephen 1930:99)

Overcome with sexual frenzy, members of both genders routinely began to abuse their reproductive powers. According to the various accounts of Navajo oral history, women attempted intercourse with a variety of strange objects other than corncobs. Some used long smooth stones (Haile 1981b:25; Zolbrod 1984:63), thick feather quills (Haile 1981b:25; Zolbrod 1984:63), hooked-spine and other cactuses (interview with Chavez; Haile 1981b:27; Zolbrod 1984:63), or bone (Zolbrod 1984:63). The women also masturbated with the leg muscles of game animals (Haile 1981b:25), the tongues of deer (interview with Chavez), or with the penises of male deer (interview with Walters, 1995a). The men attempted to appease their passions with mud (Haile 1981b:26; Zolbrod 1984:63) and the flesh (Zolbrod 1984:63) or livers of freshly slain deer (interview with Chavez; Haile 1981b:26; interview with Walters, 1995a; Yazzie 1971:30; Zolbrod 1984:69), antelope (Stephens 1930:99), or other game animals. In addition, some men used the vaginas of freshly slain mountain sheep, antelope, or deer to relieve their longings (interview with Chavez; Haile 1981b:26; O'Bryan 1956:8; interview with Walters, 1995a). Those who attempted these or other such inappropriate acts with game animals offended the supernaturals to whom authority over each particular species belonged; as a result, they were punished as in the following account, by lightning (Haile 1981a:68; O'Bryan 1956:8; Stephen 1930:99; Yazzie 1971:30), snake, or bear. "When they killed an antelope they cut out the liver and made a hole in it and artificially performed the sexual act. Some who could overtake a doe would copulate with it, but these lightning struck and burst open. Some in like manner with an antelope doe, and the rattlesnake bit and killed them. Another man would do likewise with mountain sheep and a bear killed him" (Stephen 1930:99). As First Man heard of these activities he warned each offender that he was "indulging in a dangerous practice" and that they would all be killed, if these actions continued (O'Bryan 1956:8).[4]

Being acutely aware of their dwindling numbers, First Man called the men together to discuss the possibility of reconciliation with the women. After considering the beneficial and harmful aspects of life apart from the women, the men concluded that if it were allowed to continue indefinitely the separation would ultimately result in their demise (Haile 1981b:31; Matthews 1994 [1897]:72; Stephen 1930:100; Zolbrod 1984:67). For, as one man put it,

"Suppose we survived while they all perished?" he asked.
"Could we possibly sustain life without them? Can mud bear our
children? Can the livers of slain deer raise our offspring?

"If this present disorder continues, the world as we know it will come to an end." (Zolbrod 1984:69)

Eventually, the men agreed to leave the ultimate decision up to Nádleehé, who said that she would be content to have the women come across to join the men because she was "tired of cooking for them all" (Stephen 1930:100). At this time, "First Woman went to First Man and begged him to let the women rejoin the men. They were hungry, without clothes and were lonely for companionship" (Fishler 1953:26). He consulted with the other men and they agreed to rejoin and live as one group for, as one leader proclaimed, "Now we can see for ourselves what comes from our wrong doings. We will know how to act in the future" (O'Bryan 1956:8). First Man said, "Very well, all will be forgiven and you can go back to your men. But I shall make a law: The male shall rule and whatever your chiefs say, that must be done" (Fishler 1953:26).

First Woman supposedly replied, "'My Dear, my Babe, my Son,' and embraced First Man. 'It is true, you are the one by whom things do exist, not I. Not through me do they exist,' she said. 'It is true, you are indeed the holy highest one, while I am not that,' she said. 'Now exactly as you may direct, that same shall be (done), just following you it shall be,' she said. 'At no time will I take the decision away from you,' she said. 'All right, I hope you really mean this,' said First Man" (Haile 1981b:33).

The hardships and failures of life during the separation ultimately proved that neither sex can exist without the other, and this reunion symbolizes the complementary roles of men and women. The "rules" established by First Man at the time of the reunion form the base paradigm for the complementary nature of gender relations. As pointed out by Harry Walters (interview with Walters, 1993), women were given control of the domestic realm (household, livestock, and agricultural fields); men were given control of hunting and the ceremonial realm. The women agreed, "Very well, we will keep the home clean, cook the food, and care for the children" (Levy 1998:204). Thus, the division of labor was made clear and permanent (Levy 1998:204). Once the guidelines for their lives together were instituted, the women were taken across the river to join the men. Before resuming sexual relations, the men and women purified themselves for four days with emetics and sweat baths, after which they dried themselves with cornmeal (Haile 1981b:35; Matthews 1994 [1897]:73; Stephen 1930:100); the men dried with white, the women with yellow (Goddard 1933:129–130; O'Bryan 1956:8).

After purification, the women rejoined the men. "They looked much healthier now and each made herself useful about the home by putting things in order and cleaning up, sorting the meat, and so forth. And when their husbands entered, they extended their hands in welcome: 'How are you, my husband? You were right. We are not in a position to provide for ourselves but must rely on you'" (Haile

1981a:99). Interestingly, when I asked Navajo women about these events and outcomes, they saw things a bit differently.

"THEY SAID 'NO' AND WE STEPPED OVER IT!"

> **EM** And since then [the reunion of men and women after the separation], you know, the man has taken the position that, you know, "You females cannot be trusted. Because of what has happened, you really can't be a practitioner or a leader." But that's not true! The wrongdoings were equal on both sides. There were these damages that were done to one another. So that is basically what the whole dividing was all about.
>
> **MS** And that was what is often referred to as the separation of the sexes?
>
> **EM** Yes.
>
> **MS** That episode, right.
>
> **EM** Mm-hmm.
>
> **MS** So that's where, that was the point in time when men began to deny women the right to . . .
>
> **EM** Mm-hmm.
>
> **MS** . . . practice their full roles?
>
> **EM** Right. (Interview with Manson)[5]

Navajo women with whom I consulted on these matters had a variety of responses to queries about the roles of men and women in the political and ceremonial realms. Pearly Yazzie of Newlands, Arizona, claimed complete ignorance on the subject (interview with Yazzie).[6] Without disputing the standard account, Betty Begay, of Red Valley, Arizona, simply stated: "I think a woman is entitled to do these things too. Like Lightning Way and all of these other sings like Night Way, Fire Dance, Blessing Way, and whatever. Ladies are entitled to do these ceremonies because they learned them. Not just men. That is how I know" (interview with Begay).[7] Other women such as Grace Emerson of Smith Lake, New Mexico, and Nettie Nez of Saltwater, Arizona, adamantly disputed the standard account told by male consultants. For example, Grace Emerson told me: "I have heard all the stories about our history, but I never heard that. No, I never heard that. I haven't heard anywhere, anybody saying that a lady cannot perform a ceremony" (interview with Emerson).[8] Nettie Nez also said these claims were contrary to what she learned. "Way back, when I was young, the men and the women would get together in the winter and they would tell stories about what has happened in the Navajo history, 'A woman can become a medicine woman,' that is what they said" (interview with Nez).[9]

By way of clarification, Louella Deswood of Goosenest, Arizona, pointed out that the notion that men must control the ceremonial and political realms is a misinterpretation or misrepresentation on the part of men.

> **LD** Back in the oral, the oral section, over there, you have your four beings and your four beings always had to be like ah, maybe the first man and then the first woman. In this type of ceremony, it was always understood, even the men practitioners, it was always understood.
>
> **MS** What was always understood?
>
> **LD** It was always understood that there was a man, maybe because they, because he was the one that was named first. Just like Cain and Abel, or Moses and Adam, or whatever. Know what I mean? And then, and then next came Eve, OK? It is something like that, it is the, it is the same nature, it is the same nature. So the practitioners, the genuine practitioners that you will come across, would be the ones that would fully tell you that it is not a male dominance world just because the man was named first. And it is, and it is very right for a woman to be able to do a lot of these ceremonies, too. That would not be bending the rules. That would have been the way the perfect world would have been. That dominance, that male dominance where the male decided that "Since we're the ones that are going off into battle, mostly," remember back in the older days? "Since we are the ones that are going in there, then I think we are the ones that should have the most control." Kind of like slavery, you know, where, where the women just to be the, just to be the housewife and all of that. . .
>
> **MS** I guess at a certain level the understanding as it has been explained to me was that this was the men's domain, largely.
>
> **LD** Yeah, that was *their* idea. That was the idea that, that *they put into their own heads.* (Interview with Deswood)

When her grandson posed the question, "Grandma, how do you like the way the man was supposed to be head of a household and he was doing the singing. Did you like it that way or not?" An anonymous woman from Canyon Del Muerto, Arizona, replied, "Yes, I like it that way because they are the ones that are supposed to do all the singing. It was given to the man! The Holy People gave them the singing. Only the men used to do the singing" (interview with anonymous woman, 1998).[10]

Other women such as Laura Nix of Tuba City, Arizona, Elizabeth Edison of Bear Spring, Arizona, Jean Mariano of Mariano Lake, New Mexico, and Gaye Shorthair of Pinon, Arizona, acknowledged that this is how things were originally intended to be but that things have changed. Laura Nix explains:

> Yes, it happened and the lady is supposed to be taking care of the home, whatever needed to be done around the home. The man is from outside on. Like taking care of the fields or whatever, and ceremonies, and hunting. That was supposed to be the man's job. That is the man's work. Some of them say that a woman can perform ceremonies too. They said it is just questionable right there. Both men and women knew how to perform ceremonies though. They knew the songs and prayers necessary to the continuation of life—without this knowledge, they would not have been able to continue life after the separation. My father told me about that, he said, "That is how the Navajo people came about. After that [the separation], they got back together." That is how he told me. (Interview with Nix)[11]

Elizabeth Edison agreed that this is how things were initially established, but she noted: "Sure, they probably said that, but up to this day there are a lot of women who are singers. Yes, when they came from the underworlds, they were told that. Over time, our ceremonies were becoming extinct. We were losing them, but now the ceremonies are being revived and so a lot of us women are encouraged to learn" (interview with Edison).[12]

Jean Mariano believes fundamental differences between men and women explain why things have changed:

> Yes, it was said that women could not be leaders or perform ceremonies, but I think that we think harder than the men do today. The women have more willpower and they manage things better and they accomplish more than the men do. That is why it is like this today, women are singing and all that. They said that in the underworld but today I don't think it is like that anymore because the men do not think that hard now. That is how it is now, that is how I am thinking about it. Just look at how Window Rock [the Navajo Nation Government] is running! There are a lot of things going on that are not supposed to go on! (Interview with Mariano)[13]

While, with the assistance of Amelda Sandoval Shay, Gaye Shorthair and I had the following conversation:

> **GS** Yes, that is what they said at that time. They said a woman is not supposed to do this or that. She wasn't even supposed to beat the basket. Up to today, we do everything. There isn't anything that we do less. *They said "No" and we stepped over it!* And now we are doing all the things that were forbidden. We are doing them. That is how it is.
>
> **AS** What do you think about it today?
>
> **GS** I don't see anything wrong with it. There is nothing wrong with it. That is how I see it. There is nothing wrong with it. (Interview with Shorthair)[14]

Instead of focusing on statements made by men and women after the separation of the sexes, other consultants discussed key events that occurred afterwards when Navajo ancestors moved on to establish a newly created world.

THE EMERGENCE

> Locust is the first one that came out. Behind him, the others came up. So the women said, "How will we build a home? A house or what?" But, before they even did that, here there were tall sunflowers, and it was already made, someone had already made them a forked-stick home. That home was already there and people were already there. Inside, they were doing stick game and shoe game. There must have been somebody else who had already come up because when the ladies came up the forked-stick hooghan was already there and they were playing games already in there. It was the animals, like lizard and things like that. At that time, they were talking; they were the ones that were playing those games. The women were still talking about how to make the hooghan, but it was already there. And, after that, they just gathered the bigger poles and they made a hooghan of it. And that one, the forked-stick one became a male hooghan. The round hooghan is female. They put together the songs as they built the hooghan. Then they started putting bark in between them and mud on them. That is where they put all the songs together. And this is how they built the Blessing Way ceremony; they began the songs with the gathering of materials and added more and more gradually over time until

the hooghan was built.[15] . . . Since the Blessing Way began with the building of the first female hooghan, it is essentially a female ceremony. (Interview with Nix)

At the rim of the place of emergence, First Man and First Woman built a sweathouse in which they thought and sang into existence the world as the Navajo now know it (Witherspoon 1977:16–17). Once their plans were made, Holy People directed them in the construction and consecration of two distinct styles of traditional dwellings. A *hooghan biką'*, the "male hooghan," was constructed first in which to create prototypes for all life on the earth's surface (Mindeleff 1898:489; Wheelwright 1942:62). Hooghan biką' were designed to be used exclusively for praying, singing, making plans, and ceremonial purposes (Aronilth 1985:179).

The second type of dwelling, *hooghan ba'ááá,* or the "female hooghan," soon followed. Hooghan ba'ááá were designed as places for children to be born and nurtured, as well as locations in which families might eat and rest (Aronilth 1985:180). Female hooghan have special roles because they are considered to be mothers (Aronilth 1985:183). According to Laura Nix, the construction of the first hooghan ba'ááá was of pivotal importance because it marked the beginning of the Blessing Way ceremony (interview with Nix)—the core ceremony of the Navajo religious system (Wyman 1970).

As a microcosm of the larger world, the prototype world constructed on the floor of the first hooghan biką' serves as a paradigm for Navajo cosmology. Seven points are specified in the Navajo worldview: east, south, west, north, zenith, nadir, and center. To strengthen the earth, First Man and First Woman made and placed a mountain at each of these critical points constructed of soil gathered by First Man from the corresponding sacred mountain in the last underworld when all life forms were forced by flood to escape into this world (Matthews 1994 [1897]:74–75; Goddard 1933:130; O'Bryan 1956:23; Wyman 1965:91; Yazzie 1971:13). The following mountains mark these directions in Navajo sacred geography: east, Sisnaajiní or Blanca Peak; south, Tsoodził, Mount Taylor; west, Dook'o'oosłííd, San Francisco Peak; and north, Dibé Nitsaa, La Plata Peak, with two additional landforms in the center. The distinctive shapes of male and female hooghan are modeled after these central features of Navajo sacred geography. The peaked roof of hooghan biką' mirrors the profile of Ch'óol'į́'į́, "Gobernador Knob," the place where Changing Woman was found, and the more gently rounded roof of hooghan ba'ááá is an image of Dziłná'oodiłii, Huerfano Peak, or the landform "around-which-moving-was-done" (Williamson 1984:152; Nabokov and Easton 1989:326).

After the mountains were placed, the Diyin Dine'é went on to create and place the sun, the moon, and the stars, as well as to determine all aspects of life and death within this sacred geography. As Eunice Manson of Rocky Ridge, Arizona, explains through Percy Deal who graciously served as interpreter, femaleness was an essential component of this new world.

> My uncle taught me that every Navajo ceremony, every Navajo song and prayer, there are four basic connections that it has. There are ceremonies and songs and prayers that are directly related to the earth, which is Mother Earth. A female. And then there are other songs, prayers, and ceremonies that are connected to the surrounding mountains. Each one of these mountains is a female mountain. And then there are prayers, songs, and ceremonies that are connected to water. These are female waters. And then there are other songs, prayers, and ceremonies that are connected to corn, female corn. And he used to tell me that "Everything that exists has a feminine aspect as its basis. Feminine is basic to this whole thing. That is very basic to our existence. We all came from female, everything that is living and breathing today." I don't see why anybody would say that females couldn't perform ceremonies and be leaders. Only after a female learns all these things, can she be whatever she wants to be. She can perform whatever ceremony she can. And she can be whatever leader she wants to be. Because everything is connected to female. . . . If they know the legend and the songs that are outlined here, that my uncle outlined, if they know these things, there's really nothing that a female cannot do. (Interview with Manson)

At the moment of its completion, the newly created world was in a state of "natural order" in which all living things were in their prescribed places and in their proper relationships with all other living things. But, this order was not destined to persist.

CHANGING WOMAN

> Changing Woman was the one who re-established order, uhm, told the people how they must live, gave them rules, and gave them Hózhǫ́ǫ́jí [the Blessing Way ceremony], and she was our first leader. And uhm, she was the one who told the men that their, that their role and responsibility is in the dá'ák'eh [cornfield] and in the other fields, and in hunting, you know, and that the woman, her

responsibility was in the home. And that both of them together, they take care of the children. And, and the women were the ones who were instructed, you know, like, you are gonna be here to teach men and women, little boys, little girls what it's like to be human, you know, to be humane. And that was, and that, and that's when she gave us, uhm, the sash belt. Her *sis łichí'í* and wrapped it around all of our waists so that we would remember every day when we wrap our sis łichi'í around us that we, we are the foundation of society. Society in the sense that there is order, that there is love, that there's peace, and that there is a sense of unity, and community. (Interview with Dooley, 1998)

As a direct result of the sexual abuses of the previous world, the newfound order was not fated to continue. According to Madalin Chavez of Coolidge, New Mexico, "From the deer vagina [used by men for masturbation during the separation], big snake was born from this" (interview with Chavez).[16] Monstrous creatures were also born to the young women who had abused themselves with objects such as petrified wood, fuzzy elk horn, feather quills, deer sinew, or whittled sour cactus (Haile 1981b:25–27; O'Bryan 1956:8; Stephen 1930:99; Yazzie 1971:30; Zolbrod 1984:63). Furthermore, because they had developed new carnal desires during the separation of the sexes, many women continued to practice aberrant sexual behaviors after the emergence (Fishler 1953:38–39; Haile 1938:77). Monsters were born to these individuals as well. One of the most fierce, Yé'ii Tsoh (Giant Monster), was born to a young woman after she masturbated with a stone while menstruating (Haile 1938:79).[17] When the women saw that their newborns were deformed, they abandoned them, leaving them to die where they were born. At first, the women did not even tell the men about the birth of these deformed beings. The monstrous babies, however, did not die. Instead, they flourished, grew huge, and began preying on healthy children, pushing Navajo ancestors to the brink of extinction.

Taking pity, the Diyin Dine'é intervened. They arranged for Asdzą́ą́ Nádleehé, "Changing Woman," the most highly revered of all Navajo Holy People, to be found at Ch'óol'į́į́. According to most published accounts, it was Talking God who found the baby and gave her over to First Man who took her home to First Woman. But Eunice Manson told me that during the time of peril, "First Man and the First Woman, particularly the First Woman, decided to go out and, and do something. It was she who found a child, this particular child" (interview with Manson). And, according to Laura Nix,

White Shell Woman was born like Jesus, the way they talk about Jesus, that was the way she was born. Early dawn, they heard a baby crying on top of Ch'óol'íí; they heard a baby crying. There was nobody around and they said, "Where is the crying baby?" Two of them took off early in the dawn and they went up on top of the Ch'óol'íí. On top of Ch'óol'íí there was a big round hole filled with water and with a cattail in the middle, and it was surrounded by mist. The baby was floating around in the water. So, "how will we pick it up and what will we wrap it in?" They started looking around and they found cliffrose. On the outside the cliffrose was rough, but inside was soft fiber. They picked the baby up folded in that fiber. They left and went home with the baby. When they brought it back they said, "This is what was crying in the dawn." They found out that it was a girl. So she became White Shell Woman. That is how the Blessing Way began. Every other day, they had Blessing Way for her, four times. (Interview with Nix)

They raised her in a "miracle way." Under the direction of the Holy People, they fed her sunray pollen, pollen from clouds, pollen from plants, and flower dew so that she matured miraculously. Some accounts reckon this growth in days, whereby in two she walked, in four she talked, and in twelve she began to menstruate (interview with Aronilth). Her menstruation symbolized the restoration of healthy reproduction on the earth and was cause for great rejoicing. The first Kinaaldá was celebrated in honor of the event. Others, such as Laura Nix, reckon her growth in years: "Within twelve years she had her *kinaaldá* [first menstruation]. That is where they tied her hair when she had her Kinaaldá [puberty ceremony], and then she ran four different directions—east, south, west, north. Up to this day we can't copy her. We can just run two directions, east and west, not four because White Shell Woman is the only one that did the four (interview with Nix).

Eunice Manson adds, "She became mature enough and she had her Kinaaldá, you know on the fourth day. And a, a ceremony was conducted for her then again, then again, and again, and until after the fourth time. There were four different Kinaaldá that were performed for her. Only then did the sunshine come back. And it was through a female's effort that it was brought back" (interview with Manson).

Shortly after this ceremony, Changing Woman took the next step necessary to restoration of order. According to Eunice Manson, "There were monsters and creatures that were on the land and their sole purpose was to destroy human beings. Well, it took a female to give birth. Changing Woman got pregnant, she got pregnant first for the sun, and then she got pregnant again, before she gave birth, for the water. So she bore two sons, a set of twins, and their sole purpose was to destroy the monsters, the creatures. And they became known as the monster slayers" (interview with Manson).

Irene Kee, of Crystal, New Mexico, maintains that the Navajo ancestors needed direction from the Holy People when Changing Woman went into labor because this marked the first childbirth, which established a precedent for all future Navajo births:

> This is how my story goes. When the children were about to be born, First Woman and First Man were confronted with what needs to be done. They wanted advice and were creating confusion amongst themselves. When their first child was to be born, they did not know that it was going to be twins. Talking God came to their front door. He instructed First Woman and First Man to place a beam inside the west side of the hooghan. "Place a sash belt over it, draping it evenly on both sides of the beam. She will hold onto the belt and will give birth doing that. I cannot be involved as I am afraid of the menstrual blood!" With that statement, he left and went on his way. They don't know where, probably went back to his own home. The first was a boy. Then another boy fell out. First Woman bathed the baby boys and placed them within the softened cedar barks. Just like what they did with their mother when they first found her. (Interview with Kee, 1992b)[18]

Changing Woman kept the boys close to home while they grew and hid them from the monsters so they would not be eaten. When they reached adolescence, the twins went on a quest to find their father. Once found, he made them endure several trials to prove they were his children. They persevered, and finally Sun supplied them with powerful weapons to slay the monsters. They worked together to slay all the monsters except Hunger, Poverty, Old Age, and Lice. The world was saved.

Over time, Changing Woman grew lonely for companionship and decided that there should be more people, so she created the Nihookáá Dine'é here on the earth's surface. By most published accounts, she did this by rubbing skin wastes from her breast, from her back, and from under her arms. She mixed this substance with ground white shell, turquoise, abalone, jet, and corn of all colors. Then she molded these materials into cylindrical forms that were ritually transformed into human beings. These beings were animated either by the breath of Changing Woman or by the entrance of Holy Winds (Matthews 1994 [1897]:147–48; Franciscan Fathers 1910:356; Goddard 1933:168; Wyman 1970:447–48; Yazzie 1971:74).

Many accounts, such as the following version told by Eunice Manson, detail the specific part of Changing Woman's body from which each clan was formed.

When the Holy People got together, they discussed the possibility of there being man, human beings. And there was only one person, one spirit that could create man, which was the White Shell Woman. She took the responsibility to create man and the way she did that was she traveled to the east in that spirit world. And while she sat there facing the east, she took a bit of her skin from between her breasts. And she made a man, a male out of that and she said, "You're going to be of the Towering House Clan." While sitting there, she also took a piece of her back in between her shoulder blades. She took a piece of that and she created the second man, a male. And she said, "You're going to be of the Water's Edge Clan." While sitting there, she also took a piece from her right arm and she created a woman. And she said, "You are going to be of the Chííshii Dine'é (Mescalero Apache Clan)." And she did likewise to her left arm and she created a female, another female. And she instructed her that she was then "of the Big Water Clan"[19] . . . Well, it was the White Shell Woman that did the special songs for the Diné to be in existence. That's why you cannot tell a female that she cannot perform certain songs. It was, after all, the White Shell Woman that sang these songs to create these first four basic people. (Interview with Manson)

These first Nihookáá Dine'é were not made to live as individuals; rather, they immediately were matched and paired to found the Navajo social order. It is generally agreed that Changing Woman selected men and women from the first Nihookáá Dine'é to live as husband and wife and thus established the four original clans of the Navajo and the practice of clan exogamy (Matthews 1994 [1897]:148; Reichard 1950:28; O'Bryan 1956:167; Wyman 1970:458, 634; Yazzie 1971:74; Aronilth 1985:83). When the first-born girl of the Nihookáá Dine'é came of age, Changing Woman instructed her relatives in performance of the Kinaaldá. It is she who dressed, molded, and guided the young woman through every step in the ceremony (Frisbie 1993 [1967]:13–15).

Shortly after, the Diyin Dine'é decided to give the world over to humans and then take their places as the inner forms of the features of Navajo sacred geography. Changing Woman became the inner form of the earth.[20] In preparation for turning the world over to them, Changing Woman and the other Diyin Dine'é arranged for the Nihookáá Dine'é to learn all necessary components of their ancestral knowledge—songs, prayers, ceremonies, and stories.

In the following account, Eunice Manson points out that when two children were sent to Changing Woman's home in the west to learn the Blessing Way ceremony (Fishler 1953:100; Wyman 1970:226–237), a boy *and* a girl were sent.

Two kids were sent, one was a little boy and the other one was a little girl. They were sent to the mountain back where the White Shell Woman existed. The White Shell Woman took time and she received the two children, the boy and the girl, and she took the time to teach them everything that she knew. And she sent them back and eventually the two children performed the ceremony that the White Shell Woman used to perform. And the rain came back, the people finally saw the clouds and the rainbow and the thunder and so forth, and it restored the land. A female can perform ceremonies that are meant to restore life, restore beauty, and all these other wonderful things. A woman, a female can perform all the ceremonies that a male can perform. You cannot accuse a female practitioner today that she is not supposed to be performing those. Nor can you accuse a woman who is today a leader that she is not supposed to be a leader because it is Changing Woman that brought back through her ceremonies and through her songs, that restored everything after the drought to bring back all these beautiful and wonderful things. (Interview with Manson)

Not only was a female child involved in the acquisition of Changing Woman's ceremonial knowledge but, as Elizabeth Edison explains in the following account, establishment of the first mountain earth bundles also has special import for Navajo women.

After we came out onto the surface of the earth, they made the mountain earth bundle for us Navajo women—Kinlichíi'nii [Red House People Clan], Tótsohnii [Big Water Clan], Bit'ahnii [Leaf Clan or Under his Cover Clan], Tł'ááshchí'í [The Red Bottom People Clan], and Chííshii Dine'é. This is how the mountain earth bundle was made for us. Anáályééł was also made at this time for the men. Dziłná'oodiłii, that is where twelve mountain earth bundles were made. That is where the first Blessing Way was performed. It was done for the mountain earth bundles. The twelve mountain earth bundles were taken by women from the clans, a woman from each different clan took one. Because of this, I don't believe in them saying that a woman cannot perform a ceremony. The mountain earth bundles were made for us women. Whether they like it or not I am doing my ceremony. . . . We are the ones that bore them, the men and boys. They are supposed to respect us and consider us leaders. We have songs and prayers within our hearts. We are entitled to learn to be singers. When they first made the mountain earth bundles, it was given to us way back there, so we have been able to become singers since then. (Interview with Edison)

"I MUST HAVE BEEN CHOSEN"

Women can perform because *it is a gift that is given to them from the Holy People* and that is how they learn to be performers. So women can do it. There is no way they can eliminate women singers. It is within their hearts that they learned. (Interview with Mariano)

AS How did you become a singer?

GD *I must have been chosen by the Holy People* and that is why things come to me easily. When I was helping my husband, probably the Holy People were watching me and I guess I did everything right and that was why I was chosen to do what I am doing. (Interview with Denny)[21]

Regardless of the precedents enshrined in Navajo oral history, several women with whom I consulted maintained that in the end, whether a woman learns a particular ceremony or not is up to the Holy People because the ability to become a ceremonial practitioner is dependent on receipt of a gift from them (interviews with Bekis, 1993; Denny; Edison; Mariano; Nez; Shorthair; anonymous woman, 1998; anonymous woman, 2000).[22] When an anonymous woman from Sanostee, New Mexico, asked her father if she could follow him he told her, "It's a gift that is given to you. Not something you just can take because you want to be known as a medicine woman!" (interview with anonymous woman, 2000). And, as Gaye Shorthair points out, ceremonial knowledge is a gift only given to select individuals by the Holy People.

MS OK, ask her why it is that she is interested in becoming a singer?

AS Mother, why did you become interested in learning?

GS I didn't want to learn, I just keep following my husband around and that is how I am learning. And all of a sudden, I started singing, so that is it. . . . It came to me by itself. *It is a gift from the Holy People to me.* . . . The Holy People choose them to be the singers. That is how it is. They are being surrounded by the Holy People. That is how they are performers. If the Holy People do not come to you, it is not going to happen, you won't learn. They are being selected by the Holy People to do this. That is why they are doing it. If you were not chosen, it wouldn't happen. (Interview with Shorthair)

In special cases, an individual's gift is indicated by a physical mark on the body. In a particularly eloquent account, Sara Ruth John, of "Between Black Butte and the Salt Water," near Indian Wells, Arizona, recalls how she was chosen and marked to perform the Tóee, "Water Way," and the 'Ats'osee, "Plume Way."

> **SJ** When I was a child, when I was five years old, I went into a coma. For nine days I was unconscious, when I was five. And they did a ceremony for me. That is when I came out of it. While I was unconscious, I went to the underworld and back. And I saw people down there. After I came back I was struck by lightning. From two o'clock to five o'clock I was unconscious again when the lightning struck me. I was struck by the lightning from above. My nálí (father's father) said, "You went both places, you were initiated both ways, down under and up. So it comes back together, and so you can do the ceremonial things that other women are told not to do, you can do them. You can do all things because you went both places. You are a lady, you can do all the things that you are capable of doing right now." So that is why I am the only one that knows this ceremony. I was unconscious. Here I am marked with it, the lightning. (Sarah exposes her left leg to show us a scar on her calf). . . . That is why I am doing all of these ceremonies. . . .
>
> **MS** Um, OK. Tell her that according to the Navajo oral history, some say that the men are supposed to control the ceremonial and political realms. And ask her if she thinks this is true.
>
> **AS** In the Navajo history, they say that only men are supposed to perform singing.
>
> **SJ** No, that is not true. Because nobody knows what I do now. Nobody else knows the ceremony. My nálí told me that "You went both places, that is why you are the one that is supposed to do this sing." . . . My nálí told me, "Whoever is struck by lightning and whoever had the same unconsciousness like you had, these are the only people that you can apprentice. You have been marked by the lightning. When you were struck, you were marked and then when you were unconscious, that is another mark on you. So that is why you can apprentice those who are like you." My nálí said, "You can apprentice a man, he doesn't have to be marked." But if I am going

to apprentice a lady, she has to be marked like me—struck by lightning and suffered unconsciousness. If they don't have those marks, I cannot apprentice them. (Interview with John)[23]

Collectively, these accounts imply that anyone who is performing a ceremony efficaciously has been chosen by the Holy People and is thus automatically sanctioned to be conducting the ritual.

CHAPTER III

"THE CEREMONY ITSELF
GOT A HOLD OF ME"

I did everything, even the drypaintings [commonly referred to as sandpaintings] and all that needs to be done in Hóchx̨ǫ́ǫ́'jí [Evil Way]. I did everything, and that is how I got it from the Holy People. It was as a gift for me from the Holy People. (Interview with Edison)

My uncle was the only one that was doing it. He was doing the Blessing Way. He was blind, so I helped him. I learned how to wash people and do other things, because he was blind. He sang while I did these things. The songs placed themselves in order, and I learned it that way. After that, I learned all of it. I never did follow him that much, just for a little bit. The songs, they just got in place by themselves while I was helping him. That is how I started. And some people say, "I can't learn these songs." And they can't pick them up. (Interview with Mariano)

I helped every way, in everything that he did [her husband Billie Emerson], I helped him. When he would make tsibąąs [ceremonial painted hoops], I would assist him. Four different hoops, on each day. Four white hoops are placed from the east on the first morning, four blue hoops are placed from the south the next morning, from the west on the third day yellow hoops are placed, and from the north on the fourth day four black hoops are placed. I did the drypaintings in between them while he was singing as the patient went through them. They put white material over the patient and she goes through the hoops, squatting down real low, at the last hoops I pulled the white material off of her and dropped it right there. The patient and whoever else wants to go through there can do it. Then they go inside. The purpose is, she is leaving all that is ailing her behind. That is Hóchxǫ́ǫ́'jí. I did all the helping in those areas—making hoops and drypaintings. On the fourth day, after the patient goes through the hoops and then inside the hooghan he washes his patient, that is where I help too. I do the drypainting for him and all of this I learned. I work for him on this. And when he is singing, I sing right along with him. . . . While I was doing the drypainting, he never said "Do it this way" or "that way." I just learned it the first time he taught it to me and from then on I was just doing it on my own. After I did all of the drypainting, I would say, "Now, I am through doing the drypainting." He would tell me, "Go ahead and put water and medicine in the shells. Go ahead and do that." When I tell him, "I am through now again." Then he tells me, "When I am singing, there will be a special song. When I start that, put the medicine in the patient's mouth." So that when he was singing, he would just motion for me to do this. At first I did not do this, in my fourth or fifth year of learning, I started recognizing these songs and what each one was for. So that when I was told to put medicine in the patient's mouth, I would know when to do it. I must have learned it pretty fast. That is how I learned the songs, I worked on them and I worked on the drypaintings, and I did not realize that I had learned everything. (Interview with Emerson)

A fundamental principle of Navajo pedagogy dictates that one must initially learn by doing; that is, attending an event and learning through silent observation, rather than verbal inquisitiveness or deliberate instruction. While this is followed by direct instruction, usually at the mentor's home, becoming a ceremonial practitioner is largely a complex process of observing, listening and, eventually, performing. As a result, on the continuum from performance to performativity, performance is dominant during the lengthy period of "following," or apprenticeship, wherein an individual attends ceremonies being conducted by a particular singer who subsequently becomes a mentor. Apprentices gradually do less observing and more of the acts integral to ceremonial practice. The women with whom I consulted provide narrative after narrative of time spent following a singer to distant ceremonies to "help out," learning songs, prayers, precise procedures such as the proper washing of a patient or the construction and placement of tsibąąs, and every detail of the complex oral traditions associated with the ceremony. For some, the process of following and performing tasks for a mentor begins at a very tender age.

Six out of the seventeen women practitioners I interviewed recalled following a parent or grandparent who was a ceremonial practitioner before she reached the age of seven. Helen Olsen Chee, of Many Farms, Arizona, remembers "When I was a young girl I was always with my grandmother who did the five-day ceremony so I knew what was going on and that is when I started learning" (interview with Chee).[1] Similarly, Juanita Mace recalls, "When I was small, as a child, I traveled with my father and my mother while he conducted [Blessing Way] ceremonies. During that time, I learned. He taught me from that time what the songs were about, which songs to sing" (interview with Mace). The account of Ramona Ettcity of Round Rock, Arizona, of traveling with her grandfather Roland Johnson, provides insight into the unstructured nature of such learning.

MS At what age did you begin learning the ceremony?

RE I don't know how small, my grandfather was a medicine man, he did Blessing Way. . . . He was always going out places, I don't know why, I guess there was no babysitter, that's why sometimes I had to go with my grandfather on a horse, down that way, they call it "Liktó'." Those people, he makes ceremony down there, sometimes, uhm, he makes a ceremony, it takes two days, and then if another lady or somebody else around there [needs him], we have to stay there and go to the next. Stay there and then we wouldn't go home until I sit on the back of the horse.

MS So this was before you started going to Shiprock boarding school?

RE Yeah, at that time we didn't have no truck, my grandfather didn't have no truck, just a horse and wagon.

MS Right.

RE So . . .

MS Yeah. So you started following your grandfather when you were very young.

RE Yeah, he didn't say, "Learn this," but he'll, I guess I was just being babysat by him.

MS Uh-huh.

RE And he sing all the songs over and over, so it just seemed like a Christmas song to me, I remembered, and what's next, and . . .

MS Yeah.

RE I started real small. (Interview with Etcitty)[2]

Nettie Nez's description of watching and listening well captures the means by which ceremonial knowledge is acquired by children following parents or grand-parents.

> From when I was a young child, my mother performed the Enemy Way Blessing Way and prayers, there are different types of prayers, and offering of precious stones (Nt'liz ni'nil). I used to watch her do these things from when I was a young girl. I watched her do the prayer and I learned all of that by listening and watching the way she was doing it. I followed her, she does prayers and all that, and I go follow her. After she died, I started performing. I am still doing it up to today. I am performing the Enemy Way Blessing Way, I do prayers, and Nt'liz ni'nil that I learned from my mother. (Interview with Nez)

Agnes Begay Dennison, of Round Rock, Arizona, recalls that she began learning sometime between the ages of six and seven:

> **ABD** Goldtooth Begay Number One is my father. I started with my father when I was six or seven years old. And when he'd do the ceremony at, at our, you know, here, with the family, he'd tell me everything, you know. So I started [getting] interested in it, and he started singing, you know, Blessing Way and I sit by him, singing, you know, with him.
>
> **MS** Mm-hmm.
>
> **ABD** So, when I about twelve years old, I knew most of the, most of the songs and most of the prayers and everything. That's on the Blessing Way.
>
> **MS** The Blessing Way.
>
> **ABD** Mm-hmm.
>
> **MS** OK.
>
> **ABD** And he, uh, he did the uh, five-days sing, too.
>
> **MS** Which five-days ceremony did he do?
>
> **ABD** How, how do you say it?
>
> **MS** What is the name of it in Navajo?
>
> **ABD** Uh, Navajo is, uh, Na'at'oyee [Shooting or Lightning Way] You know those Thunder? Thunder, thunder?
>
> **MS** OK, Lightning Way.

ABD Yeah.

MS All right.

ABD I know, I used to sing, you know, those, uh, five-days, I used to sing with him, too.

MS Uh-huh.

ABD But that one, I didn't get it all. (Interview with Dennison)

Laura Nix and Mary Ben Jones Whitney apprenticed at the youthful ages of twelve and fourteen respectively. As Laura Nix recalls:

I learned from my dad, Knox Walker was his name. I was twelve years old. They told me, "Learn it." I didn't know what they were saying in their songs and prayers, but they kept telling me to learn it. My dad said he had been doing it for a long time. I used to lie by him when he was teaching me. He did the Kinaaldá and the regular Blessing Way. That is how I started. . . . My dad did a five-day sing too. He was the only one around this area that did the Blessing Way and the five-night ceremony. I learned just a few songs at a time, in each year. Then I started putting it together. Lately, my dad went into old age at the age of one hundred. I started following my brother Frank Walker and I fixed the songs then. For nineteen years, I was following my brother and putting songs together to make it in order. Until nine or ten years ago, I was just putting it together. The prayers too. After I started following my brother around, I started putting them together right. That was my brother. He is gone. Before he died, he had it all in order for me, and he told me, "Now go ahead." (Interview with Nix)

Mary Ben Jones Whitney of Tohatchi, New Mexico, notes:

My father was a medicine man. He did different kinds of singing— Blessing Way, and others. When I was younger I used to see him do these things and then I started learning from him. I helped him. He did the Blessing Way and I used to follow him for a long time. After that I picked the Blessing Way up and that is what my title is. That is what I do. And the other ceremonies, no. I never picked up any other ceremonies. I do Blessing Way and Kinaaldá. Days or nights, all the time. . . . I started at fourteen years of age. (Interview with Whitney)

These women were essentially raised on the ceremonies they now perform or are apprenticing because, as noted in their personal accounts, they were each in the nearly constant company of a singer and thus surrounded by the ceremony during their formative years. Madalin Chavez, Louella Deswood, and Sunny Dooley took up ceremonial apprenticeship in their twenties, while many other women took up an apprenticeship after the age of thirty.

The age at which women I interviewed began apprenticing ranges from six to forty-four, with an average age of twenty-four years. In comparison to data gathered on men singers, this information reveals that, while the age at which an apprenticeship begins varies widely for both men and women, the age at which women in my study began apprenticing is older than Hastiin T'łah, roughly the same as Frank Mitchell and the men in Ch'iao's study, and a bit younger than men studied by Henderson and Sandner.[3] Since the average age of twenty-four years correlates with the childbearing years, factors such as sexual relations, pregnancy, and nursing must be taken into consideration for women apprentices.

REPRODUCTION

> You don't have sexual relations with your man. Like for example, when my mother was teaching me about the prayer, and here I am repeating that prayer trying to put it together. You are doing it now and you can't just go in and crawl into bed with your husband. You can't until after you wash. (Interview with Nez)

Women consistently maintained that sexual relations are forbidden to apprentices for a specific time period after instruction in ceremonial matters or attendance at a ceremony.[4] As noted by Nettie Nez, this can be until after cleansing oneself (interview with Nez). Other women reported longer periods of continence. Laura Nix told us, "You just don't do that until after four days" (interview with Nix). Betty Begay reiterated the four-day rule and noted that this is "because you are helping over there like doing drypaintings and things like that" (interview with Begay). The prohibition against mixing sexuality and ceremonial contexts is so strong that women must not show any affection toward their spouses or even sit near them during ceremonies (interviews with Begay; Bekis, 1993; Shorthair). In the words of Betty Begay, "It is important. You do not bother the man or have any relations. . . . You don't do sexual activity and you must be careful when doing ceremonial things, these rules my husband taught me. When I follow him, I don't bother him. He has to sit away from me. There has to be someone between us" (interview with Begay).

In marked contrast to these consistent recitations of the rule against combining sex with ceremonies, which women reported without exception, opinions vary amongst the women with whom I consulted regarding attendance at ceremonies while pregnant or nursing a child. When asked about pregnancy, Elizabeth Edison stated emphatically. "I did everything! I told you. I learned from two people, my husband and his grandfather, they taught me everything and I did everything when I was pregnant. There was nothing they kept from me. Pregnancy didn't slow me down. I did everything. I did everything!" (interview with Edison). And although the occasion did not arise, Sarah Ruth John maintained,

> I would have been able to apprenticeship [Water Way] under my father when I was pregnant, but I didn't need to. My youngest child is six years old, and my oldest is thirty-seven, and my fourth son [youngest from that father] is thirty, and my youngest boy is six years old, in between I didn't have any kids, and that is where I learned. So, I did not apprentice while I was pregnant. I had my first son, and then four children in between. I was alone for twenty-four years, then I had my last child. Twenty-four years, I was by myself. And then I had that little boy. I did all of my learning in those twenty-four years. (Interview with John)

Women generally agreed that it is acceptable for a woman to apprentice the Blessing Way while pregnant (interviews with Chavez, Chee, Higdon, Mariano, Nix, Yazzie) or nursing a baby (interview with Mariano). Yet, when asked if she was able to follow her mother to the Enemy Way Blessing Way version of the Blessing Way ceremony while pregnant, Nettie Nez replied "No. I never did that" (interview with Nez), without offering an explanation.

Like Elizabeth Edison, Pearly Yazzie, who started apprenticing for the Blessing Way while pregnant with her last child said, "I did everything!" (interview with Yazzie). Laura Nix pointed out that pregnant women who attend Blessing Way could actually benefit from the ceremony.

> When I was pregnant, I usually went along because this has nothing to do with blood. It is for a baby, to be born right, and it is supposed to have a good life too. That is why I went along and helped. It is going to be a healthy baby, it is going to speak right, when it starts growing it is going to have a better life. A boy or a girl, they will have a good future. That is why we have Blessing Way for pregnant ladies. That is why I was allowed to go. It is for the good of the baby. Yes, you are doing it for a pregnant lady, but when you are pregnant it is good for you too so you are allowed to go there. They did it for me when I was pregnant and I went there, there is nothing wrong with it. There, I was learning what they

were all doing there. If a singer has a little different prayers and techniques, that is why I went. (Interview with Nix)

Women cautioned, however, that it is not safe to perform a Blessing Way until after a certain point in the child's development, that is after four months when the child has begun to move in the womb (interview with Bekis, 2001) or after eight months when the child has fingers, hair, and eyes (interview with Agnes B. Dennison). Laura Nix and Mary Ben Jones Whitney confirmed the latter precaution (interviews with Nix, Whitney) but noted that it is acceptable for women to apprentice the Blessing Way while less than eight months pregnant. By way of explanation, Mary Ben Jones Whitney said:

> Because I am just a performer, I have a way to do that. It will not harm my four-month-old fetus. I was just helping out with the songs and the prayers. I was not having a ceremony done. I was just helping my dad. It would not harm my fetus. So, I could go ahead and perform. When I was pregnant I followed my dad and learned all these things—the prayers and the Blessing Way singing. I learned what was going on so that when my time comes around, I know what to do. I could perform the songs and prayers for others without harming my own unborn child. (Interview with Whitney)

And Laura Nix told us, "They weren't performing on me, but for the patient. I am just watching when they are performing for a pregnant woman that is to have her baby. Yes, I went over there and I tried to learn more, like on the prayers and things like that. That is why I went over there, to watch and listen" (interview with Nix).

In the view of Madalin Chavez, pregnant apprentices are free to attend Blessing Way because of the content of the ceremony.

> AS When you were pregnant, did you keep on learning?
>
> MC Yes, because in my ceremony they sing the baby songs and the cradleboard songs. All parts of the cradleboard, they sing about them. They have different names. White corn, yellow corn, whatever you wrap the baby in, these are the baby's blanket, whatever you put on the baby or wrap the baby in. That is what they sing about and that is what they pray about. I was entitled to learn, even when I was pregnant. . . . That is what they sing about, so even when you are pregnant, you can still learn. When you do a hooghan song, after you do that, that is when you sing the baby song if you are performing for a pregnant woman. (Interview with Chavez)

Irma Wheeler Higdon reported that the reason she was able to follow her father to Blessing Way ceremonies while pregnant is "Because there are no drypaintings. All he did was the sing at night. No drypaintings" (interview with Higdon).[5] Irma Wheeler Higdon's concern resonates with concerns voiced by others about pregnant women attending any ceremony with drypaintings or body painting (personal conversation with Bekis, 2001d; interviews with Chee, Agnes B. Dennison). Mae Ann Bekis points out, "When you are pregnant you are not even supposed to see a patient that is painted up. That can cause birth defects. So with the Lightning Way, Plume Way, or Water Way, you are not supposed to see patients when they are painted up, if you are pregnant" (personal conversation with Bekis, 2001c).

According to Helen Olsen Chee, neither a pregnant lady nor the father of the unborn child should see paraphernalia at Night Way or Enemy Way ceremonies, nor should they see drypaintings at any type of ceremony. "Neither the expectant mother nor the husband should see the Yé'ii Bicheii [Grandfathers of the Holy People] or the drypaintings. They should not see the masks at Yé'ii Bicheii [colloquialism for Tł'éé' jí, Night Way]. Neither should they see the staff or the scalp at an Anaa' jí ndáá' [Enemy Way]. Or any drypainting from any ceremony" (interview with Chee). Gaye Shorthair offered the following account of how an unborn child might be affected by exposure to a Night Way ceremony: "Sometimes it might be paralyzed on one side, or it can harm its hearing or its eyes. There are many, many ways that children can be affected by it. There is one that we call a clown. He runs around and does a lot of silly things. If a child is affected by it, the child would be moving all the time and its mind won't be all there. It becomes our job, we have to refix all this even though it wasn't at our singing, still we have to fix them. We do a lot of that too" (interview with Shorthair).

Grace Emerson reports that she could assist her husband in the performance of the Hóchxǫ́ǫ́'jí (Evil Way) while pregnant, but alterations needed to be made in the drypaintings:

> I was having children while I was helping my first husband. With my first husband I had four children. They were little children when I was following my husband around learning. I was pregnant too when I was following him. But when I did the snakes, I had to leave an opening at the tail so that it won't hurt the unborn child. Either way, the tail or the head, leave it open there and that way it won't affect the unborn child. They make four snakes—a black one, a blue one, a yellow one, and a white one. Each one of them has a border color, just leave an opening on one snake, not all of them. People know it. A pregnant woman can't be where they are making a drypainting. She can't watch it being made. She must stay away even if her husband is performing. And the women know that when

they are pregnant they are not supposed to go to a ceremony, even
if they live somewhere where a ceremony is going on. (Interview
with Emerson)

Leaving an opening in the snake border allows a pregnant woman to do a drypainting but she must not be there when the drypaintings are disassembled (personal
conversation with Bekis, 2001c).

Despite these precautions, in the case of an emergency, a pregnant woman may
have a ceremony performed over her that includes drypaintings. For example, a
woman from Del Muerto, Arizona, told me "I was pregnant when the Snake Way
ceremony was sung for me" (interview with anonymous woman, 1998). In such
cases, the practitioner will save some medicine from the ceremony for the mother
to give to the child after it is born to avoid negative effect (personal conversation
with Bekis, 2001c).

Betty Begay reports that theoretically she could not follow her husband, a
practitioner of the Na'at'oii bika', "Male Shooting Way," while pregnant because of
the harm that could befall the yet-to-be-born child, but on occasion it was necessary for her to assist. As she explains,

> I never went when I was pregnant because it would affect the
> unborn baby. Also, when you are pregnant, when you go to a sing,
> you cannot do any tying because it can cause deformities in the
> unborn child. That is why, when I was pregnant I stayed home and
> he went ahead and did the singing. It can cause birth defects.
> Sometimes there was not enough help, and my husband would
> need me to help even when I was pregnant. I could do drypainting,
> but I had to be sure to do it perfect and not make a mistake on it and
> that way it will not affect the unborn baby. We did it this way so all
> of our children are fine, they have no problems physical-wise. All
> four of them. My husband told me "All these things that we do like
> the drypainting and other parts of the ceremony, we have to do
> them right—the eyes, the face, the legs—everything must be done
> right. We must be careful and do it correctly, so that we won't hurt
> our children. So that our children will be fine." When making
> drypaintings, sometimes you make the eyes crooked and it will
> bother the baby. When making the body, you must make it straight
> or it will affect your baby or your children in the future. I think it is
> true. (Interview with Begay)

Moreover, she cautioned that if a woman should accidentally walk in upon drypainting in progress she could not just leave. As she explains, "When they are

making a drypainting, if a woman, a man, or a girl walks in, they cannot just walk out. Anyone who walks in upon people working on a drypainting must help out, just one line, even just a little way. They will show you how. You must help out before you leave. They are very careful about it" (interview with Begay).

In addition to cautions about drypaintings, women pointed out that pregnant women should not be present at a bundle retying because witnessing this process could bind up the child and make childbirth more difficult (interviews with Bekis, 1998a; John; Yazzie). Helen Olsen Chee explains that this prohibition also applies to the father-to-be:

> If a lady is pregnant and if she wants to learn or her husband wants to learn, either one can learn the songs and things like that [meaning go to the singer's home to learn songs at night] or attend the ceremony. But neither one can watch a mountain earth bundle retying because the bundle is going to be tied for four years before it will be reopened, so if the mother or father-to-be sees that the mother will have a hard time when having the child. We usually sew *tádídíín* [corn pollen] bags when there is a Blessing Way going on. If you are pregnant you cannot sew such a bag because the stitches will show someplace on the baby's body or the cord will wrap around the baby's neck. The same with a basket too, you cannot sew baskets while pregnant because they are sewn forever too. Anything that is sewn you cannot do it because you are sewing the baby, like he or she is part of the thread or whatever is being sewn. . . . These are the things. A lot of the pregnant ladies are doing what they are not supposed to do and that is why they are having a hard time having babies. They are just having C-sections and that is how they are having the babies taken out. If all of them knew these things, the dos and don'ts, they would not have a hard time in having their babies. I had all my kids, but I never had a hard time because I know all of these things. (Interview with Chee)

Mae Ann Bekis expands on this point by adding that tying of bundles may cause the cord to wrap around the baby's neck, for the mother to have a prolonged labor, or for the child to have a defect (personal conversation with Bekis, 2001b). She also itemized the following rules that apply specifically to the father-to-be. "He cannot sew leather horse gear, tádídíín bags, or baskets. Also, neither the mother nor the father-to-be can make a weaving fork while the mother is pregnant or the baby will have extra toes or fingers. And then a man cannot castrate calves or sheep when his wife is pregnant" (personal conversation with Bekis, 2001a). In addition, she relayed that if a pregnant apprentice beats the basket throughout an all-night ceremonial, the child's hearing might be affected (personal conversation with Bekis, 2001b).

Regardless of the age an apprenticeship begins or one's life circumstances while apprenticing, a variety of techniques might be used to build stamina and assist with learning.

TECHNIQUES

> When I was a young child I used to sing while riding a horse to help develop my voice. My grandpa told me to do that. That way you can have a voice. If you don't do that you will have a poor voice, you can only sing a little while before losing your voice. But if you sing while riding a horse your voice gets strong and you will be able to sing all through the ceremony. You have to sit up straight. You have to get up early in the morning and run. (Interview with John)

> **MS** OK, another thing was, some people have mentioned, uhm, like one woman mentioned that when she was growing up her, her father told her to always sing in order to strengthen her voice. Were there any things that John Bull told you or anyone, maybe your mother or father, about strengthening your voice when you were growing up?
>
> **MB** I have been all the time. When I was little . . .
>
> **MS** You did what?
>
> **MB** and people, you know, when I herd sheep, I would sing like a Navajo song, you know, way out there I could sing it as loud as I can, all the time. And then when I had my Kinaaldá, I yelled when I run, all the four days . . .
>
> **MS** Uh-huh.
>
> **MB** and uh, but in between, I always did, you know, like, uh, sing to little kids, you know, like, nursery rhymes, in English and Navajo, and kept my voice up that way. And then when I started following my uncle around, he said, "You have the voice for singing and you should stick to it." (Interview with Bekis, 1998b)

Women consultants mentioned various techniques such as singing while herding sheep (interview with Bekis, 1998b) or riding a horse (interview with John) used to build one's voice, and techniques such as running in the early morning (interviews with Bekis, 1998b; Chavez; John) or rolling in snow (interview with Chavez) to build the physical strength and endurance needed by practitioners who often perform for five or more days consecutively.

In addition, consultants described various means by which to aid the learning of songs. For example, Gladys Denny told us, "I have been eating the corn kernels from the yucca drumstick all along, when I beat the drum for my husband when he performed.[6] You eat the corn kernels because it makes your voice good and strong" (interview with Denny). Along a similar vein, Madalin Chavez described a special process called "eating songs" used by her mentor Kenny Begay to aid her remembrance of ceremonial songs.

> AS How old were you?
>
> MC Twenty-nine, I was learning from his mouth. I used to run and I used to undress and roll in the snow. I used to run and I roll in the snow, early in the morning. He made eating songs for me.
>
> AS What do you mean by eating songs?
>
> MC There is a song called "Twelve." That is what I learned first. With running, I got tired and sweaty. I rolled in the snow after that to toughen myself for it. You make yourself strong any way that you can. Then, he told me to get twelve white corn kernels and sand from the water that ran, a little bit of that is picked up, the dirt. That and the corn, I ate while I was singing. I was not supposed to miss any part of the song, and I ate the corn with it. You also have twelve yellow corn kernels. You eat all of that too. . . . When you are singing, they put something in your mouth toward dawn and at midnight and then during the Hooghan Songs. They put something on you during the Hooghan Songs, the midnight and the dawn. . . . The cedar trees were cut off slanted. He warned me to be careful not to miss any part of the Hooghan Songs while I ate these things. That is how they made it for me. . . . All the songs that you are singing during the night, they put something in your mouth all of the time. When you take this thing, the songs come in order for me. The Holy People provide the songs for me. They are ready to be sung. The song itself comes in front of you. (Interview with Chavez)[7]

Toward the same end, Mae Ann Bekis carries with her a small piece of turquoise that was put into a baby coyote's mouth. As she explains, "My brother Paul, who was a singer of the Flint Way, took pieces of turquoise up and put them into a baby coyote's mouth. He did that because the coyotes howl so long and strong. He gave it to me in 1981 while I was learning from my uncle" (personal conversation with Bekis, 2001f).[8]

Moreover, due to the power of Navajo language, apprentices are cautioned to only speak positively about their progress in learning the ceremony. As Mae Ann Bekis explains, if one speaks negatively it can impair one's progress or halt it entirely.

> **MB** And even when you're talking, you know, like, you can't say, "I don't know the songs," even though you don't know you say, "Oh, I do," you know, "I like that song. I like to learn it." And that's the way you put it. And you don't say, "I don't know."
>
> **MS** Why?
>
> **MB** Because you wouldn't know. It'll never come to you.
>
> **MS** Oh, I see.
>
> **MB** Like she, you know, she, she, people tell her, "Oh, you're learning." "Oh," she says, "No, I'm not learning," She says, "I'm just going, uh, after my sister to eat."
>
> **MS** So she is . . .
>
> **MB** So that's why . . .
>
> **MS** impairing her ability to learn . . .
>
> **MB** when she's, yes, uh, she's, uh, she's letting that away, like pushing it, like pushing her kids away.
>
> **MS** Right.
>
> **MB** That's why it's not staying with her. (Interview with Bekis, 1998a)

While corn, special turquoise, and a positive attitude are deemed appropriate learning aids, consultants adamantly criticized the use of recording devices. For instance, during our interview Eunice Manson noted: "I am told that there are other female practitioners that actually use recording devices to record the songs that they want to learn and that that's how they learn, but I didn't do mine that way. I did it all by heart and by memory" (interview with Manson). Mary Ben Jones Whitney insisted, "I never learned with the use of a tape recorder, or I never had it written down on a piece of paper. I learned it by mouth. I learned from my dad. I did not have it written down or tape-recorded, that is how I learned" (interview with Whitney). And, at the close of our discussion, Ramona Etcitty made a point of adding, "One more thing. I learned the hard way. My grandfather said, 'No tape recorder!' I had to learn from the ceremony. He didn't want any recorded on him!" (interview with Etcitty).

As pointed out by numerous consultants (interviews with Denny; Edison; Mariano; Shorthair; anonymous woman, 1998), age of initial apprenticeship and well-intentioned techniques are ultimately irrelevant however, because ceremonial knowledge is a gift only given to select individuals by the Holy People. Thus, whether an individual is placed in the proper context and provided with aids or not, she will only learn if chosen by the Holy People. As a woman from Del Muerto, Arizona, notes:

> If it is not given to you, you will not learn, you will not be able to remember the song and prayers. It wasn't a gift to me. That is why I never did learn. . . . My uncle wanted me to learn a horse song. I never could learn it. He sang it and I sang it right along with him, but I never learned it. I never, never learned. If it is not given to you, you can't learn it. (Interview with anonymous woman, 1998)

This account reveals that personal desire is not enough, for without a gift from the Holy People learning is impossible. Simply put, if an individual is not specifically selected by the Holy People for this role, the words and melodies of particular songs will not remain with her and their proper order will be forever elusive.

MOTIVATION

> **MS** What thoughts at first did you think, when you were first considering becoming a medicine woman?
>
> **JM** Back then, I did not consider becoming a medicine woman. The ceremony itself got a hold of me. It filled me up. I helped my father, because he was growing old while conducting ceremonies. He got old for his songs, that is where I helped him. He instructed me to help here, and he would always ask me to help here and there. That is how I got into this ceremony. He prepared me for this ceremony and he handed me his ceremony. As time continued, my father died. I helped my mother from there on, and she died, too. From there I walked out alone. I started with conducting an all-night ceremony for Kinaaldá. That is how I started and it took a long time for me to come to where I am at now. (Interview with Mace)

Like Juanita Mace, many female singers profess no personal intent to become ceremonial practitioners. Nettie Nez stated, "I never asked that I would do this. It was given to me, so that is why I picked it up" (interview with Nez). Grace Emerson told me "I did not know that the songs were coming to me too. So, I did not think I was going to learn it, I did not plan to learn it" (interview with Emerson). For Pearly Yazzie, weaving rugs was her work at home after she started having children, until two clan brothers suggested that she learn the Blessing Way. With the help of her daughter Nancy Yazzie, we had the following discussion on the matter:

> NY OK, When you were little, when you grew up, tell us about your history. Just you, when you had your puberty, and when did you get married, and how old were you?
>
> PY I lost my mother and my sister is the one that raised me. All I did was herd sheep. That was my job. At thirteen I had my puberty. When I was seventeen, I married your dad. I lived with him and I started living by myself, I had my own house, I never went back to my sister's house, I just made my own home. I had sheep and horses and cows. First we just took care of our horses and sheep, until two Kinyaa'áanii [Towering House] clan brothers named Bahozhooni Begay and Hastiin Nez Badani told me, "You need to have a Blessing Way done so that you will have strength and a better life in the future." One of them did a Blessing Way for me. . . . Even though I didn't have a dad or a mother, I did not do anything bad. I had a good life. When I got married, we had a good life together. I had children and that became my work. We had ten children that we raised. While I was pregnant with my last child, I still used the Blessing Way for my own use and the medicine men who did the sing for me told me to learn some of the Blessing Way. They showed me how to do it and told me to learn it. Your dad knew it and they told me to follow them so that I could learn. My dad knew other songs, other ceremonies, but all I did was begin learning the Blessing Way. I didn't think I was going to perform Blessing Way. But the people around me told me to do Blessing Way for them. Even after your daddy died, I still performed until two years ago. That is when I stopped. From last year, I had a health problem, my legs bothered me, that is when I started carrying a walker around. That is why I have this walker, my leg bothers me. So I raised my kids with that. (Interview with Yazzie)

When queried regarding motivation, Mae Ann Bekis and Louella Deswood each replied "I like the songs" (interviews with Bekis, 1998a; Deswood). Irma Wheeler Higdon also reports that appreciation for ceremonial song inspired her to accompany her father rather than an intention to apprentice. As she put it, "I just want to, to know. My father has a real nice song when he is singing, he had real nice songs. So I really liked it, so that is why I followed him" (interview with Higdon). And when I pressed her she continued:

IH I never think that "I'm gonna be a, I'm becoming a medicine lady." I just loved that song and loved to hear it. That is all [why] I was doing that. . . .

MS So, while you were apprenticing, you did not realize you were apprenticing?

IH Uh-huh.

MS You were just,

IH I just became a medicine woman, I did not even practice or nothing.

MS You just followed your father and learned.

IH Uh-huh, I just followed my dad, when he goes to, he is going to do the medicine for somebody and now, he told me that, "I am going over there and you come." So, I go over there, you know, sit there and watch what he is doing. This is how I learned.

MS Uh-huh. (Interview with Higdon)

In like fashion, Louella Deswood told me that she never intended to become a practitioner. Rather, she always enjoyed being involved in ceremonial contexts. She especially liked it when she was given a gift in exchange for her assistance. She recalls using such items in an attempt to appease her mother over the fact that family expectations for her were lowered after she refused to participate in the Kinaaldá they planned for her. As she recollects, "I liked the feeling of being able to bring something from the ceremony, that was given directly to me, and bring it home to my mother and say 'Look, I got this from the ceremony.' Again, you know, make her feel proud because back there I did not do Kinaaldá and then everybody was just kind of frustrated with me so [chuckles], and then I was, maybe I was trying to prove to them that I would still be able to accumulate and accomplish a lot of things even though I did not do that [a Kinaaldá] there" [Chuckles] (interview with Deswood).

At the time that she began following her would-be mentor, Louella Deswood did not even realize that she was apprenticing. As she explains, her initial intention was to provide needed assistance to an elderly relative. As time went on, however, her motivations shifted.

MS Now, um, in a way you have talked about this but you didn't really address it directly. Why did you want to become a ceremonial practitioner?

LD I didn't want to be the practitioner.

MS You didn't want to be a practitioner?

LD No, I wanted to be able to, to be able to know the songs. I wanted to be able to be there and then know that I am going to sing, just express, you know, just express my emotions through singing. I mean, you don't know how much pleasure we get out of singing and then being out there. And, I wanted to be able to do that. . . . But um, I got forced into it because my grandfather [Harvey Johnson] got sick. . . . I liked the feeling of being there and then having people, you know, bring out the corn pollen and show respect. . . .

MS So in other words you knew what type of prestige you could expect as a ceremonial practitioner?

LD Yeah, they had the best, they had the best spot in the hooghan! [Chuckles]. And then, they had the best spot in the hooghan, and they had the best cuts of the meat.

MS And you sought that?

LD And I sought that yeah. And then, everybody, everywhere, he commanded a lot of respect; he commanded a lot of people and told them that his word was it. And, just one word, just maybe the second word he would tell them, "Look here!" you know, maybe he'd use a little profanity there. And then you will, you cannot feel offended by it, you have to do it regardless. And I liked that. I liked that superior attitude. [Laughs]

MS You felt you could walk in those shoes?

LD I felt I could. And I knew I would, I felt I could and I will. That didn't come until after four years, after being an apprentice. I didn't even think of myself as an apprentice. I was just only helping him out.

MS I understand.

LD I wasn't even saying that I was an apprentice. (Interview with Deswood)

When she found herself at a crossroads regarding her career, Louella Deswood's grandfather urged her to become a singer, because as he put it, "This is stability. This is stability. If this is the stability and also the calm that you need in your life then you would go this way, but it is up to you" (interview with Deswood). In similar fashion, Madalin Chavez recalls, "Way back there, my grandfather said, 'It is good that you didn't go to school. If you had gone to school you would only get paid a little bit every two weeks and you would be hungry. Since you learned all of this [the ceremonies], you will never be hungry and always have all the things you want, cows, sheep, jewelries, blankets, material, and money. This is what it is'" (interview with Chavez).

This rationale correlates with that used by Frank Mitchell's father-in-law while trying to convince him to become a practitioner (1978:193–194), it echoes the advice given to two men in Ch'iao's study (1971:19),[9] and it is what community leaders sought for Lucky when they decided his best option would be to become a singer (Griffen 1992:14, 15).

Regardless of how random one's initial involvement is, one form of personal motivation or another ultimately becomes an important factor for most apprentices because acceptance of such a gift from the Holy People requires the taking on of a difficult lifestyle, which includes numerous hardships and enormous responsibilities. When I asked women why they wanted to become ceremonial practitioners, they responded with a variety of reasons for deciding to accept the gift. Madalin Chavez replied, "Because I didn't go to school, my sisters and my children, they are the ones that went to school" (interview with Chavez). And, Nettie Nez told me "Because my mother was a medicine person, that is why. I wanted to be like her" (interview with Nez). The passing on of ceremonial knowledge through generations within a family or a clan is a common theme mentioned by consultants for choosing this role in life. Helen Olsen Chee stressed the importance of carrying on a family tradition by continuing the ceremony of her grandfather "The No Talk Man." As she explains,

> My grandfather's song that is, and then my mother learned it, and then me. . . . My mother learned it first and she started doing all of this and then it came down to me and I started doing it. Even though my grandfather did all of these and then my mother learned it from him, and then I learned it from my mother, it is still coming down from my grandfather. The five-day sing is my grandmother's. She learned that. My grandmother is the one that learned how to do the Hááhóyátééh [Restoration Prayer] and then the rite for someone struck by lightning. . . . My grandfather [Red Mustache] and his father did the singing too. The songs were brought down from my great-grandfather and my grandmother and it is all brought down, the singing, through the family and it came down to me. That is what my mother [Daughter of Red Mustache] is doing. The Blessing Way is from my great-grandfather [No Talking Man] and he is the one that taught me and then my mother does the same thing too and we are all doing the same thing that my grandfather told us to do. . . . These songs came down from my great-grandmother, the Singing Lady, to my grandfather, to my mother and to me. This is four generations now. That is all I know. (Interview with Chee)

Laura Nix resonates these concerns while recalling being motivated to continue her father's ceremony for the benefit of her children and grandchildren:

> My other brother, Tommy Walker, my brother Frank Walker and me, all three of us, we carried on that tradition from our father [Knox Walker]. It was just brought down. After we brought that down from my dad, I said to myself, Who is going to do it for us? So, I might as well do it. That is why I am doing it now, the Blessing Way. It is going to be good, I am going to do it for my kids, my grandkids and for my people, that is what I thought. So I just picked the whole thing up. I am doing it for my children, some are in the service, and in school and a lot of them are working. That is how I use it. I stand for them with my prayers and ceremony. They have dangerous and important jobs. (Interview with Nix)

Fulfillment of family need is another consistent theme of women's reasons for seeking ceremonial knowledge. For example, Sunny Dooley describes her motivation to learn about ceremonial matters:

> My mother got really ill, and when she did, I realized that nobody in my family really had the traditional knowledge or wisdom for my family to con-, to continue because my mom, she has this basket full of stuff, full of bundles and, you know, what-nots and, and nobody knew what was in there. And, uhm, I sort of had an idea what the things were 'cause some of them were for the horses, some of them were for the sheep, some of them were for the house, and some of them were for the family. And when we had the first ceremony, all my sisters, you know, they just kept kind of looking at each other and I was kind of like the one saying, well, that's what that one is for. So, that's sort of like how it started and, uhm, and then I really started looking around and I thought, nobody in my home right now would know a lot of the meaning to all of this. And so that's sort of like where I got really serious. (Interview with Dooley, 1998)

Mary Ben Jones Whitney recalls, "My dad used to really do a good job in doing the Blessing Way. I was thinking of myself, that since my dad did it, someday I could use it in turn to help myself, and my children and others. That is why I started practicing" (interview with Whitney). Along a similar vein, while discussing her motivation for taking on the Blessing Way, Agnes Begay Dennison recollects her father's advice regarding ceremonial matters.

ABD My father told me what's, you know, all the songs about it, which song belongs to this and this and that, all the Holy People. And then he told me that, "Whenever you grow up, when you have a family, when you get married, when you have children, and then you're gonna have to need this, you're gonna have to need this prayer, songs." And then he says, uh, "If you have children, if you don't have this [a ceremonial bundle], then the things that you like [will be] like the paper, you know, when the wind blows, it just blows away. But when you have this [ceremonial] bundle and other things, if I make this [bundle] for you, it's gonna help you. In your life when you have children. They're gonna, if you don't have this and then, the, the things that, [say] the paper was here and then when the winds blow, then it just blows away."

MS Mm-hmm.

ABD "When you have this song and the prayers and all these things, then there is something heavy, like, like a rock it sits on that paper or whatever. And then it stays there, it don't blow away. That's the way your future is gonna be, like that." That's what he told me. So he make all these things for me and he give it to me and he teach me how to sing and then all of these prayers and everything. I don't know if you understand what . . .

MS I understand. I think.

ABD . . . I'm trying to say.

MS So what you're saying is that your father was explaining to you that giving you the bundle and the ceremony to perform would stabilize your family and make things secure for you.

ABD Yeah, and everything good, their future, you know, my children.

MS The future of your children.

ABD Mm-hmm.

MS Excellent. (Interview with Dennison)

Agnes Begay Dennison's father's advice correlates with beliefs that dziłleezh (mountain earth bundle), the paraphernalia essential to Blessing Way, ensures goodness in life and is therefore the most sacred article a Navajo family can possess (Frisbie 1987:69–70).

Helen Olsen Chee became motivated to learn the familial ceremonial traditions out of concern over upon whom family members will be able to rely after her mother is taken by old age. As she explains,

My grandfather was getting too old and my mother was getting old too. And that way I would still have something that they knew. That is why. Now my mother is really old and she can't hear now. That is why I want to know what they learned from grandfather and down to my mother and now it is down to me. I want to keep this knowledge in the family. My mother is very old. After my mother goes, whom are we going to lean on? That is why I learned this. I wanted to keep the ceremony in the family and keep on doing what I am doing. Who is going to help us? That is what I am thinking about. (Interview with Chee)

In addition to the needs of her immediate family, Elizabeth Edison sought to fulfill those of fellow Navajo. As she put it, "I took it because I wanted to heal people. For healing purposes, that is why I learned. It was a gift to me for that. From here on [after my husband passed], I was going to use it to raise my children. I used to weave, but that is a lot of stress and strain and I quit doing that. So since I picked the ceremonies up, the money allows me to provide for my children. I help other people with my healing. That is how I help my people with it too" (interview with Edison).

LENGTH OF APPRENTICESHIP

In my younger age, one day we learned that my uncle was going to be performing a ceremony not too far from here in a place called Horse Spring, we found out that he was going to be performing a ceremony over there. So, I suggested to my sisters that we ought to go over there and witness him performing the ceremony. So we went over there and my uncle was happy to see us. We went into the ceremonial hooghan and he was going to be performing the Blessing Way ceremony. We witnessed him, you know, bathing the patient in a basket to begin the Blessing Way ceremony. And then following that, you know, the patient's relative brought in all these foods and we enjoyed a nice meal with him at which time I said to my uncle that, "You know, I really don't know any of those songs that you sing. I'd like to learn at least one little one. The one that would bring me wonderful things that I can have in my household and for my family and so forth. That's the one little song that I'd like to learn from you." He responded saying that, "You know, there is not one little, single song that I can teach you that can bring you those wonderful things that you're dreaming about. You have to learn it all, that's the only way that it'll work. You can't just take a little piece and expect for it to bring forth all these wonderful things." So, he said to me, "I'm getting old and no one has ever said anything like that to me, nobody has ever expressed an interest in learning these things that I know. You're the first person. But I'm not going to teach you just one little song. Instead, what we're going to do today is, I'm going to teach you the first four basic songs that you have to learn. These four basic songs are what are known as the four basic lead songs, these are the lead songs. After you learn these four lead songs, then all the others will begin to build around those four songs. And that's how the Blessing Way ceremony is learned." So, he took the entire day teaching me each one of those basic four songs. He told me what they were, he told me the legend behind it, the stories behind it and how each verse is connected to life, real world life. And it took me a while, it took me all day at first, you know, it was hard, I couldn't remember those verses and I had a hard time singing them. But by the end of the day it began to all come together. After learning those, the four basic songs, thereafter whenever he was performing other ceremonies nearby, I used to go over there and just join him because I knew those four basic songs, the lead songs. And the more I followed him around here and there, the more that he taught me, as if I was in school, he would teach me more and more songs. Then all of a sudden, the whole thing just came together for me. There were things like songs for the hooghan and then there were things like songs for the early dawn songs. I mean these were the very basic Blessing Way ceremony songs. And they just all began to come together and these songs were very, very sacred songs. And then as time went along, as I learned these songs, he knew that I knew them. Then sometimes when he was going to perform ceremonies, he would send somebody for me, so that I could join him at a certain patient's residence, so that I could per-form the ceremony for him while he sat there and coached me. And I would then sing all these songs for him and perform these cere-monies. After going to the ceremony at which he taught me the four basic songs, from that moment I guess I used to follow him around, when I had time and he was performing the ceremony nearby, for about two years. (Interview with Manson)

An apprenticeship involves years of routinely following one or more singer to per-formances, helping out during ceremonies, and spending countless hours at the home of the singer learning prayers, songs, procedures, and relevant stories.

Length of apprenticeship is influenced by various factors including the length and complexity of the ceremony under study, personal proclivities, life circumstances, and seasonal restrictions. The latter guide when oral traditions can be told, as well as when certain ceremonies can be performed, which by extension govern when ceremonies can be learned and paraphernalia for them made. The length of time for Eunice Manson's apprenticeship under her uncle Hastiin Tsédą́ą́, "Gentleman at the Edge of the Rock," is, therefore, about the minimum number of years that it takes for an apprentice to master a ceremony.

It took Jean Mariano three years of apprenticing with her mother's brother Chee Johnson before she gained command of the Blessing Way (interview with Mariano). Before the age of thirty, Madalin Chavez spent a total of six years learning the Blessing Way and a variety of other ceremonies from Kenny Begay. As she explains, "my grandmother's brother taught me. He was blind. I led him around for fifteen years. . . . He taught me other things, like prayers, the basket turning ceremony, footprints, and how to place nt'łiz [precious stones]. These are all the things he taught me" (interview with Chavez). Louella Deswood recalls apprenticing for about four or five years under her grandfather Harvey Johnson to learn: "The Male Shooting Way, it consists of ah, three nights, five nights, nine nights. One is an indoor ceremony, a nine-night ceremony and then one is an outside, Fire Dance ceremony" (interview with Deswood).

It took four or five years of assisting her husband before Grace Emerson had a complete grasp of the ceremony:

> **GE** Nineteen fifty-nine is when I began to learn Hóchxǫ́ǫ́'jí and a few other things from my husband. Blackening is what I learned. I do that to today. That is all I know. . . .
>
> **AS** Just Blackening? Is that all you know?
>
> **GE** Yes. That is all I learned to do. . . .
>
> **AS** How about your husband, did he do the Blackening? Did he learn some prayers?
>
> **GE** Yes, he used to do Hóchxǫ́ǫ́'jí, five days, and did the Blessing Way also. Billie Emerson was his name, he used to be a singer of the Hóchxǫ́ǫ́'jí. He builds the fire for four days so that the patient and whoever else is inside the hooghan could sweat out or purge themselves of all that is ailing them. He did the Blessing Way and he did the Protection Prayer. But me, I didn't learn that. I didn't learn any of that. (Interview with Emerson)

Sarah Ruth John reports a decade of apprenticeship under her father Joe Hayes before his untimely death. She began to perform shortly after this loss. As she explains, "My dad told me, 'I can't do any more sings. You already learned so twenty days after I am gone, you can start if anyone wants you to do a sing'" (interview with John). Pearly Yazzie, who began learning the Blessing Way in her early forties, was initiated at about age fifty-one (interview with Yazzie). Mae Ann Bekis followed her uncle John Bull for nearly ten years to learn the Blessing Way (interview with Bekis, 1993). Irma Wheeler Higdon apprenticed for over a dozen years under her father 'Áshįįhnii Wheeler to master the Blessing Way. She began practicing on her own two years after he passed on (interview with Higdon). Her father Goldtooth Begay Number One initiated Agnes Begay Dennison at the youthful age of twenty-one, approximately fourteen years after she began following him (interview with Agnes B. Dennison). Elizabeth Edison reports a fifteen-year apprenticeship under her husband Billie Emerson. As she recalls,

> I was learning for fifteen years. I learned for fifteen. I am seventy-four now. I was thirty when I began learning. . . . In fifteen years. I fixed the songs then. They were in order after fifteen years of following him. . . . I know the Blessing Way, Evil Way, Hand-trembling, Ha'a'gaa' [extraction of things from the ground] and Aąh ha'iishnííł [extraction from a patient's body]. All of this, I learned from my husband. . . . I just learned a portion of it [Hóchxǫǫ'jí]. What I know can be used any time, winter, spring, summer, fall. It can be used any time in the year, there are no restrictions on that one. The five-day Hóchxǫǫ'jí, I have not done yet. The five-day singing, I have not done, yet. Just all the smaller portions of it, that is all I learned. I learned all the prayers and procedures that are part of Hóchxǫǫ'jí. I know the prayer for a Navajo who goes into a coma. If someone goes unconscious, I know the prayer to bring him back. I know the prayer that must be performed if a child dies in a woman's womb. And, I know the smoking, too. It is just for emergencies that I do these, like if a baby dies in the womb, or when someone goes unconscious. Not every day, just when an emergency comes up. (Interview with Edison)

Betty Begay, who learned from her husband, does not remember exactly how many years she followed him:

> **BB** The four children that I have, their dad was a medicine man. That is who I learned from. Three months ago, he died. He was in a home and that is where he died. That is who I learned from. When he went out to sing, I followed him and that is where I learned. I used to follow him, and that is how I learned the songs from him.

AS What ceremony did you learn?

BB Na'at'oii bika' [Male Shooting Way], I didn't learn all of it. Many, many years I went with him, but I didn't learn all of it. I don't know how many years. (Interview with Begay)

Gladys Denny also followed her husband for years to learn the ceremony:

After I married my husband, we started having children. I usually just stayed home with the children and he was doing the singing. He would come home when he was done. My children all went to school and finished school. Now, my husband is sick. He has been very ill. He got better for a while. When we were younger, my husband got sick. After he got well, [my son] Avery told me, "Mom, you should follow my father around all of the time." So, that is when I started following him around when he was performing. Avery told me that so I started following him. . . . I help him do drypaintings and all of these things that he needed me to do. We sometimes spent five days, and sometimes nine days away from home. That is Fire Dance. For many years we have been doing that. I used to help him and we helped people with that. I didn't know that I had learned all of these things. It did not occur to me that I would be a singer. I didn't even think about learning it. I started learning all of these songs and then here I would be singing all by myself. And, my husband would be sleeping while I was singing. And he probably thinks that, "She knows all of it." I did the dry-paintings and all these things. . . . I never thought about it. I wasn't even thinking about learning. I stayed home and he did the singing. After he got sick that one time, after that I started following him. I just did this and that for him. Then he got sick, then he got sick. I didn't even think he was going to get sick. He told me, "You do it." I didn't realize that I had been learning it all along. He said, "Go ahead and do it. I will not do it." That is what he told me. Then I just started. That is how I started. He said, "There is my parapher-nalia, use it. It cannot just be there, use it." That is what he told me. Another man had done a sing for me before I started learning from my husband. (Interview with Denny)

Many of these women spent a much longer time following than the average length of apprenticeship experienced by men in Ch'iao's study, which was just over six years (1971:32), or the average length of apprenticeship for male Night Way singers in James Faris's study, which was seven years (1990:98)—approximately half the average length of time for apprenticeship among the women that I consulted, which is just over fourteen years. Apprenticeships of women can in fact be quite protracted. For example, Mary Ben Jones Whitney who began following her father at age fourteen was not initiated until age thirty-seven, so she was an apprentice for twenty-three years. Although Laura Nix began learning the Blessing Way from her father at age twelve, she did not receive a bundle until age forty-nine and was not initiated until age fifty-five. She was essentially an apprentice for forty-three years. Nettie Nez, who began following her mother before the age of six, said that a bundle was not specifically prepared for her until she was fifty-one years of age. Helen Olsen Chee reported that although she started following before the age of six, she did not start performing on her own until 1993; she was following for approximately fifty years before beginning to practice on her own. Apprenticeships can be protracted for any number of reasons.

Apprenticeship was prolonged for Betty Begay, Helen Olsen Chee, Elizabeth Emerson, Nettie Nez, Laura Nix, and Mary Ben Jones Whitney, because as the principal assistant to a spouse, parent, or other close relative who is a singer, these women frequently do not begin to practice on their own until after the mentor is incapacitated due to illness or death. For example, as Betty Begay explains, when poor health resulted in her husband taking up residence in a nursing home, she felt obligated to fulfill the needs of community members requiring her husband's ceremony.

AS Why did you want to become a medicine woman?

BB When the children's dad was over at the home, men and women came by the house asking "Do you do a little portion of the Lightning Way?" [Meaning making drypaintings and putting medicine on them.] They needed these done for them. "Yes, I know how," I told them. "Then, do that for us," they said. I always said yes, and so I went and did it. When I visited my husband, I told him exactly what I was doing for these people. "OK," he said, "You know it now—the drypaintings and all of the songs. Now keep on doing it on your own in the future." After he told me this, he went really down and he did not know what was going on around him. He couldn't even talk. When he was still talking and remembering things, that is when he told me to do it right, and that I knew all of these things. Then, later he couldn't talk anymore. From there on, I started doing these things myself and I am very careful about carrying on his ceremony, by doing things just the way he taught me to do them. (Interview with Begay)

Although she knows the full ceremony and had performed it on at least one occasion before our interview, Gaye Shorthair still considers herself to be her husband's apprentice and helper because she has yet to master one component of the ceremony. As she and her husband Juan Shorthair explain,

AS What ceremony are you performing?

GS None, my husband does the Night Way and I just follow him and I just learned small portions of it. For the ceremony that my husband does, whenever there is a Fire Dance, I have a team of dancers and they dance for me. That is the only part I know. I am known all over for this. My husband is a medicine man.

AS When did you start learning?

GS I didn't. All of a sudden I was doing what I am doing right now with my dance team. My husband learned from Fred Stevens. That is who he learned from. After he learned, he got the bundle made for him and now he is performing. I just follow him when he does the singing. All of a sudden I was called upon, they told me to make up a team of dancers. They like to see the teams dance. I did, I put the team together and they danced for me and from there on I have been known for that.

AS Where does this Fred Stevens come from?

GS I don't know where he is from, but he used to live down at Chinle [, Arizona], that is where we got to know him. He lived next door and we used to follow him when he was doing the ceremony and that is how my husband learned from him. That is how we learned. We didn't actually want to learn, we just followed him but the songs and all just came to us so that is how we picked it up. . . .

AS Do you want to become a medicine person? For the nine-day ceremony, do you ever think of that?

GS Yes, I think about it. I want to become a singer.

AS She said yeah, she's interested in it but she just helping him along with it. That's—

JS She did a sing, one time. I just watched her. Down below Chinle [, Arizona]. She did the sing for a woman down there. She knows all the songs, but she is still having a little trouble with the prayer. She did the sing.

AS He said that,

JS Only the one time. . . .

AS Whose bundle did she use when she performed?

GS Our bundle, we used our bundle. Juan Shorthair's bundle. (Interview with Gaye and Juan Shorthair)

An apprenticeship can also be interrupted by school attendance, work demands, or the loss of a mentor. For example, as she explains, although she began following her grandfather at a very young age, Ramona Etcitty's apprenticeship was interrupted by attendance at an off-reservation school and by her grandfather's untimely death.

> **RE** I was young and I could have learned more, but I was young, I wasn't really ready to, you know, and my grandfather passed away. . . . The last song he, he, he told me to learn was the Kinaaldá, the ceremony, he keeps singing, I was washing with, at that time we used to wash with our hands [do laundry by hand] . . .
>
> **MS** Mm-hmm.
>
> **RE** . . . I was washing and he keep asking me and I just put it away and I listen to him. And then he went to Lukachukai, the man named John Bull, and he got sick there when he came back he just went straight to the hospital, he passed away.
>
> **MS** And did you learn the Kinaaldá songs?
>
> **RE** Yeah, you know, briefly I learned. And then after, I didn't want to sing all these songs 'cause it was sad until way about five years later, I kinda forgot some songs, and I went to my uncle, Harry [Anthony], and then I brought him home to do a ceremony on me.
>
> **MS** Mm-hmm.
>
> **RE** I gave him a long turquoise earring.
>
> **MS** Uh-huh.
>
> **RE** That is what my grandfather used to say, "If you want to learn or ask question, you give something to the person"
>
> **MS** Mm-hmm.
>
> **RE** "that's gonna tell you."
>
> **MS** Mm-hmm.
>
> **RE** So I gave him long earrings, my uncle Harry Anthony.
>
> **MS** Mm-hmm.
>
> **RE** And then I asked him questions [pause] and I sang that song. And he said he, "Your grandfather made it short." And it's a long, there is a long one, too, but . . .
>
> **MS** Right.

RE he made it short for me.

MS Right.

RE And then he, he, he just told me what it was called. He said, "Asdzą́ą́ biyiin nisi'lá'" [Within yourself you have the women's song]. (Interview with Etcitty)

At the time of our interview, Ramona Etcitty was apprenticing under her uncle Harry Anthony and hoping to be initiated the following year.

PRESTATION

There are four pieces of blue cornbread that are cooked in the ashes. . . . That is used in place of money. It can be used as a form of payment when someone requests a Blessing Way or any ceremony. That is what I used. I used four loaves of blue cornbread as a payment, that is how I learned. (Interview with Edison)

MC My grandfather, everyone was working over in Blue Water and he was by himself. So, I took care of him. He didn't have anything to give to me for my care. He said, "I will teach you these songs." And, that is how I learned. And Big School Man, they left him with me also. All of his family went to Idaho to pick potatoes and sugar beets. He taught me how to sing the weaving songs, the pressing board [weaving fork] songs, and the batten stick songs. He knew all of that so he taught me all of that. Sometimes they spent the whole winter with me and the whole summer with me.

AS Did you pay them? What did you give them?

MC Yes, I cooked for them, I made their beds, I washed for them, I mended for them, I dressed them, I put silver buttons on their vests, that is how I took care of them. That was the payment. And they all went back into old age. I cared for all of them, they were not poor when they left this earth. (Interview with Chavez)

As pointed out by Ramona Etcitty when recalling her grandfather's advice, it is customary for seekers of knowledge to give something in exchange for it.[10] This is so because to Navajo people, knowledge is a source of life-enriching and life-sustaining power, because in the Navajo world an individual's knowledge can be used to exert power on reality. "Any particular item of anyone's knowledge is therefore a part of that person's power. Transfer of knowledge is, by consequence, a giving away, and so a loss, of power" (Pinxten and Farrer 1990:249). A prestation of some form—livestock, jewelry, cash, or blue cornbread—must accompany every exchange of knowledge in the Navajo world as a form of protection for all parties involved (interview with Tso, 1991). The protection attained through the exchange extends beyond the individuals directly involved, to their families (interview with Roessel).

In the cases of several of the women with whom I consulted, compensation was not made in standard form but rather in intangibles. Mary Ben Jones Whitney's father told her "Follow me so someday when I go, you can do the same thing, you can have the same things that I have [meaning the ceremonies and the paraphernalia] for the sake of the family" (interview with Whitney). In other words, he wished to share his knowledge with her so that she could replace him for the family.

Women such as Madalin Chavez, Gladys Denny, and Nettie Nez each offered care-giving in exchange for knowledge. As she pointed out, Madalin Chavez's uncles taught her because she cared for them during old age (interview with Chavez). In response to my query about payment for learning, Gladys Denny replied, "No. I didn't pay him. I just took care of him. I guess it is for taking care of him. He cannot do for himself, I have to feed him, I have to wash him, I have to stay with him all of the time. I am not performing now because I am just taking care of him" (interview with Denny). And Nettie Nez painfully recalls,

> I took care of her. When she got sick. My mother spent two years in the hospital in Tucson. She comes back for a short time, maybe three days or two days. And she was at Fort Defiance [, Arizona] sometimes. Then she went to Durango [, Colorado] to the hospital again. She was very sick when she came back. She died three days after she came back from the hospital. We were living down here and I took care of her, I was by myself here, only my kids were here, and she got very sick. So, I just put her in a blanket and started carrying her on my back. My children were holding the blanket too from the back. When I went over the hill, I put her down and she was gone. (Interview with Nez)

Compensation in one form or another must continue through every stage of apprenticeship and initiation.

MULTIPLE MENTORS

MC My grandfather's brother, Chee Johnson was his name, he knew the same ceremony also. He knew how to perform for Kinaaldá and other things like that. These paraphernalia came from them. There is another one, Big School Man was his name. All these men, they got together and they built the whole ceremony up for me in four years. . . . They were all brothers. Kenny Begay is a brother to Big School Man and Chee Johnson is the brother to Big School Man. . . .

AS Who taught you the Hóchxǫǫ́ʼjí?

MC My dad used to do that. He taught me. . . .

AS How old were you when you started learning?

MC After I learned the Blessing Way, my grandfather learned how to sing these and then my father learned it from Antonio Silversmith. He was an in-law to Antonio Silversmith and that is how he learned. I used to run after my father when he was singing the Big Star Way. I learned another ceremony that is almost the same as Big Star Way that I learned from my uncle Jimmy Largo. That is to blacken people and for washing them outside, that is how I learned from them. I just do those two parts.

AS Who did you learn the washing outside and the blackening from?

MC My dad taught me the Big Star Way, one of my uncles knew it too. So I learned from both of them.

AS How long were you following your dad and your uncle?

MC Two years. (Interview with Chavez)

To further complicate the apprenticeship process, learning from more than one mentor is not at all uncommon. As she explained, Madalin Chavez's complete knowledge did not come from Kenny Begay alone, for she learned from four other men as well (interview with Chavez). Elizabeth Edison learned from her husband and his grandfather (interview with Edison). At twenty-eight, Sunny Dooley began following Frank Tom and Nevvie James, two clan brothers, to learn the Blessing Way and the Naʼatʼoyee [Shooting or Lightning Way], respectively. She followed for about four and a half years before deciding that she did not want the responsibilities of being a singer (interview with Dooley, 1998). Helen Olsen Chee learned from her mother as well as both paternal and maternal grandparents. As she explains,

HC My grandfather was Red Mustache and my grandmother was Singing Lady. My father was Joseph Olsen and my mother is just known as "Daughter of Red Mustache" or in English as Mrs. Olsen. I am the oldest of the children, ten children. Way back, my grandfather was a medicine man. My mother told me that his name was Doyáłtii' "The No Talk Man." That is where the Lightning Way begins is way up there with my grandfather, "The No Talk Man." And, the Blessing Way is from my grandfather (Red Mustache, her *cheii* [mother's father]). My mother learned the Blessing Way from Red Mustache and I learned it from my grandfather too, and then from my mother. I did sing with my grandfather, sometimes. I sang with him several times. And he showed me how to do these things, and then my mother told me the same things, too. My grandmother did a lot of things like certain drypaintings as part of the Lightning Way. She only taught my mother part of it, it was hers and she did not want to give all of it away. My grandmother gave me two parts of it to do. When Red Mustache's wife passed away, my mother told me to do just those two things. One that is for those who have been affected by lightning, and then a prayer, it is called Hááhóyátééh [Restoration Prayer], these are the only two things [parts of Lightning Way] that were given to me. I learned from my grandmother. After that my grandfather and my mother told me, "You have sheep, you have a lot to do around the home and the only thing that is good for you is the Blessing Way." I was told not to do the five-day sing, just the Blessing Way because you have sheep and lots to do and with that you can use the songs wherever you go, when you are herding sheep, like when you are traveling you can sing the mountain song. So that is all that I am doing is the Blessing Way. With what I learned, I can do the Blessing Way for ladies that are pregnant, that are going to have a baby, so that they can have an easier labor. And I do the Kinaaldá. And Hózhǫ́ǫ́jí [Blessing Way] done on an annual basis to renew our past and our future. So, there are several different ways, at least four— for the baby, Kinaaldá, regular Blessing Way, and then a smoking Dįnáál'yaa' [rite to restore the patient's mind, so that you won't be afraid when traveling or homesick]. These are the four things that I know and from the other way (the Lightning Way) I can do the prayer on that side and I can do Náá'ha'nįį', that is place "nt'łiz" hard goods where lightning has struck with a prayer. That is all I learned. That is what my mother told me, she is still living. She learned from her dad and her mother. My grandfather did the Na'at'oii biką' [Male Shooting Way] and my grandmother did the same thing, and my mom did both, and so I learned from each of them. I asked to do both ceremonies and my grandfather [Red Mustache] said "No. She can just have the Blessing Way." My grandfather didn't want me to do the Na'at'oii biką' because I have sheep and everything. Just only my mother was told everything about the Na'at'oii biką' and I was told just to do the Blessing Way, my grandfather said "You can use that everywhere." There is also a regular prayer that I do for placing of nt'liz and a prayer done for them. My mother is still alive and my mother learned from her dad. My grandmother used to do the Blessing Way too, and my grandfather did the Blessing Way too. My mother is the one that really put it together for me. And I learned from my mother also the five-day Lightning Way, but I do not know all of it, just the two things that were given to me. That is all that I learned, that is all that I learned, that is all that I can tell you. (Interview with Chee)

Ramona Etcitty learned from her grandfather, her father, and her uncle Thomas Anthony (interview with Etcitty). Pearly Yazzie learned from several male relatives, as she explains: "It started with a policeman named Hastiin Belly. That is where it started. That is where they all learned. They used to get together, and I used to see them do that when I was a little child. These songs are all the same, I had an uncle named Goldtooth, he lived in Taachii, and there are others that did the Blessing Way and they told me to follow them so I used to go with them and that is where things came to me clear" (Interview with Yazzie).

Mae Ann Bekis recalls, "I just started going to where he is doing the sing, my uncle. . . . And then we followed Willie Redhouse. He died, uh, about five years ago, and he used to call us, and then we used to follow him. And then Archie Begay is another one that we followed and whenever he is singing somewhere he'll let us know" (interview with Bekis, 1998a).

In addition to what her mother taught her, Nettie Nez learned many things from her husband Hastiin Nez who was also a Blessing Way singer and knew quite a few ceremonies:

> NN Blessing Way and Small Wind Way and Flint Way and prayers and Hááhóyátééh [Restoration Prayer] and smoking of mountain tobacco. From him, I took some Blessing Way things [meaning she learned some songs, prayers, and procedures from him] like smoking. He showed me how to do and use some of these things like the smoking and prayers. . . .
>
> AS You are doing the Blessing Way now, do you know any others too? What else do you know?
>
> NN Mountain Tobacco Smoking, Blessing Way, another Dį-nááł'yaa', specifically used on youths who have been involved in

marijuana or other mind-altering drugs. These substances twist their minds so they need this smoking done. There are two sides to smoking. Mountain tobacco is *dził nát'oh*. They are both referred to as Dįnáál'yaa' but the first is only dził nát'oh and is used for protection, the second is dził nát'oh and four other substances and it is used for substance abuse. It is all pertaining to Blessing Way. (Interview with Nez)

Having multiple teachers is not a phenomenon restricted to women apprentices. Frank Mitchell reports learning parts of the Blessing Way from several different men (1978:194, 198), Lucky claims to have learned several different ceremonials from four teachers (Griffen 1992:199), Franc Newcomb reports that Hastiin Tł'ah had knowledge of at least four separate ceremonials learned from no fewer than five teachers (1964:84–85, 96–100, 103–106, 108–112), and Ch'iao notes that the twenty-one singers he interviewed had an average of 2.62 teachers each and that one had seven separate teachers (1971:27).

SEASONALITY

As noted by Eunice Manson (interview with Manson), a critical element in the apprenticeship process is the learning of all oral traditions associated with the ceremony and its individual components. It is easier for an apprentice to remember all the songs, prayers, and ceremonial procedures being learned once the stories associated with them have been shared because the stories associated with each ceremony provide a framework into which an apprentice can fit the songs, prayers, and procedures (Roessel 1981:123).

Acquisition of this important element of ceremonial knowledge is complicated by the fact that the telling of these stories is seasonally restricted. An apprentice can ask questions in any season but, "the whole story can't be told to her until the winter," that is "from the bear's hibernation . . . until the thunder is heard" (interview with Bekis, 1995).

MB All these they tell you in the wintertime not in the summertime because of the lightning, even though it's hot, you know, they say there's lightning and crawlers and the bears, you never know if you tell these stories that something will happen, you know, so that's why you don't, you don't tell those stories in the summer and when you're singing in the winter, you're, and you're learning the song, that's when they tell you all these stories about each song, not / in the summer.

MS Right, so during your apprenticeship in the winter months . . .

MB Uh-huh.

MS that's when the person from whom you're learning will . . .

MB tell you

MS tell you the stories . . .

MB Yes.

MS associated with the song or associated with the prayer?

MB Uh-huh. (Interview with Bekis, 1998a)

This restriction aims to protect growth and development of all living things, "because of the coming up of a new, new herbs and the flowers and the new birds, of babies, you know, and the lambing and all this. That's why it can only be done in the winter" (interview with Bekis, 1995).

Seasonality plays a critical role in apprenticeship as well as acquisition of oral traditions, because while some ceremonies can be performed year round, the performance of many ceremonies is restricted to either the winter or the summer season (Kluckhohn and Wyman 1940; Sandner 1979:27). As Mae Ann Bekis explains,

MB Well there is, ahh, mostly like the Wind Way, the Small Wind Way, they call it Diné binílch'ijí, and then, that is the Big Wind Way and then they call Nílch'ijí, just the Small Wind Way. And then Lightning Way, and they call that Na'at'oliijí [Shooting Way] and then Hóchxǫǫ'jí, which is winter. These are all winter and summer.

MS Winter and summer?

MB Unhuhn, and the Blessing Way is, you know, all the time in the winter and summertime. And part of that Fire Dance [Iizhnii-dááh] just half could be done in the summer, which is the Lightning Way, part of it. And then the other part, you can do a nine-day sing, but you have to leave out the dancing and all that.

MS In the summer?

MB In the summer.

MS OK.

MB Where you do just the painting and all that. But, you don't do the, you know, the dancing, the dancing part you leave it off. And ahh,

MS The dancing. That dancing can only be done in the winter?

MB Unuhn. That can be done only in the wintertime. And then the Yé'ii Bicheii [Night Way] is only done in the wintertime too. From frost till, well right now [March] there is nothing going on as a Yé'ii Bicheii. And, or Fire Dance. Those two.

MS Because you have already had the first thunder?

MB Unhuhn. And the others, they can be done all the time, but the Enemy Way, the Enemy Way one, it can be done like for emergencies in the wintertime because I heard in the fall they weren't reporting any, ahh, any Enemy Way. They said, they're not because that's not a winter, but it is a winter too, for emergency. Like if the person really needs to have that done, they can do it in the wintertime.

MS Unhuuhn. Do they have to do anything different to do it in the wintertime?

MB No. It is just like the way it is done in the summertime. It is just done that way.

MS Can they have the dancing?

MB Yeah.

MS Huh?

MB And they go three nights in a row like the first, second, and the third. So it is done, the whole thing, it is done even in the wintertime [for an] emergency if a person really needs to have it done. And so it is done that way. (Interview with Bekis, 1995)

A ceremony's seasonality limits when an individual can apprentice (Newcomb 1964:109–110) and when appropriate equipment can be made or renewed (Mitchell 1978:207). The process of apprenticeship is further complicated by the fact that apprentices must also carefully navigate restrictions against the combination of certain bodily functions and fluids with ceremonial matters.

CHAPTER IV

BLOOD—
DANGEROUS AND
OTHERWISE

AS Could you follow your father while on your *aadi'* [common euphemism for blood shed during the third and all subsequent menstrual cycles]?

MBJW No. You cannot do that. It bothers your voice, that is why. You get hoarse. It gives you a hoarse voice. When you are like that, any ceremony, you cannot go. (Interview with Whitney)

AS When you were learning while young, if you had your aadi', what did you do about it? Did you go ahead and perform?

JM No. After I am over my monthly I can attend ceremonies and all that. When a ceremony is going on, you don't go in there when you are on your aadi'. All the ladies are like that, we don't go in when a ceremony is going on if we are on our aadi'. (Interview with Mariano)

I never helped my husband when I was on my aadi'. When I am doing a ceremony, if anyone comes around and has an aadi', I don't let them come into the hooghan where I am performing. I tell them that they must stay out, because I am very careful with my paraphernalia. For myself, now I have no aadi'. (Interview with Edison)

Before my mother had her hysterectomy, she could not perform a ceremony when she was on her aadi'. When they came for her to do singing or drypainting she told them she could not do it because she is on her aadi'. And when she is over it and washed up they can come for her. (Interview with Chee)[1]

It has been said that when you are *diligii* [with blood] you cannot walk in where a ceremony is going on when you have a *dił* [blood] on you. When there is a sing inside, you are not supposed to go in there when you have blood on you. That is very important. When a person is sick, if you go in there when you have your period, you can harm that person with your odor. If a person on her period is inside, it will bother the medicine person's singing. There are Holy People there and they don't want you in there when there is a ceremony going on. We are really concerned about a person on her period being around when a ceremony is going on because it can take away the voice of the medicine man and there are Holy People there and they are afraid of it too. That is why you don't go in there. It is just the voice that they are concerned about. . . . The family hired a medicine man so that he can heal the patient and if you have your dił on and went in there, you are doing damage. That is why you are not supposed to be where there is a ceremony going on. If you are with blood, you don't go in there. . . . When you have blood on you are not supposed to be in a ceremony because the patient is trying to be healed and if you have blood on and are inside it will prevent the cure from occurring. (Interview with John)

With only one exception, the women with whom I consulted agree that women cannot attend, apprentice for, or practice a ceremony while menstruating because to do so would destroy the efficacy of the ceremony (interviews with anonymous woman, 1998; Begay; Bekis, 1998a; Charley; Chavez; Chee; Agnes B. Dennison; Denny; Dooley, 1998; Edison; Etcitty; Emerson; Higdon; John; Jones; Lynch; Nez; Mace; Mariano; Whitney; Yazzie; see also, Bailey 1950:19; Wyman and Harris 1941:59).[2] This prohibition extends to patients as well as to the spouses of patients or visitors with aadi'.[3]

Strict rules also govern how soon a woman can attend, apprentice for, or practice a ceremony after childbirth. Jean Mariano notes, "You cannot perform or learn while you are still bleeding and all of that. After the bleeding stops, it takes three months for us, then we can go back to performing or learning again. You can perform or practice again after that" (interview with Mariano). This was confirmed by Nettie Nez who said, "When I had my baby, I took it with me to sings. . . . After about three months, that is when you are clean" (interview with Nez), and Madalin Chavez who said, "After the baby is born, after my aadi' is all over and the baby is talking, then I could go back to helping and performing. Up to there, I didn't go" (interview with Chavez).

This cluster of rules and prohibitions can only be understood within the wider context of Navajo views on blood in general. Navajo accounts reveal that not all blood is deemed dangerous. While certain types of blood are associated with abnormal growth and development such as *arthritis deformans* and bone growths (interviews with Mariano; Nix; Shorthair; see Schwarz 2001a for an in-depth analysis)[4] and precautions are routinely taken by hunters to protect vulnerable individuals from contact with blood shed in the process of butchering game animals (interviews with Billie; Dooley, 1992a; Harrison; Walters, 1995a), other types of blood are considered benign or even beneficial. For instance, no concern surrounds the shedding of blood in the process of butchering domesticated animals or at a Kinaaldá, a mother's blood is believed to nurture a fetus while in the womb (interviews with Knoki-Wilson; Walters, 1992), and warriors obtained protection through ritualized contact with an enemy's blood (interview with Ashley, 1993). It is necessary, therefore, to ascertain exactly what types of blood—human as well as animal—are given special consideration in the Navajo world in order to gain a fuller understanding of why menstrual blood and postpartum discharge are believed to be so problematic.[5]

NAVAJO PERCEPTIONS OF MENSTRUATION

MB The first one [menstrual period] and the second one. And the third one, it's, they said it, it's strong, you know. And it lasts longer, but the first one you just see for a while.

MS Yeah.

MB And the second one is the same way. And from there on it's different.

MS Right. So wha-, how do, what's the word that you use to say, to refer to that blood that is the third one and on?

MB Uh, the first one, it's supposed to be a healing part of the blood, and to, you know, when they stretch and they try to massage the older people [at a Kinaaldá ceremony] to restore their strength and all that. And they said these two are the main two parts that are, uh, holiest. It's holy, and from there on it's not.

MS OK, so the blood that the girl passes during the first two . . .

MB Mm-hmm.

MS it's holy?

MB It's holy.

MS and you said it has healing . . .

MB That's healing.

MS And wha-, ho-, what do you, what's the word you use to refer to that blood?

MB We, uhm, I wouldn't know, I don't know how it would be explained because it's not as powerful as the third . . .

MS I understand, I'm just trying to get the terminology. One woman said it is *kinaaldstá*?

MB Kinaaldá, aoo [yes]. Or kinaaldstá. . . .

MS What does that mean?

MB That means that she started. She started her menstruation. (Interview with Bekis, 1998b)

Despite worthy efforts by many generations of scholars, Navajo views on menstruation remain a challenging conundrum that has never been fully explicated by any of the numerous ethnologists who have written about them (see Bailey 1950; Dyk 1966 [1938]; Franciscan Fathers 1910; Keith 1964; Kluckhohn 1944; Ladd 1957; Leighton and Kluckhohn 1947:87; Morgan 1936; Reichard 1950; Wright 1982a, 1982b; Wyman and Harris 1941).[6] Building on the work of these previous experts, this analysis represents my attempt to grapple with this puzzle and propose a new perspective on the problem.

The Navajo people with whom I consulted clearly indicated that, as occurs elsewhere (Buckley and Gottlieb 1988:39), in the Navajo world menstruation both purifies and pollutes. The menstrual flow is perceived to purify the Navajo woman from whom it flows (interviews with Bekis, 1995; Alfred E. Dennison 1998; see also Wright 1982b:57) and to pollute those who have contact with it after excretion. Thus, the literature and my field notes are replete with lists of restrictions placed on menstruating Navajo women and their spouses.[7]

Navajo accounts reveal, however, that not all types of menstrual blood are deemed potentially harmful. The blood shed during the first and second menstrual cycles is not considered to be dangerous, while that shed during all subsequent periods is deemed to be potentially very dangerous. This difference is linguistically reinforced by means of specific terminology. The terms kinaaldá or kinaaldstá (interviews with Bekis, 1998b; Agnes B. Dennison; Alfred E. Dennison; Mariano; Nix; Yazzie; see also Franciscan Fathers 1910:451) are used to refer to the blood shed during the first two menstrual cycles. As Jean Mariano explains, "Changing Woman had it first so when the girl has her first or second period, we just call it kinaaldá or *kinaaldstá*, so it has always been called that" (interview with Mariano). That shed during all subsequent cycles is referred to as *chooyin* (interviews with Bekis, 1998b; Dooley, 1992a, 1998; Emerson; Mariano; Tsosie; Yazzie; personal communication with Shay; see also Franciscan Fathers 1910:451), which is euphemistically referred to as aadi' in everyday conversations. As Grace Emerson explains, "It was in the First World that they came to call it chooyin. It is not us, it was the Holy People that named it when the separation of the sexes happened" (interview with Emerson). The amniotic fluid in which a fetus lives is called *bich'íítoo'*. It is not considered dangerous but the blood that a mother begins to discharge shortly after delivery is considered to be chooyin, so it is very dangerous (interview with Yazzie). This explains Talking God's fear of the blood connected to childbirth (interview with Kee, 1992b).

Differential treatment of menstrual blood, depending on when it is shed, was not acknowledged by some prior researchers (Reichard 1950:173; Wright 1982a:385) and not fully explained by others even when it was recorded (Bailey 1950:10; Wyman and Bailey 1943:6). Noting this distinction, Leland Wyman and Flora Bailey concluded that menstrual blood becomes increasingly dangerous as a Navajo woman matures "because she has children" (1943:6).[8] Subsequently, Flora Bailey posited that perhaps "[i]t is possible that this expression of fear only *after* the first two menstrual periods have passed may be due to the fact that according to the old pattern the Blessingway songs were sung for the girl on these first two occasions [that is, during her Kinaaldá] and that in itself may counteract the danger" (Bailey 1950:10, emphasis in original).

The time depth of inquiry, coupled with these unanswered questions, makes the Navajo case ideal for a fresh approach to menstruation. A carefully rendered analysis of Navajo menstrual rules and taboos, such as the type of study called for by Buckley and Gottlieb (1988:3–50), must begin with Navajo exegeses about the power and effect associated with menstruation and menstrual substances. The Navajo people with whom I consulted had quite a bit to say on these matters.

WHAT MAKES IT DANGEROUS?

MS Umm, what is, I am trying to figure out a way to ask this question. It is having to do with menstrual blood, and the danger. Some people call it danger. What makes it dangerous?

MB I don't know, I think it is just that, umm, in Navajo, like the Kinaaldá. We are back to Kinaaldá. Ok, umm, a kinaaldá. *She is pure, she, nobody bothered her.* But her first blood that you see? You are not supposed to put a pad on her. That is supposed to have been just, that is pure for two times, the first one and the second one. And then the third one, and then that's that. She is a woman, she can conceive now! (Interview with Bekis, 1993)

The distinction made by Mae Ann Bekis is reinforced by explanations given by other consultants for why different terms are used to refer to the blood shed during the first two menstrual cycles and that shed during all subsequent cycles and for a period of time following childbirth. For example, Agnes Begay Dennison and her son Alfred of Round Rock, Arizona, and I had the following conversation:

> MS Well, then let me ask you this question. Is the word, is that word [chooyin] used to refer to the fluids that a woman, a young girl passes during her first and second [menstrual period]?
>
> AED No.
>
> ABD No.
>
> AED No.
>
> MS What word is used then to refer to the fluids [discharged during the first and second menstrual period]?
>
> ABD That's just . . .
>
> AED *That's more of a pure, pureness about it, because it, assuming that person has never had a sexual relationship.*
>
> MS Right, so what word is used in Navajo?
>
> ABD Kinaaldá.
>
> MS They refer to the . . .
>
> AED They refer . . .
>
> MS . . . blood as kinaaldá?
>
> ABD Yeah, yeah.
>
> AED They refer to it as kinaaldstá. (Interview with Agnes B. and Alfred E. Dennison)

Pearly Yazzie and Mary Ben Jones Whitney offered further glimmers of understanding when they tied aadi' directly to reproduction. Pearly Yazzie noted, "The first one is not bad blood, the second is also not bad blood, the third one is when it becomes aadi'. The first and the second, we call that kinaaldá. And then from there on the babies start coming. After the first two, she will have children in the future" (interview with Yazzie). While Mary Ben Jones Whitney said,

> On the Kinaaldá, the first and second, there is nothing wrong with it. After it becomes aadi', all these other dos and don'ts come into it. . . . From there on, when she starts her regular period then that is supposed to be bringing children. I don't know how long she will be having children and then it will stop on its own again. After that, you are not going to have any more children, after your period

stops. You will start going into old age, no more children. From the third on, that is for the children, to have children. (Interview with Whitney)

Madalin Chavez further clarified the reason for the distinction made between the blood shed during the first and second cycle and all subsequent cycles when she stated bluntly:

MC The first kinaaldá *there isn't a penis yet.* A man hasn't opened it yet. That is a *kinaaldá's* [the pubescent girl] blood and she makes the *chííh dík'óózh* [antidote for chooyin] because she is a virgin. She does the chííh dík'óózh with the salt and chííh mixed together, that is why it is called chííh dík'óózh. After that, the third one, 'acho' [penis] rolled in the blood, and that is why the cho is first and then yin. It is called the way it sounds cho-yin. The first two are holy because they are from a virgin girl, the third one, the penis is rolling in the blood so that is called chooyin, the way it sounds, cho first and then yin. That is how you call it. Nobody is ashamed of this.

MS Um, ask her what the blood is called during the, when the girl has the first two. It's not called chooyin? What is it called?

AS Uh-huh. What is the blood of the first two kinaaldá called?

MC The first two are called kinaaldá or Asdzáá Nádleehé ni'ha-ani'yá' (Changing Woman came), that is what it is called. (Interview with Chavez)

Keeping Pearly Yazzie, Mary Ben Jones Whitney, and Madalin Chavez's explanations in mind, the full significance of the timing for the shift in terminology from kinaaldá or kinaaldstá (interviews with Bekis, 1998b; Agnes B. Dennison; Alfred E. Dennison; Mariano; Nix; Yazzie) for that shed during the first two menstrual cycles, to aadi' (interviews with Bekis, 1998b; Dooley 1992a, 1998; Emerson; Mariano; Tsosie; Yazzie; personal communication with Shay) for that shed during all subsequent cycles, becomes clearer when views on the special powers possessed by a kinaaldá and rules for marriage eligibility are taken into consideration.

The blood she sheds during her first and second menstrual periods signifies a young woman's reproductive capacities and energies. Mae Ann Bekis (1993), Madalin Chavez, Nettie Nez, and Mary Ben Jones Whitney said, "It's holy," while Oscar Tso of White Valley, Arizona, told me that this blood is considered "Very precious. It is looked upon as very sacred. This first blood from your period is considered 'life blood.' So you have a real special ceremony" (interview with Tso,

1992a).[9] As Mae Charley from north of Rock Point, Arizona, notes in the following account, young women are acknowledged to have a unique power while experiencing their first and second menstrual periods. To maximize its positive effects, family members make every effort to have as many preparations as possible completed well in advance, so that the puberty ceremony can be performed while the young woman is still in this special state. "The kinaaldá [pubescent girl] at the time of her actual kinaaldá [first menstruation] she has something unique. It's acknowledged and celebrated days later when the power of the kinaaldá has already begun to change, then do we prepare her. When she has her power, she is not to eat with sugar or salt. She cannot eat hot meals. In that sacred manner she is to tend only to her corn grinding work. She is supposed to be in this condition throughout her Kinaaldá, dressing, and final day" (interview with Charley).[10]

To take advantage of these special powers, every Navajo girl is ideally supposed to have Kinaaldá at the time of her first and her second period. "Back at the dawn of time, when Changing Woman was picked up as a baby from the crevices and when she had her ceremony. It was done for her four times, we are told. We are told not to do it four times, but only two were assigned to us" (interview with Charley).[11] As Nettie Nez explains, "You have to make a cake for her. This is the first step. This ceremony makes her start walking into her future life. She is going to pick up things, jewelry, turquoise and all of these things. That is why she came of age" (interview with Nez).

An antithetical relationship exists between aadi' and the blood shed during a Kinaaldá. As Laura Nix points out, "When somebody else comes in, if they are on their aadi' that is a no-no, too. Even at a Kinaaldá ceremony. The two types of blood don't like each other. It bothers their voices, they lose their voices, those who are singing in the ceremony" (interview with Nix). In fact, as Nettie Nez explains, such mixing will ruin the entire ceremony for a kinaaldá:

> When you are doing the Kinaaldá ceremony, anybody that is having an aadi' cannot go in there. Even though they both have blood, they don't like each other—these two different types of blood. That is how it is. When there is a ceremony going on for a kinaaldá, if you have aadi', you don't go in there. If you go in there while on your aadi', you are going to take everything away from her, all that she is being blessed with, the jewelry and all of those things. The ceremony won't be effective for her. The first blood she sees, that is holy and you put all kinds of jewelry on her and fix her up good. In return she will have all those things in the future. In the future she will be like that, dressed up nicely. That is why we have Kinaaldá, make the cake and have the ceremony for them. That is for all girls. (Interview with Nez)

Formerly young girls were considered to be eligible for marriage after their second Kinaaldá (Bailey 1950:12; Leighton and Kluckhohn 1947:77; Frisbie 1993 [1967]:348). Thus, the distinction between different kinds of menstrual blood theoretically correlates with the pre-sexual and sexual phases of a woman's life. That is, the blood shed before a girl *ideally* marries or otherwise becomes sexually active is not dangerous; the blood shed after the young woman *ideally* becomes married or otherwise sexually active is very dangerous.

It is while a girl sheds blood during the pre-sexual phase of her life that she has the ability to foster growth and development of children (interviews with Bekis, 1992; Dooley, 1992a; Kee, 1992a; Walters, 1993); to heal problems related to exposure to menstrual blood shed during the sexual portion of a woman's life by means of massage, or the laying on of hands (interview with Bekis, 1998b); and to produce an essential component of chííh dík'ǫ́ǫ́zh (interviews with Bekis, 1993; Agnes B. Dennison; Alfred E. Dennison; Mace), an antidote capable of neutralizing the effects of menstrual blood shed by women after their second monthly cycles.

According to Ursula Knoki-Wilson, of Ganado, Arizona, chííh dík'ǫ́ǫ́zh is ingested or aspirated to "contain the power of the menstrual blood" (interview with Knoki-Wilson).[12] When used correctly, it forms a barrier to protect vulnerable individuals from menstrual blood. It is sprayed from the mouth into the interior of a room where a vulnerable person is, or it is put on, or ingested by, individuals to correct several different problems.[13]

For instance, chííh dík'ǫ́ǫ́zh is placed in the mouth and blown on a person to "help him or her to come out of unconsciousness" (interview with Chavez). Menstruating women use it when they are tending to the needs of assailable individuals such as infants or ill persons. Breastfeeding mothers are told that when menstruating they must put a tiny bit of chííh dík'ǫ́ǫ́zh in the infant's mouth as well as in their own mouths and then "blow around in your house" (interview with Bekis, 1993) before feeding the child. Alternatively, "when the kids are sick and someone who is like that comes to you, you put it on the ill child" (interview with Denny). All menstruating visitors use it in the homes of the terminally ill (interview with Bekis, 1993). In the case of hospitalization, it is used to counteract any potential ill effect from menstruating nurses and other medical personnel (interview with Chavez).

A woman helper who unexpectedly begins to menstruate during a ceremony also uses chííh dík'ǫ́ǫ́zh, as Betty Begay explains:

> If one of the outsiders, the ladies who are cooking outside the hooghan while a five-day sing is going on, if she gets her menstruation, she can come in and do chííh dík'ǫ́ǫ́zh on all four sides of the hooghan, and the patient, and the singer, and the paraphernalia, and blow it on all of the people in there. That way, she can go in and out of the structure in which they are conducting the cere-

mony. She can go in and out. . . . The medicine man will be singing while she is blessing the hooghan with chííh dík'óózh. There is one particular song that is used for this. . . . [A menstruating woman's husband can also attend] if he takes the chííh dík'óózh, he can go in there too. They pass it around just like tádídíín [corn pollen] and everybody inside the hooghan takes some. [Those in attendance put it in their mouths four times from the tip of their fingers.] He [the helper's spouse] can go inside if he takes chííh dík'óózh too. (Interview with Begay)

Administration of chííh dík'óózh is not enough in such cases, however, for as Irma Wheeler Higdon notes, those who use chííh dík'óózh in order to help with cooking or to watch a ceremony must be careful not to touch the patient or tádídíín. She told me, "The one that is helping or something like that and uses that chííh dík'óózh and then she can help. But she don't bother the patient, and she don't bother the tádídíín, you know. She don't eat that. She sits there and somebody has to do it for her [as the tádídíín pouch is passed clockwise for personal blessings during the ceremony], she don't put her hand in that bag" (interview with Higdon).

Blood is the most concentrated form of the power contained in aadi' but it is also externalized as an odor, which can negatively influence people subjected to it. Chííh dík'óózh is used to counteract the odor of menstrual blood, which can cause trouble with mental concentration (interview with Lynch), dizziness (interviews with Jones, Lynch), headache (interviews with Chavez, Deswood, Jones, Lynch, Mariano), aching (interviews with Charley, Chavez, Jones, Mariano), arthritis (interviews with Bekis, 1998a; Charley; Kee; see also Bailey 1950:19; Wyman and Bailey 1943:6; Wyman and Harris 1941:59), deformity of bone growth (interviews with Deswood; Tso, 1992a) or for one to become hunchbacked (interviews with Lynch, Tsosie). It is also used "to reduce fever" or to counteract "frenzy disorder" brought on by guilt over sexual incest (interview with Knoki-Wilson).[14]

The making of the powerful protective medicine known as chííh dík'óózh is a complex multiple-step process, which begins in the weeks and months preceding a Kinaaldá. Although a kinaaldá cannot thwart the effect of aadi' during her Kinaaldá (interviews with Nez, Nix), she has the ability to collect a component vital to the making of this medicinal substance.

Collected during her first or second Kinaaldá ceremony for this purpose, the saliva of a kinaaldá constitutes an essential component of this medicinal mixture (interviews with Bekis, 1993; Charley; Chavez; Dooley, 1992a; Mariano; Whitney). At her Kinaaldá, a girl is directed to spit into a pouch containing a combination of ground chííh (red ochre) and natural salt at the conclusion of each morning, noontime, and pre-sunset run (interviews with Bekis, 1993; Charley; Agnes B. Dennison; Dooley, 1992a; on the Kinaaldá see Begay 1983; Frisbie 1993 [1967]; and

Schwarz 1997:173–229). As Laura Nix clarifies, "A kinaaldá makes it. Natural salt and the red powder together are on the kinaaldá's belt. She spits in it after each run, that is what chííh dík'ǫǫzh is made out of. . . . The red dirt, salt, and some medicines if they are available, if not it is just chííh and salt. And this one, when she turns when she is running, when she turns around a tree, she opens it and spits into it and then runs back. For four days, she spits into it. On the fourth night, they have the all-night sing for her" (interview with Nix).

But, as Grace Emerson makes clear, "She just makes part of it during the Kinaaldá and from there on you add other things to it yourself. If you know the medicines that are needed for chííh dík'ǫǫzh, you can gather them and then mix them with the chííh and salt from the kinaaldá. If you know it" (interview with Emerson). Women across the reservation mentioned a variety of substances that need to be gathered and dried in anticipation of making chííh dík'ǫǫzh. These include "bloomed flower parts" (interview with Charley); "red berries" (interview with Mariano), "chokecherries and dogberries" (interview with Bekis, 1993), or "berries of all different kinds of shrubs" (interview with Shorthair); "Flint Way medicine" (personal communication with Bekis 2001c; interview with Emerson); "the root of some medicine" (interviews with Bekis, 1993; Shorthair); "any flowers that are yellow, blue, and red" (interview with Shorthair); "dirt gathered from the ocean floor" (personal communication with Bekis, 2001c; interviews with Emerson, Shorthair); "cedar tree pollen," and "a medicine called ł'azéé, 'the medicine from the earth,'" (interview with Mariano; see also Wyman and Bailey 1943:11–12). As Grace Emerson explains, "If you have gathered and dried the medicines ahead of time, then you can grind and mix it on the last morning of the Kinaaldá while the cake is being cut. Once it is mixed, it is passed out to the medicine people and others who need it who are at the ceremony. All the things that are needed for chííh dík'ǫǫzh, they are hard to gather" (interview with Emerson).

If, on the other hand, all is not ready before the Kinaaldá, the chííh, salt, and saliva mixture from a kinaaldá's pouch is divided and distributed to all who request some on the last morning of her ceremony, "after the cake is cut out of the ground" (interview with Whitney). This substance is saved until it can be converted into chííh dík'ǫǫzh through combination with the other requisite substances, songs, and prayers.

MB Like if J.D. was singing, and the final night of the Flint Way is going to be tonight. And then they will take all these chííh and then the salt and then the herbs, you know the dried herbs and the berries. They will take it over there. There may be about that much,

MS Hmm, a foot and a half high.

MB Unhuuhn,

MS Ok. . . .

MB And they have salt added, too. That rock salt. And then like a young girl that is not married or anything, she grinds first by hand on the stone tools. And then after that other strong ladies can grind it with a grinding stone. And then he will sing while they are grinding it. And that is how it is made, the chííh dík'ǫǫzh. After they grind it, they have to put it out and he has to sing all night. He puts it out with all the personal belongings such as purses and car keys to be sung over. . . . And he has to put the chííh on his patients and then the next morning, that is when people who want to buy some and they buy it and then that is when it does its job. What you buy at the flea market, I don't really go for that. That is not done right. They are just doing it for the money. (Interview Bekis, 1993)

Later Mae Ann Bekis added, "It is very precious." When an individual's supply is running low, "You can stretch it by adding some of the salt, chííh, and saliva from a kinaaldá's pouch. That way it renews itself and lasts, and lasts" (personal communication with Bekis, 2001c).

While enlightening in regard to making and using this substance, this information left me wanting a fuller explanation regarding the source of chííh dík'ǫǫzh's unique ability to protect vulnerable individuals against aadi'. When asked about this, Betty Begay replied: "It is made for it. Kinaaldá is the one that makes chííh dík'ǫǫzh so that it will be effective. . . . You go to the Navajo Flea Market, they always have a big jar of chííh dík'ǫǫzh that they are selling, but this won't work. It is not effective because it was not made by a kinaaldá. It must be made by a kinaaldá, to be effective" (interview with Begay). In interview after interview, I consistently pushed for further insight into chííh dík'ǫǫzh's efficaciousness. In one such case, Madalin Chavez retorted emphatically: "It kills the dirty blood! . . . She hasn't been kissed yet and a man has not put a hand on her, that is why it is effective and it heals when she makes the chííh dík'ǫǫzh" (interview with Chavez).

Taken collectively, these various accounts offer insight into why a girl's menarche is celebrated yet strict guidelines aimed at controlling the potential danger of menstrual blood from subsequent periods exist. The fact that sexual purity is the distinguishing factor between menstrual blood shed during the first two cycles and that shed during all subsequent cycles indicates that Navajo views on the relative danger of menstrual blood center on sexuality.

Navajo people are taught that it is inappropriate to dance with a clan relative in ceremonial or social contexts (Kluckhohn and Leighton 1974 [1946]:201) or to hold hands with, kiss, or fondle a sexual partner in public (personal communication with Billie; interview with Tso, 1992b). Extreme personal modesty is the ideal with emphasis on concealment of body parts, especially the genitalia. Even among sexual partners, exposure of the sexual organs is considered shameful and embarrassing (Dyk 1951:108–110, 112). To insure privacy and protect personal modesty, "sex relations take place during the hours of darkness" (Kluckhohn and Leighton 1974 [1946]:91). Indulging in sexual intercourse during daylight hours is "said to cause damage to the sperm" (Csordas 1989:478). Sexual excesses are no exception to the norm that excess of any form is dangerous. "Excessive sexual activity by a man or a woman is deplored. . . . Excessive sexual activity with promiscuous partners for whom one takes no responsibility is labeled 'just like dogs'" (Shepardson 1995:168). Furthermore, it is deemed improper for Navajo people to engage in oral sex or to use certain positions during sexual intercourse (personal communication with Billie; interview with Tso, 1992b).

Statements made by Mae Ann Bekis (1993), Betty Begay, Madalin Chavez, Agnes Begay Dennison, Alfred E. Dennison, and Ursula Knoki-Wilson link sexuality with the dangers associated with menstrual blood shed by women after their second cycles. But, we are still left wondering why sexuality makes blood dangerous. Clues are available when we consider that the connection made between the menstrual blood shed by women after their second cycle directly parallels with Navajo views on the inherent danger of butchered game animal blood, which is believed to derive from ancestral immorality.

MANIFESTATIONS OF ANCESTRAL IMMORALITY

HW Game animals, the deer, you know, the deer, mountain sheep and so forth, like that. They are not given to man. Different deities belong to those and they have authority over them. So when you take those animals, when you hunt these animals, there is, ahh, you do it in a way that you do not offend. The deer for example, there is a strict procedure of hunting. And then, also, in the butchering and preparing the meat. And there are strict procedures. In the third world when the people, when the men and the women were separated, they used parts of the deer. The women used the male deer parts. The men used the female deer parts. And this is where the monsters came about. So, the deer has, still has these capabilities in it. So, this is why you never sleep with your wife, you never have intercourse, you know, while you are hunting. When you are butchering a deer and you want to go to the bathroom, you have blood and hair on your hands, you wash it first. And you don't touch, you know, your private areas with that, and so forth. And so everything, you know, like that is still related to that [to the sexual abuses in the last underworld]. . . . The same way with menstrual flow. Those kind of things are Naayééʼjí. And ahh, the reason for it is that ahh, anything to do with menstrual blood and things like that are things that are, they can be used for evil purposes, witchcraft and things like that. This is how the monsters came about. And that, this is what causes birth defects, retardation, you know, hunchback and things like that.

MS Unhuhn.

HW So, you are very careful how you, how you discard those. And then so there is power, you know, that is, emits from that. When a girl is like that. You know, she is instructed to, you know, how to clean herself very carefully. And that the material that she used to wipe herself off, she is to dispose of far away from the, you know, where there are children, you know, livestock and things like that. It can affect livestock too. When you are, when someone who is like that enters a hooghan where a ceremony is, it contaminates.

MS Unhuhn.

HW The ceremony. And where, you know, that it can affect the, it affects the people, the patient, in numerous ways, you know, one of them is the medicine man's voice. (Interview with Walters, 1995a)

This statement by Walters contains the linchpin for unraveling the mystery surrounding Navajo views on the danger associated with some types of menstrual blood. Restrictions exist to control the flow of blood in hunting activities that are dominated by men. Deer and other game animals must be butchered away from the home, deer parts must be carefully disposed of, and all by-products of the butchering process—blood and hair—must be carefully cleaned off of the hunter and the meat before returning home. As David Harrison of Wheatfields, Arizona, makes clear: "Sheep and cattle we can butcher, yeah, blood all over, and don't [matter]. But the deer is different. You have to do it not too close to the house, and take it somewhere and butcher it over there. Remove all the hair and whatever and leave it like that" (interview with Harrison).[15] Contact with butchering by-products from a slain game animal can cause severe health problems. For example, Steven Billie of Wheatfields, Arizona, told me that "leaving the skin and the hair around can make you get cancer[16] . . . That is what they said, you get sore later on" (interview with Billie).[17]

Furthermore, strict continence rules remain while men are hunting, because severe effects can result from exposure to the deer blood and hair (interview with Dooley, 1992a). Hunters are not to have sexual relations for two to four days after the hunt (interview with Billie) or until the hunter has cleansed himself (Luckert 1975:18). Steven Billie and David Harrison told me that should a hunter engage in sexual activity while he still has any of the blood or hair of a recently slain game animal on his body or clothing, the blood and hair will alter his mind so that he will become prone to "wandering" from home in search of sexual exploits. As they explained it, men are told:

> **SB** Don't sleep with ladies, you know. Just stay by yourself you know. Especially if you have blood on your clothes. You're gonna clean yourself, you know. . . . All the hair will get on you too. So kind of put it, clothes changed, you know. And don't sleep with a woman you know, for at least two or four days.
>
> **MS** After you kill the deer?
>
> **SB** After you butcher, yeah. . . .
>
> **MS** Did they ever, anybody ever tell you why you had to do these things?
>
> **SB** Yeah, because if you sleep with a woman, you know, sometime it will bother your mind. You will go like have fun with women.
>
> **DH** Like thinking about going to have fun, their minds go like, they don't want to stay home, they want to be on the road all the time.
>
> **SB** Bother your mind. . . . It will make your mind twist a little bit. . . . They [the deer blood and hair] gonna bother you later on, not right then, you know, when you grow older. . . . I guess that is what the law in Navajo culture is like. (Interview with Harrison and Billie)

As noted by Harry Walters, these precautions must be taken when handling the remains of butchered game animals in the contemporary world in part because deer parts were used by men and women overcome with libidinous desires during the separation of the sexes (Fishler 1953:38–39; Haile 1981b:25, 26; Stephen 1930:99; Yazzie 1971:30; Zolbrod 1984:63) and by women overcome with such desires afterwards (Fishler 1953:38–39; Haile 1938:77, 79). In addition, some men used the vaginas, penises, or livers of freshly slain deer to relieve their long-ings (Haile 1981b:26; interviews with Chavez; Walters, 1995a).[18] Contemporary hunters must carefully follow rules delimiting the length of sexual continence following a kill, due to the fact that the association between the anatomical parts of butchered deer and sexual arousal through masturbation remains (interview with Walters, 1995a).

Knowing that ancestral sexual abuses are the source of the danger associated with deer hair, entrails, blood, and other substances (interview with Walters, 1995a), and that sexual activity is the factor distinguishing dangerous menstrual blood from safe menstrual blood (interviews with Bekis, 1993; Chavez; Agnes B. Dennison; Alfred E. Dennison), I concluded that Harry Walters equates the rules surrounding handling and disposal of aadi' with the factors contributing to the birth of monsters in the underworlds (interview with Walters, 1995a) because in some episodes of the origin story, *menstrual blood,* rather than butchering by-products, is linked with aberrant sexual acts (Fishler 1953:26; Haile 1938:79).

The lasciviousness and inappropriate sexual acts documented in the Navajo origin story resulted in strict rules for men in regard to the butchering of game animals, and for women concerning the care of oneself during menstrual periods and the disposal of menstrual blood. Understanding that its connection to ancestral sexual impropriety is the basis of prohibitions against the mixing of aadi' with ceremonial matters allows us to place these restrictions within the broader context of concerns over mixing of other types of sexual activity and ceremonial matters, which are reflected in strict rules regarding behavior at ceremonials.

When I inquired about the rules against mixing sexual relations with ceremonial contexts, the women with whom I consulted stressed that all involved in a ceremonial—patient, practitioner, helpers, and visitors—who partake of the tádídíín used in communal blessing, must be cautious regarding sexual activity. As Mary Ben Jones Whitney explains,

> When there is a ceremony going on at your mother's or any other place, you just go there and sit and help. If you take tádídíín when they are having a ceremony, when you go home, you don't crawl into bed with your man. You must keep yourself holy. The same rules apply to everyone—singers or visitors. If you go to a sing and take tádídíín, you cannot sleep with your husband, anybody, they are not supposed to do that. When you still have corn pollen on you, you don't crawl into bed with your husband, you have to wash up before you do that. Maybe a day or two after the ceremony, you wash up. My singing is this way and all of the singing is this way. After you come back from performing, you do not sleep with your husband. (Interview with Whitney)

Laura Nix points out that a rule of four days of continence applies while apprenticing or practicing. As she insisted, "You don't do your sexual relationship when you perform, for four days. When I was learning or when I am performing, it is the same way too. You just don't do that until after four days" (interview with Nix). Betty Begay was able to answer our queries on this topic as both the wife of a singer and an apprentice of a ceremony. Asked whether she and her husband could have sexual relations when he was singing, she replied:

> **BB** No. You can't do that. It is important. You do not bother the man or have any relations. . . . You don't do sexual activity and you must be careful when doing ceremonial things. These rules my husband taught me. When I follow him, I don't bother him. He had to sit away from me. There has to be someone between us. . . .
>
> **AS** For how long must you not bother your man? When can you do your sexual activity?
>
> **BB** No, you cannot sleep with your husband. Any ceremony that is done for you, you cannot sleep with your husband for four days. Four days, you keep yourself holy for four days. You must keep yourself holy, you can't cook, you can't cut, you can't handle raw meat, for four days. And then, after four days, you wash your hair and take your bath, you wash up. And then add one or two more days and then you can have your sexual activity. But they usually refer to four days.
>
> **AS** What I mean is like you are just following him around. Is that the same?
>
> **BB** Yes, it is the same. Four days, because you are helping over there like doing drypaintings and things like that. (Interview with Begay)

In contrast to Laura Nix and Betty Begay, Nettie Nez claimed that, according to what she was taught, cleansing oneself is the critical factor required before resumption of sexual relations rather than a set number of days:

> **NN** Like for example, when my mother was teaching me about the prayer, and here I am concentrating on that prayer trying to put it together. You are doing it now and you can't just go in and crawl into bed with your husband. You can't until after you wash.
>
> **AS** Do you have any specific number of days.
>
> **NN** Maybe overnight. (Interview with Nez)

As Grace Emerson points out, these rules are aimed at safeguarding the health of the apprentice and practitioner as well as ensuring a cure for the patient.

AS When you were apprenticing or when your husband was performing could you have sexual relations with your husband?

GE No. It will bother you, not right now, after several years. That is what they say, they take care of themselves. They know to avoid sleeping together. You have to be careful with the patient, if you have relations the patient will not heal properly. So it is both sides, the singer and the patient. (Interview with Emerson)

Women who carefully navigate these rules throughout their apprenticeships reach the next step towards becoming a ceremonial practitioner: initiation.[19]

CHAPTER V

"IT'S YOURS NOW"

When people came and asked for someone to do a singing, sometimes my husband would have me do it by myself. When they gave
him money for singing, he would just give it to me. And when I
would do the whole sing myself, he would watch me. The first
time, I remember thinking, "He must think that I have learned it,
that is why he is just sitting and watching me do it." (Interview with
Emerson)

RE I have to be initiated. At a place, my uncle has to make me sit in
front of him. He'll sit behind me, by me, throughout the ceremony.
Like we are doing our final test!

MS Yeah, yeah, there you go, the final exam. Well, I hope that you
have your final exam before we see you next year.

RE But right now I guess I'm, I'm already ready 'cause he goes to
sleep and I'll be singing.

MS And you keep going.

RE Hey, and I keep going, yeah, about twelve songs up until the
main, what needs to be next, and I wake him up. Then he wakes up
and starts singing and I know where I'm at. Then he can sleep.
Then I sing again. (Interview with Etcitty)

As apprenticeship continues, proficiency improves until a complete shift has occurred from observing to performing the ceremony. As noted by Ramona Etcitty, at
this point the mentor often feigns sleep during the ceremony in order to evaluate
how well the apprentice has mastered the requisite songs, prayers, and procedures.

Once the mentor is convinced that the apprentice knows every facet of the ceremony, it is time for the next step—initiation. Initiation is a multipart process including performance of the ceremony by the apprentice in front of the mentor, acquisition of essential *jish,* or "medicine bundle(s) containing all requisite paraphernalia
such as prayer sticks, feathers, masks, arrowheads, pollens, bullroarers, or fire-
drills," and performance of the ceremony by the mentor over the apprentice. An
important performative moment occurs in the latter, when the mentor verbally calls
the initiate's new status into being.

Once a mentor has determined that an apprentice is ready, he or she waits for
the next available occasion to begin the initiation process. When the opportunity
arises, he or she asks the apprentice to perform a ceremony. Consultant testimony
indicates that having performed a full ceremony in front of one's mentor lends
credence to one's right to be a practitioner. For example, Elizabeth Edison told us:
"My husband was right there when I did the prayer. He was there while I did
everything. I did everything in front of him" (interview with Edison). Juanita Mace
recalls, "When I turned twenty years old, my father asked me to complete a certain
part of the song in the ceremony. He would observe me, while I sang the songs. I
sang in front of him. He said, 'You have learned the ceremony well'" (interview with
Mace). And Louella Deswood noted: "He was here, still alive with us when I did all
the ceremonies in his presence. And I got his stamp of approval in each one of
them" (interview with Deswood).

An apprentice's first performance of a ceremony in front of her mentor is a
pivotal event for two reasons. As what Ramona Etcitty called "our final test" (interview with Etcitty), it is an occasion for an apprentice's self-doubts to surface.[1] In the
following account, Mae Ann Bekis captures the nervous anticipation and joy that
accompany an apprentice's first full performance in front of her mentor.

> The first one I did, it was empowering. . . . We were at an Enemy
> Way down at Round Rock [, Arizona], all of a sudden my uncle
> drove up. He sent his wife over to me, and Elizabeth came and then
> she said, uh, "Your uncle wants you." And so I walked back over
> there. And he said, "I was supposed to do a Kinaaldá over at Wheat-
> fields [, Arizona]. I want you and your husband to go over there,
> and you are going to be the head lady over there," you know. "You
> are going to be performing the Kinaaldá. This is the first time." I
> wasn't really sure of myself, and so, even then, I didn't say, "I don't
> know how to do it yet," or anything. I just say, "OK, I'll do it" . . .
> And he said, "Just be over there around about seven." And he said,
> "You go over there, park close to the door," and he said, "We'll be
> sitting outside or inside." He said, "Either we'll be eating or not," he
> said, "but we'll be over there. I won't help you. But," he say, "Eliza-

beth will sit there with you, and I'll sit by her, and your husband will be sitting there, too," and then I said, "OK." So he say park, and then walk inside just usual, you know, and sit down, and put your tádídíín down. Just take your tádídíín. That's all I had at that time. I didn't have my bundle yet. . . . And then, so, I walked in. And from here (motions to her stomach), I was, I had butterflies, you know, for like doing a program or anything like that, you know, you have butterflies. And I had the butterflies. I sat down where the medicine man sits, and put my tádídíín down and so they started running around. They brought food over. . . . At about 11:30, they start putting the blanket down and they put their things down, you know, and then, so I started. And, it was really interesting. It seemed like, it, this is really something. It seemed like somebody was behind me, guiding me. And then I did the first song, second song, third, fourth, fifth, sixth, seven, eight, nine, ten, eleven, twelve. So this all came, just, you know, no problem. And I performed all night, sang all night, up to when the kinaaldá ran in the morning. And then the last song, then I let out (sighs). [Laughs] And he was just proud of me. And whatever it was, it was right here [holds her hands behind her head] with me. Afterwards we refixed her, redressed her. They served us coffee and then they cut out the cake and they gave us the cake and we came home. And I was really surprised, for the first time, I did something like that. And, oh, I felt so good within me, you know. And I thought, well, this is gonna be it, this is, how I'm gonna do it. And that stayed with me. (Interview with Bekis, 1998a)

More importantly, this occasion marks the first public acknowledgement of the apprentice's emerging career and this can lead to role conflict.

Gaining a mentor's approval does not necessarily alleviate the awkwardness that some women feel at taking on a role generally deemed most appropriate for men. Because where and when an apprentice will perform this ceremony depends on the happenstance of who next asks the mentor for a ceremony, the apprentice will more than likely be entering a crowded hooghan full of strangers. After entering, she must circle clockwise around the fire and take the seat of honor on the west side of the hooghan reserved for the ceremonial practitioner. As Eunice Manson recollects this experience,

I had a brother-in-law, his name was Thaiji, he was married to one of my older sisters. He also learned from him (her uncle), he taught him everything. And one day, there was a ceremony, a Kinaaldá again, being performed by Thaiji, my brother-in-law, at the same location, at Horse Spring. Then I thought, "Well, I think I'll go over there this evening and just help with some basic little songs that I know." So I went to the ceremony and I sat by the doorway and when the ceremony was to begin, you know, Thaiji said to me, "You come over here, you sit in my place." And it was difficult for me to, to get up there and sit in his place and perform the entire ceremony. And that's when I actually did my first full ceremony. I did that only in the presence of Thaiji, not my uncle. He wasn't there. . . . It was really difficult for me, because I was afraid of making a mistake in front of one or the other of these two gentlemen. It was difficult for me to even find a comfortable way to sit because I'm a woman. And it was just, you know, really, really difficult for me for a long, long period of time. (Interview with Manson)

Eunice Manson was not alone in her sense of awkwardness. As a woman from Sanostee, New Mexico, recalls in the following, she felt uncomfortable even accompanying her sister to her first performance as a ceremonial practitioner. As she explains,

We had a Kinaaldá over here by Morgan Lake [, New Mexico], and they couldn't find a medicine man, so they asked my sister. And all these, here, around here, on this side (indicating what would be half of the hooghan), there was only my sister and myself that were on this side, and all these were men (indicating the other people present on this occasion). And it seems like we switched them. *The ladies got over where the men are supposed to be!* We were taking their place and I felt uncomfortable. That's the first time I felt like that. I felt like I shouldn't be right there with my sister as a lead singer. (Interview with anonymous woman, 2000)

Understandably, full acceptance of this new role takes a period of adjustment for women. During this time, the mentor and apprentice are busy making arrangements for the next step in initiation, acquisition of proper paraphernalia.

PARAPHERNALIA

We were singing mountain songs, and I was sitting right by my uncle there. . . . And then here, uh, I went to sleep. You know, I'm supposed to be learning, but somehow I dozed off. In my dream I saw my uncle holding La Plata Mountain. I thought, He has it, it's a miniature; he was holding it like this [holds her hands out with palms up]. And then I, in my dream I was thinking, Oh, they have mountains like that, they hold on to them, that's why they know so much. And then, so, all of a sudden I woke up. He was just sitting like this [mimics him] singing, and then here I try to wake myself, you know. . . . [After the ceremony] I told my uncle, I said, "I had this dream about you last night," and after I described the dream he said, "Do you have a mountain earth bundle?" I said, "No." He said, "You're learning without that, that's why it is showing you that you need to have that done." And then, so, we came back over here, and on Sunday noon . . . all of a sudden, my sister calls. She said, "I want you down here" . . . So, we walked down there, and I thought, Oh no, what did we do? You know, I wondered what she wants. And we got over there and then here, just as I walked in and sat down, she got up and she said, "The people from Tsaile [, Arizona], brought this back," she said, "I have no use for it. You can have it." And she handed that [mountain earth] bundle to me that was our uncle's. "Mom wanted it back and she never got it back, but now we have it back. Now you're learning, I want you to take care of it." So she gave it to me, and then I said, "Well, you can have all my sheep that are in the flock." "OK," she said, "thank you." And I said, "Thank you." (Interview with Bekis, 1998a)[2]

Paraphernalia for an initiate is secured by two primary means—inheritance of existing jish as in the case of Mae Ann Bekis, or as illustrated in the following account from Juanita Mace, creation of an entirely new jish and other equipment.

JM My father prepared a medicine bundle for me, himself. He gave it to me. "From here now, it is yours. You can conduct ceremony during a Kinaaldá," I was told. I conducted my first puberty ceremony before him and I conducted a Blessing Way ceremony over him, too. From there on, he instructed me, "You can practice the ceremony."

AS What about the Night Way chant?

JM The Night Way chant, my older brother conducted that ceremony. We would just help him at each ceremony. I would assist him, that's how it was. He told me that since I knew everything about the ceremony, that I should practice the Night Way ceremony on my own. "How come you do not?" he asked. They met one time and they all prepared a Night Way medicine bundle for me. From there they gave the bundle to me and I started practicing that ceremony. . . . That was about twenty years ago. (Interview with Mace)

Madalin Chavez recounted how her three teachers, Kenny Begay, Big School Man, and Chee Johnson, made a mountain earth bundle for her that contained different pouches for specific purposes—sheep, horses, and jewelry—and three other bundles (interview with Chavez). Alternatively, as is pointed out by Nettie Nez and other women in the following accounts, paraphernalia is secured through a combination of the two above-mentioned processes.

The bundle used to belong to my husband, he died forty-three years ago. Forty-one years ago, I received his mountain earth bundle. The talking prayer sticks, he had that too. That is called, anáályééł. That represents the First Talking God and there is an arrowhead with it. That part, thirty-one years ago they refixed the talking prayer sticks for me. Before that, I used my mom's Blessing Way paraphernalia. What my mother had, that is the mountain earth bundle. My mother's brother Norris Nez took that one. After he took it, they made one for me. Before that, my uncle and I shared our mother's bundle. Now, I have one so that we don't have to share. . . . So after my mom died my uncle Norris Nez and I, we just shared her paraphernalia. When one of us did the Blessing Way, he or I just borrowed it from the other. My dad told me, "You better have one fixed for you." Then, I had one made for me. . . . And my mother's arrowheads, we just divided them between us. Then I started using the bundle that was made for me. (Interview with Nez)

Although she inherited her mountain earth bundle from a deceased clan uncle, Mae Ann Bekis was directed by John Bull to gather the required materials for construction of a prayer bundle and two other pouches.

MB In October, when you see the first moon, real thin, you know the moon?

MS Unhuuhn.

MB That is when he told me to try to gather things to make me a bundle for prayer. . . . He made the bundle for me, then he gave me four arrowheads to start with, for my prayer. And it is called *ókeed* *sodizin* [requested prayer], that is when your patient, you know, when they want you to do a prayer for them, you know like protect their work and like somebody's talking against them, or something like that. . . . And then two bags of tádídíín. And one to use in my, like four sacred stones that we put out for, we call it *Náá'ba'nu̱'*. We go out and give it to the Mother Earth or the sacred trees. You know we put it under them and do the prayer. And ah, and then one bag is for you to put on your patient or to eat when, you know, when, to pass it around [during ceremonies].

MS Yeah, right.

MB And so I have two bags and a mountain earth bundle, and my prayer bundle that I have to carry. (Interview with Bekis, 1993)

In like fashion, Agnes Begay Dennison told me that her daughter has a mountain earth bundle but that she will need a prayer bundle constructed for her before she can be initiated (interview with Dennison).

A ceremony's seasonality limits when appropriate equipment can be made. As Louella Deswood explains below while discussing poor planning on the part of one of her apprentices, this means that apprentices who want to be initiated must plan to secure materials for needed paraphernalia in advance so that requisite items can be made in the season when the specific ceremony is performed.

He is lacking the paraphernalia. And during the time that I was doing the nine-night ceremony he should have consulted me about two months ahead of time so that we would of had everything ready. . . . So, right now he is shorthanded. Maybe he can do the ceremony, but he doesn't have the right tools. . . . Because these paraphernalia, you can't just draw them up, you know, on your own free time. It has to, it has to go through like if you are adopting a child, you have to go through court to get all of the necessary papers and get the judge to sign it, OK? And that is the only way that it is going to work, with any of these, with any of these establishments if you have guardianship papers. And this is the same type of procedure here within the ceremonies. (Interview with Deswood)

Most of the women with whom I consulted inherited paraphernalia (interviews with Bekis, 1998a; Chee; Denny; Edison; Emerson; Etcitty; John; Nez; Nix; Whitney; Yazzie). For example, in response to a query about when she received her paraphernalia, Pearly Yazzie recalled, "About thirty years ago, my brother died, the one from whom I received the mountain earth bundle. He made it for me. Later, another brother named Hataałii Nez died and he left me a bundle called 'Oratory Divinity' [commonly referred to as Talking God]. He left it to me when he died" (interview with Yazzie). This type of inheritance is not at all uncommon; in fact it can go on for generations within a single family of practitioners. This is a conscious choice on the part of Helen Olsen Chee, who told us: "I want to keep all of my grandfather's paraphernalia in the family. His paraphernalia for the five-night Lightning Way, it is still here with us, and the Blessing Way bundle, it is still here with us. And so we are keeping it in the family. That is what my grandfather wished. I want to keep it in the family. And I have my own daughters that follow me when I go do my singing. I don't want it to stop" (interview with Chee). Sarah Ruth John reported the longest recounted continuous inheritance of paraphernalia amongst the women I consulted: "My nálí had the Water Way bundle first and so from there it came down to me. This is the fourteenth time in the family. The first one that learned went back into old age. Then another one took over. From there it just went on and I am the fourteenth one. . . . I am the fourteenth one to have the paraphernalia now. It just went down through the generations within our family. With my dad it is thirteen. My dad was the thirteenth so I am the fourteenth" (interview with John).

In most families there are not as many practitioners as in Sarah Ruth John's case, so if previous arrangements have not been made, when a singer dies family members have to make careful decisions about to whom paraphernalia should pass. Mary Ben Jones Whitney recounts how a decision about the transference of paraphernalia was made within her family:

> All the paraphernalia that my dad had, after he died, my mother had it for a long time. After my mother died, my sister gave me my father's paraphernalia in a basket. My sister said, "I don't know anything about this and you do the Kinaaldá and you go to sings and do some songs, and you can have it. Now you can have it and you can use it. I don't know any songs or anything about it, so you can have it because you do the Kinaaldá and the Blessing Way. And people used to say that if you don't know any mountain songs or anything like that, you cannot have it. (Interview with Whitney)

Family members work diligently to find the best qualified relative to whom they can entrust the paraphernalia, because as Mary Ben Jones Whitney's sister noted, one must know something about a bundle in order to properly care for it (interview with Whitney). Mae Ann Bekis points out that when you are a bundle's caretaker, "you have to sing for the bundle every day. That is why you have to know something about it and some songs" (personal communication with Bekis, 2001d).

Strict rules govern the care and inheritance of bundles because they are considered to be living entities "with feelings and needs" (Frisbie 1987:9). According to Mae Ann Bekis, the passing on of ceremonial materials within families is mandatory because bundles are inextricably connected to particular clans.[3] For example, in the case of her deceased uncle's bundle:

> It was his and finally he was married to, uh, a lady over in, uh, Tsaile [, Arizona], and they kept it until they were told that it wasn't theirs. . . . They had a crystal, crystal gazing done and the crystal gazer told them that "This is a Táchii'nii [Red Running into the Water People Clan]. It's," they say it's a body, you know. "This is Táchii'nii's body, this is not yours! You guys are Kinlichíi'nii [The Red House People Clan], you're Redhouse people. And this belong to Táchii'nii, 'Red Running to the Water,'" and so they finally gave it back to us, after mom died, so many years. (Interview with Bekis, 1998a)

Consistent with this logic, bundles can only be properly cared for by their clan relatives.[4]

Regardless of their source, initiates are given specific instructions regarding the care of jish. Laura Nix notes that, this includes proper decorum: "If you have the mountain earth bundle they tell you not to be angry at anybody and not to talk about other people. You must keep it holy, you have to think about your bundle" (interview with Nix). Elizabeth Edison recalls that at the time of her initiation, "I gave him six hundred dollars and I gave him a turquoise necklace, one of the old ones, not this new stuff. And, he put it on himself, right there. When he gave me the paraphernalia he told me, 'Now, take care of it. Treasure it all through your life. Do not abuse it.' That is what he told me. That is how I keep it now" (interview with Edison). In recollecting what her husband had to say on proper care for her bundle, Elizabeth Edison shared the following views: "When I take my bundle somewhere, I am very careful with it. I treasure it. I care for it. My husband told me, 'Take care of the bundle with your life. I am giving it to you. You learned it, all the songs, so now it is yours. So, take good care of it. You can't drop it or abuse it. You are going to heal people of all ages. Now, I put down the sheepskin for you, now I put down good food for you. With all the good things that are in it, I give that to you, I made a good future life for you. You are doing it for your children too' (interview with Edison).

Mary Ben Jones Whitney received the following advice regarding care of her bundle from Nathan John at her initiation: Mr. John cautioned, "Don't just keep this, it gets lonely too. So you must use it. Don't keep it in a suitcase. You keep it on top, in the basket or in a pouch where it can get light and air because it needs to breathe. Don't keep it in a trunk, or don't keep it in a suitcase, be sure to have it on top in a basket" (interview with Whitney).

In addition to the points made by Mr. John, as living persons bundles are in need of regular renewal by means of a Blessing Way performance.[5] Laura Nix explains:

> The mountain earth bundle, it was made for my dad a long time ago. My mother and dad, that is who it was made for. After my father died, it was given to me. So from there on, I have it opened every so often. I had to pay the medicine man a lot and I have to have a lot of materials and blankets down, on top of that, that is where they reopen it, and then re-clean it and retie it. From sixteen years on, I had it opened four times and that is what I use for Blessing Way. The four sacred mountains are presented in the bundle. There are six [because there are two for doorways]. (Interview with Nix)

As Ramona Etcitty makes clear, in the case of mountain earth bundles, this ceremony also benefits the bundle's caretaker because of the intimate connection extant between caretaker and bundle. "You have to have it renewed. It's your life, you stretch it. You kind of get sick and then it's that way also. So you have it have it renewed and reopen it. Afterwards, you feel better again. You get a relief" (interview with Etcitty). The profound connection between bundle and caretaker was the rationale offered by Mae Bekis's uncle's wife for not wanting to part with his mountain earth bundle after his death. She reportedly said, "I hang on to it, because of my husband, keeping his bundle keeps him near me all the time" (interview with Bekis, 2001).

Attention to proper etiquette and special care are warranted because well-cared-for jish provide blessings to their caregivers. Laura Nix points out, "I have my mountain earth bundle, I have that and that is holding us together as a family. That makes me feel good and it gives me strength too" (interview with Nix). In like fashion, Madalin Chavez notes that because they share caretaker duties, her bundles provide security to everyone in her extended family. She said, "These four that are made for me, my sister has one, another sister has one, another sister has one, and I have one. That is why we are living really good and our kids are not drinking, they are all taking up school and all of that. They were blessed with it too" (interview with Chavez).

Owing to the intimate connection established between jish and caretaker, inherited items must be ceremonially purified before use because bundles of the recently deceased are tainted by the death of their most recent caretaker. Such materials are usually purified by means of a Hóchxǫǫ'jí, "Evil Way" (interviews with Bekis, 1998a; Edison; Whitney; see also Frisbie 1987:95). Mae Ann Bekis explains:

> **MB** Because it had belonged to my uncle that died. . . . And his wife had it, she died, too. So I had to have that five-day Hóchxǫ́ǫ́'jí done for me before I started singing with it. . . . Every day I had to go through something like wagon wheels.
> **MS** Oh?
> **MB** It's called *tsibąąs*. And I have to take my pouch through there, four times, and then after that it was blessed to me. And then I picked it up, and then I started using it from there on. (Interview with Bekis, 1998a)

As noted in this account, once inherited paraphernalia has been purified, the next step is for it to be ceremonially blessed. Given that the timing is correct for the ceremony under study, this will occur at the next step in the process of initiation, when the mentor performs a full version of the ceremony over the initiate.

PERFORMANCE OF CEREMONY OVER INITIATE

> I paid him [Wayne McCabe], he came that night, he did a prayer for me and in the morning too, he did a prayer again. Then the soap weed was brought and dirt was brought in from the field. They spread the dirt out inside the hooghan, and on top of that they put the basket. Then they put the soap weed in the basket and he made the soapsuds. He put tádídíín around the edge of the basket and made the footprints and the handprints for me. He fixed all of this up. From your hair all the way down you have to rinse yourself off with the soap weed. He picked up the basket and put that away. Then somebody got over there and picked up the dirt and they put it back in the Mother Earth. Then they put another blanket down. I sat on the blanket again, he blessed me with yellow cornmeal and I dried myself up with it. If it is a man they use whitecorn, but if it is a woman they use yellow corn. So, that is what I did. I dried with yellow cornmeal. Then they did the prayer at noon. The prayer is called Mother Earth Prayer. Father Sky, Mountain Woman, Water Woman, Darkness, Morning Dawn, First Talking God, Second Talking God, White Corn, Yellow Corn, Corn Pollen Boy, Corn Beetle Girl, Holy Man, and Holy Girl—this is the prayer they did for me. They have to start from the feet and move all the way up to

the head with the prayer. From the east, south, west, and north it goes around in all directions, clockwise. He put cornmeal on me again and corn pollen. There is a song he used, that song belongs to the field, it is where you plant. The song is called the field song, and that is when they blessed me with corn pollen. "This is what you learned, what you learned is like this now [planted]." That is what I was told. "This is what you learned and you do it this way now," I was told. After that, he had to have the smoke with mountain tobacco again. He opened the tobacco again and he rolled it in cornhusk and he lit it and I started smoking. There is a song that goes with it, so they can make you feel good, and make all your thinking positive thinking, for the strength too. That is used, cornhusks rolled with tobacco. I had to smoke that and blow the smoke on the mountain earth bundle that was refixed for me. And all what belongs to me, I had to blow it on that. All these things that were given to me or fixed for me, that had to be renewed. That is how it was made for me. When that was finished, that night, from about after twelve o'clock up to dawn, they sang for me. (Interview with Nix)

The final step in the initiation process is for the mentor to perform a full ceremony over the initiate. Louella Deswood referred to the Fire Dance performed over her by Harvey Johnson as "a graduation ceremony" (interview with Deswood). In some cases, the ceremony is performed over the initiate more than once (Chisholm 1975:87; Sandner 1979:27). For example, Grace Emerson shared the following account:

> **GE** I had the sing twice and he did it himself. He sang for me twice. And he initiated me.
>
> **AS** Your husband?
>
> **GE** Yes, he did it twice over me before he died. Another man sat between us, and he helped my husband to sing. [In other words, this man was hired to initiate her under her husband's guidance since a spouse is not allowed to do it himself.] The one that sat between us died also. The man that sat between us was called "Black Streak Wood Man." He was my nephew by the Táchii'nii clan. He was from Twin Lakes. My husband had sugar diabetes and kidney failure, that is how he died. And then he had heart failure too." (Interview with Emerson)

Initiations must be scheduled to conform to the previously cited seasonal restrictions that apply to particular ceremonies. Many things occur during this all-important ceremony, including ritual preparation of paraphernalia and, as described by Madalin Chavez, the construction of new paraphernalia when needed.

> They made three bundles for me. One to herd the sheep into the corral, one for when the horses are herded into the corral, they made one for horses, and they made one for my jewelry and all that. So, they made three for me. Dibé badaadelkaa was performed for me. I was holding that basket [containing her jewelry and all three bundles] while they did the prayers for me. All three did this for me—Kenny Begay, Big School Man, and Chee Johnson all did this for me. That is a mountain earth bundle. Three they made for me for all these things, horses, cows, sheep, jewelry, and all of that. I put down this much [motions three feet high] material and blankets for them. That is how they did it for me. That is how I got initiated. . . . They jointly performed for me. (Interview with Chavez)

As stated beforehand, after purification, inherited paraphernalia must be ceremonially blessed. Elizabeth Edison remembers that in her situation, "They refixed the paraphernalia for me a month or two after the Evil Way and they blessed me with it at that time. It was mine after that" (interview with Edison). As pointed out by Mae Ann Bekis in the following account, renewal requires bundles being opened. In the case of her paraphernalia she recalls, "We got buckskin, we got some blankets, and a shawl, robe, and all these, then we put that out for it and then he opened it, and then he made an extra, he made my little pouch bag. I had to do it myself anyway, but he was singing when I did all this" (interview with Bekis, 1998a).

Although, unlike many ceremonies, Blessing Way can be performed year-round, as Ramona Etcitty points out, seasonal restrictions govern when a mountain earth bundle can be opened for renewal, thus initiations for Blessing Way are seasonally restricted.

> **MS** Do you have a mountain earth bundle?
>
> **RE** Yeah. My mom did. . . . And my mom told me "We'll just share. See, it is both of ours," she said that then she passed away, and I, it's mine.
>
> **MS** So it's yours. So, so can you be initiated, or have you been initiated as a singer?
>
> **RE** I was planning last summer but I didn't, they have to have some

money and some baskets, and materials that cost a lot of money. *'Abaní* [unwounded buckskin] and all that, to have that done and pay the medicine man. . . . So I didn't have enough money, so it looks like it's just gonna go by again this winter.

MS When do you do it? What time of year do you have that initiation done?

RE Oh, end of June, July, August.

MS That's the only opportunity?

RE Yeah. . . . Some people do it in October, September, but they told me in fall you're not [shakes her head] supposed to. . . . They did it to my mom. I told her no, but they did it to her [renewed her mountain earth bundle]. Months later, two months later she passed away. (Interview with Etcitty)

Once all routine preparations for the particular ceremony are complete, the formal initiation takes place.

INITIATION

Joe Nelson initiated me. He did the ceremony for me. He is my brother by clan. He is the one that initiated me with all of the paraphernalia. He performed the ceremony for five nights. And from there everything that was his is mine. During the initiation, I sat on the drypainting on the last day. He mixed medicine with honey and rolled this into a little ball. He made beads for me. These were put from the feet to the head on the drypainting. Then he raised them to the sun, one, two, three, four. Then he tied them onto my hair with clay. Then he used the paraphernalia and blessed me with it from my feet up. He touched each of my feet, knees, elbows, my heart, and then my head. Then he gave me all of the paraphernalia that William had in the basket. I received it. I raised the basket toward the sun and then breathed in the air by the basket, this I did four times. He was singing throughout. That is how he initiated me. Five nights, he sang. He did the painting on me and he blessed me with the paraphernalia two times. (Interview with Denny)

As Gladys Denny vividly describes in her account of initiation by her clan brother Joe Nelson, the initiate is treated like a patient throughout the ceremony. Various techniques—similar to those used by some mentors during apprenticeship—may be used at this time to secure the songs, prayers, and procedures meticulously learned by the apprentice. For instance, as described by Mae Ann Bekis, some mentors give initiates names during the ceremony. "It was in that hooghan over there [pointing southeast with her chin] and my husband was in there and he told my husband to step out because 'I'm gonna give her a name so she won't, she won't forget the songs.' And there was, uh, another medicine man came, too, uh, he told him to leave and so they abide, they left. And then so he told me, 'This is gonna be your name now.' And so I was given that name and none of the songs, you know, they just, they just all stay with me. I remember all of them" (interview with Bekis, 1998a).

Alternatively, initiates may be asked to consume corn, in the form of kernels, mush, pollen, or a combination of these. As Laura Nix explains, "White corn, yellow corn, black corn, grey corn. Eight of them, they picked out. They ground it and put it in water and I drank that. . . . Just one kernel from each color. They ground it up, added water and I ate that. That helps you, the corn that you eat helps you to keep the songs in place so that you won't get mixed up" (interview with Laura Nix). After bestowing her special name, John Bull also asked Mae Ann Bekis to eat corn. As she points out, he explained what song each kernel represented as he reiterated the rationale for the specific order of the songs in Blessing Way. "He just told me like this is for the three, and then I ate it" (interview with Bekis, 1998a). As she recalls,

> There's about seventeen, seventeen corn kernel, corn kernels that you have to eat. Like the first one is for the first song of the hooghan, there's one [pinches her fingers as if holding a kernel], second song, third song, and the road that you walk to the door, and there's three more and then there's, uh, a road from your house on, like, into town and all that. And then, uh, there was always a coyote, he says, when they sang three, they say, "Oh, this is the beginning, the foundation of a hooghan," and they say they sat there and they were thinking quite hard, "How shall we make more songs? This is just only three." And then coyote comes along, he said, "You guys, you don't have a thinking cap on." And he says, uh, "Here, you're building a hooghan! How about that!" So they start building up again, and they finish it, and then, and then they say, "Well, there's six now." And then he said, "How about the roads? You're gonna walk out to the door, and around your hooghan." So there was three more. And then he said, "How about the roads to, away from your home?" So there was three more. And then he says, "How about me? I'm gonna add three for you for my song." So he has three in there. And then after the hooghan is built, and then

they bless the roads and everything and then they have, they added four more songs to it. That's where you bring in your, like, you build a fire, and you brought in your poker and you brought in your bedding, your utensils, and your grinding stone, all these that you brought in and those are four right there. And then after that is, uh, we call it, uhm, the last song for the hooghan. And then that's when your patient goes out. And then she comes back in and everything is set now in the hooghan. That hooghan is ready now to live in and, uh, so it's blessed. And then from there on it's different songs that, it's for your, yourself the way, like, uh, if they were going into the service, they have songs for them. If you're going to go into the service, and then they are going to travel in the airplane, there's some songs for that. And, oh, all different kinds. (Interview with Bekis, 1998a)

Jean Mariano recalls when the Blessing Way was sung over her:

White and yellow cornmeal mush, and corn pollen were fed to me when my uncle was singing. And corn pollen too. That is what they do. Both and tádídíín. He was singing while I ate these. He told me to pinch the mush from each [cardinal] direction in the basket. I did this as he sang east, south, west, north. And, he put corn pollen in my mouth after each pinch, and sometimes water. Then I ate from the center and the rest. Four things, I ate white cornmeal, I ate yellow cornmeal, and I ate pollen, and he was singing. That makes four. . . . When he was singing while putting pinches of corn mush and pollen in my mouth, that is called *Sinbíliiyaq'*, "I ate the songs" . . . The bundle was in a basket with my beads and other things [jewelry]. He gave it to me as he sang. (Interview with Mariano)

Echoing Laura Nix on this point, Mae Ann Bekis explains that during these procedures, "The singer is planting the songs and prayers in your body and mind. Eating the songs means, all the songs and prayers that you have learned are in the cornmeal mush. You eat these. They feed you a little water with it so that you will remember the songs, and prayers, that way they won't leave you until you get back to old age, then you forget them" (personal communication with Bekis, 2001e).

Toward the same ends, special turquoise can be used. For example, Elizabeth Edison describes how turquoise "from a bird's mouth" was used during her initiation to help with her future singing.

All different birds. *Azéé'nast'ą́ą́n,* they put it in my mouth [a piece of drilled turquoise on a string that has been swiped through the mouth of a blue bird or a yellow bird]. They told me to move it around in my mouth, pull it out, and then to swallow my saliva. They did this to make my voice strong like the bird's and so that I will not forget the songs given to me by my husband. Afterwards I tied it onto my most special necklace. I keep it with me all the time. I wear it all the time, I tie it on to whatever necklace I am wearing, as time goes on. They did Azéé'nast'ą́ą́n when I was initiated. I have it with me all the time. (Interview with Edison)

Initiates are sometimes offered the option to employ alternative mnemonic devices such as notebooks listing the names of songs in proper order (interview with Bekis, 1998a) or sketches of drypaintings (interview with Emerson).[6] Afterwards, the ceremony is officially passed to the initiate in what some term a process of giving (interviews with Agnes B. Dennison, Mariano, Nix).

For example, after making her paraphernalia and performing over her, Madalin Chavez recalls that her mentors "told me 'Go ahead, it's yours'" (interview with Chavez). Similarly, Pearly Yazzie recollects, "At my own house, Hastiin Nez Bidoni did a sing for me and that is when he told me, 'It is all yours now. Now you can perform Blessing Way on your own'" (interview with Yazzie). And Laura Nix remembers, "Wayne McCabe reopened my bundle. He just gave it to me. I gave him a belt that cost two thousand dollars. It had a lot of turquoise on it. I had a lot of blankets and things that I put down for him. On top of that he reopened and retied it for me. And, after that he said, 'Now go ahead. It's yours. You have learned, now you can go ahead and perform with it for Blessing Way and Kinaaldá.' This was eight years ago" (interview with Nix). In these cases, and in every other case, in his very enunciation of this illocutionary speech act, the mentor accomplishes an action that effectually transforms the woman's status from apprentice to practitioner.

While the point at which her mentor says "it is yours" may appear to be the quintessential performative moment in the life-course of a Navajo women becoming a singer, the element of witnessing is crucial here. As witnesses, the Holy People must hear the mentor give the ceremony to the initiate, after which they must ratify and legitimate this act in order for the newly invested singer to be efficacious at every step of her career. One could thus argue that the significance of this speech act is not so much the saying as the hearing. For if the Navajo Holy People do not hear this speech act, and feel compelled to thenceforth take notice of the newly initiated singer's pleas for assistance whenever she calls them through song and prayer, then she will be impotent to help her patients. It is imperative that the practitioner's plea for assistance at the beginning of each ceremony, and all prayers and songs throughout the ceremony, be heard by the Holy People in order for a cure to occur, for as the women with whom I consulted repeatedly pointed out, the success or failure of a ceremony is ultimately "all up to the Holy People" (interview with Shorthair), because "the Holy People hear you and in turn they help you" (interview with Bekis, 1998a). Thus, the witnessing of this declaration by the Holy People is as important as its being said.

CHAPTER VI

COMMUNICATING
WITH THE
HOLY PEOPLE

Even if there is nobody but you and the patient there, when you start you say, "I am starting, I want you to be with me when I am singing." That is how you pray before you start the sing and that way the Holy People will hear you. "I want to do a good job," you tell them. (Interview with Nix)

ABD Before you start to sing, you know, you talk to the Holy People up here [raises her hand above her head]. You pray, you pray to these Holy People who belong to the songs. To these Holy People you talk. And then you start it. It's automatically, I don't know, I can't really explain how, but you could feel it, you could feel it, your voice, you know, you could feel it. It's easier, and uh, makes it a good song and, you know, uh, you could, you could say the next word. . . . It's just like, uh, uh, automatically you get, you get your voice real clear and kind of, uh, real soft and all these things. So, that's the way it is, but, I don't know how, but I think it's from the Holy People. . . . You know, you offer this, ah, corn pollen before you start it?

MS Yeah.

ABD You, you pass it around, all the way around [amongst those assembled for the ceremony].

MS Right.

ABD And then when you put it in your mouth, and you put it up here [touches the top of her head], and then you give some to Holy

People [motions out in front of herself as if she were making an offering].

MS Right.

ABD That's when you pray. You don't have to pray out loud.

MS I see.

ABD It's just, you know, thinking about it.

MS Right.

ABD That's, that's the way it goes. (Interview with Agnes Begay Dennison)

When you are getting ready to sing, that is when you say aloud "All the people that are in here"—you are not really saying it to the people in the hooghan, you are really saying it to the Holy People—"help me to perform this singing tonight." The Holy People are present. They are in there. They are here. They are the ones that are in charge of the songs. They are the ones that you are really talking to. When I say, "help me perform the singing to-night," the Holy People know that I am not saying it to the Navajo there. They know that I am asking them to help me keep every-thing in order and keep my voice strong. And that is the way that they help you. That is the way you do it and that is the way that the songs come in the proper order for you. (Interview with Denny)

The multiple issues discussed thus far converge in the action of ceremonial perfor-mance. As pointed out by Laura Nix, Agnes Begay Dennison, and Gladys Denny, as a ceremony begins, the practitioner beseeches the Holy People for their help. This is necessary because as was stated repeatedly by women, "It all depends on the Holy People" (interview with Mariano), or "It is the Holy People that do the healing, I am just a shell, I am doing it for the Holy People" (personal communication with Bekis, 2001g). This sentiment is so strong that Nettie Nez describes her practice as a process of following the Holy People. She said, "Even when I am sleeping during the night, someone comes from far away and I just take off because they want me to do something. It is the Holy People that I am following. They are the ones that I follow after someone comes. I get called on during the night, any time" (interview with Nez).

Practitioners' personal narratives reveal that they are cognizant of the Holy People's presence throughout the ceremony. As avowed by Laura Nix, "You feel that the Holy People are present and your voice, it helps you with your voice also" (interview with Nix). Elizabeth Edison noted, "You can feel the presence of Holy

People. When you are praying they put things in line for you whatever you are praying about. When you are singing, it is the same way. They keep all the songs in order for you" (interview with Edison). And Jean Mariano stated, "It is from the Holy People. One is called, First Talking God. He is from the east. They are around me. And then the Second Talking God, from the west. These are their songs. I am between them, so I can feel them surrounding me. That is how I know that I am being helped when I am singing. They help me to put the songs in place" (interview with Mariano).

Keeping the songs "in line" (interview with Edison), "in order" (interviews with Denny, Edison), or "in place" (interviews with Mariano, Nix) is vitally important because, as Nettie Nez points out, for the ceremony to be effective, the practitioner must carefully follow all of her mentor's instructions and present each song, prayer, or procedure in full, as well as in the correct sequence. "When you are singing, if you are not singing the right way, it won't be effective. What is in your songs must be sung correctly, that is the way that it is effective for your patient. When you are learning you are told, 'You do it this way. You say the prayers this way,' you are taught all of this from the beginning. 'Just sing it the way that you were taught, don't put any other things in there. You don't add to it.' That is how you get told. That is the way that they teach you" (interview with Nez). Collectively a singer's verbal and physical expressions form an incantation compelling the Holy People to assist.

Certain factors clue practitioners to the relative effectiveness of the ceremony while it is in progress. For instance, Grace Emerson points out, "You think of your patient. Is he or she going to get healed? You must think positively about healing your patient. All of this, you think about it and your voice comes out and if the patient begins to feel better, your voice begins to increase in loudness" (interview with Emerson). Laura Nix echoed this exact sentiment:

> They tell you that your voice, it is given to you by the Holy People. They are the ones that come upon you. When I start, I might have a low voice, but towards morning I have a better voice. Then I am going strong. When you are singing, you stop once in a while and pray to yourself and that is how your voice stays with you like that. It is up to the Holy People. All you do—your prayers, your songs— the Holy People are the ones that keep things straight for you. They give you a voice. It is up to them, the way they help you. . . . The songs just stay in place and you just know that you are doing a good job. You have the songs, the way it goes, you do it that way, you are not going to miss any. . . . The songs, they just come out. It is like running out of you. That is how it is. (Interview with Nix)

As personal savoir faire builds, practitioners learn to carefully watch their patients with the intention of gauging the success of the ceremony. In Jean Mariano's experience, a patient will sit very still if the ceremony is having the desired effect.

> **JM** When you are singing, your patient will sit still. That is when you know that she is getting healed. The patient is sitting still and doesn't move around. She likes it, that is why she is sitting still. You watch your patient, and if he or she is sitting still, you know it is effective. . . . And, anything that was moving on her (whatever is causing the illness), the process of my singing takes away from my patient what is bothering her. Anything that moves on her, when I sing, it all goes away. . . . In your song, you take what is bothering her away. Your patient sits still and is not nervous, so you know that the power is working on her to get healed.
>
> **AS** So that is how you know?
>
> **JM** Yes. That is how I know. (Interview with Mariano)

Alternatively, a practitioner can measure the relative success of the ceremony on the basis of the patient's reaction when he or she leaves the hooghan at dawn. As Madalin Chavez describes, "When they go out in the morning to do the prayer, they pray out there and they are crying and they are asking for this and that, and that is how I know that my voice is working on them. In this prayer they receive cars, they receive jewelry, they receive horses and cows and that is why they are praying out there and crying and all that. That is the way that it really helps them" (interview with Chavez).

Grace Emerson points out that weeks, months, or years after a ceremony, patients will return to bear testimony to its success. As she recalls,

> They get well when you sing for them. I have done a lot of sings for people. . . . Later on, they return to see me. They say, "I am the one that you sang for." And they thank me for doing the sing for them and they tell me, "Now I am feeling well." For me, sometimes I am concerned over how I am going to make them well, I worry about it, but it works. They do get well. It will work. Some of them are not walking, but after I do a ceremony for them they are walking again. Some of them are not walking, some of them are not talking, and then after the ceremony they are walking again, they are talking again. Sometimes their eyes are like this (blinking), and they get healed too. I do it for them in the evening and the next day they

are looking and seeing things. Their eyes are well. That is how it is. (Interview with Emerson)

Once a recently apprenticed woman's practice begins, she must navigate potential problems in two divergent realms—bodily functions and socially directed obligations and limitations on what a woman can or cannot do. While navigating these various rules and would-be troubles, primary concern is consistently focused on one's patient, one's paraphernalia, and in the case of pregnancy, with the vulnerability of one's unborn child. A new practitioner must also fulfill all pecuniary obligations to her mentor or mentors.

PRESTATIONS

MB I did pay him for it. But, it is not money that I paid him, it is what they put down, the people put down like shawls and robes, and baskets and things like that. And what they gave me to do the sing. And four times, I gave it to him, and that covered my obligation.

MS So you mean the first four Blessing Way that you did?

MB Unhuuhn.

MS People gave you shawls and baskets, material things, you gave those to him—

MB Those to him four times, and that is it.

MS In exchange for learning.

MB For learning?

MS Yes. (Interview with Bekis, 1993)

I paid him with whatever I brought back—baskets, blankets, materials, men's robes, and the cash I was paid. Four times, I gave him all that I was given for the first four ceremonies that I performed. . . . When I would come home. I usually only came home with two materials for myself. I give them (her mentors) the baskets and blankets and materials. Now, I bring it all home and it piles up in the corner! (pointing with her chin to a pile in the hooghan). (Interview with Chavez)

The first four times that I performed the ceremony, I gave him all the money that was given to me to perform, the basket that I used to wash the patient, and for the blankets and materials that were put down. "Four times you perform a ceremony," that was the payment that I made. "After that, it is all yours." (Interview with Mariano)

As noted by Mae Ann Bekis, Madalin Chavez, and Jean Mariano, in addition to whatever valuables are given to a mentor at the time of initiation, afterwards the newly ordained singer is obligated to compensate her mentor for the knowledge exchanged throughout the apprenticeship. In many cases, this consists of all that is given to the singer for performance of her first four ceremonies (see also Ch'iao 1971:34–35; Frisbie 1987:91; Sandner 1979:29). In addition, a singer will continue to pay her mentor whenever cases arise for which additional information is required. By way of illustration, Mae Ann Bekis offered the following examples:

And, every time somebody comes with a problem, they're different problems, they're not all the same. Like, uh, "I'm going to court Monday, can you do a prayer for me?" Like, "I had an accident" or "Somebody hit me but they're blaming me for it," you know. And then there's a different prayer for it, and then like D., uh, H.'s daughter, her kids were fighting and she whipped them and then one of them stayed home, the other one, she came to Tsaile [, Arizona] with it, and uh, when there was graduation going on. And they, the other one went to school and she had, uh, lashes on her, and said that "My mother beat me up!" And so they took her kids away and here I did a sing over at, uh, at Roundhouse Canyon, and here all a sudden here she comes, with the money in her hand she says "I want you to do something for me. My kids are taken away," and she was in tears. I said "Hey, don't cry! We just did the sing here." And uh, so she quit and then she just, she just took off outside after she hand me the money. So I say "I'll be over there at your house," and then so I came back over here, told my husband and my husband was laying there and I said "I'm going down to my uncle to ask him how to do this one." So I just gave him [her uncle] the money and he told me what to do. How to do it and everything. And then another one came an old man came from Chinle [, Arizona], he said that, uh, in his sleep he went and wet his bed. And so he gave me the money, too, so I went back to my uncle, gave him the money, I said, "This man came from Chinle and said he wet his bed." And so I gave him the money that the man had given me and so he says, "Well, do it this way," and, uh, so I did it that week. And so, every time something comes up differently you have to go back, and whatever you got paid you have to give it to him and he tells you how to do it. (Interview with Bekis, 1998a)

Thus, the pattern continues from apprenticeship through initiation and throughout practice, a prestation must accompany each instruction indefinitely.

CHALLENGES

MS Have you faced any challenges as a female practitioner?

AS From the time you started conducting ceremonies to today, have you encountered any men who questioned you about being a medicine woman?

JM There are a lot of them. There are a lot who question me and the ceremonies that I conduct. People who said that are plenty.

AS When they come to see you, do they say that to your face?

JM No, but only from a distance, from behind the hills, and those who gossip, information obtained through third parties. They say that so-and-so said this. My father forewarned me about that, [he said] that "People will be saying that to you. But just know that you did not learn the ceremony before them. They were not aware of the training you had to learn these ceremonies. They were not surrounding you while you were first learning. Just know, that people who say that will be the first for you to conduct your ceremonies on" . . .

AS Those who criticize you, are they saying that because you are a woman?

JM Yes.

AS Yes. She said, "because I am a woman and, they say that, 'She is a woman, where did she learn all of that?' "

MS Do they challenge her performing the Blessing Way? And the Night Way? Or, just one ceremony or the other?

AS Does that apply to both?

JM Yes.

AS Both.

MS Both?

AS Yes, uh-huh the Blessing Way and the Night Way. (Interview with Mace)

In response to my query, Have you faced any challenges as a female practitioner? women spoke of being forewarned to anticipate criticism and given advice on how best to handle it (interviews with Mace, Manson, Yazzie). Pearly Yazzie reported that her mentor told her "People that talk about you now, will use you for Blessing Way in the future, everybody will," and she added "That is what happened" (interview with Yazzie).

Knowing Navajo beliefs about the ability of language to call things into being, I regretted having to ask this question since consultants might think I was wishing them problems. Understandably, the women with whom I consulted had a variety of responses to this query. The quick replies of women such as Madalin Chavez and Elizabeth Edison who said "No! Nobody says anything" (interview with Chavez) and "Nobody talks against me!" (interview with Edison), let me know that they were honestly shocked at the innuendo. Betty Begay gave a more measured response when she told me, "No, nobody ever said any of those things to us. I hear of people saying things like that, but nobody ever said that to me" (interview with Begay).

Other women pointed out that such challenges never arose because their long-standing relationships with their mentors were publicly known and accepted. Sarah Ruth John noted, "People know that I followed my daddy around and I did all that my father did and I keep it up now" (interview with John). In like fashion, Nettie Nez pointed out, "From way back when I first started learning from my mom, she used to go different places and I was with her. People knew her and they used her to participate in Blessing Way. So she was known everywhere" (interview with Nez). And, Irma Wheeler Higdon had the following to say on the matter:

> IH NO! Nobody criticize me. They just, they know that I go with my dad all of the time. So when I am doing my ceremony, I just start singing. Nobody is going to say anything to me because when I was with my dad they were not there, nobody was there.
>
> MS Right.
>
> IH So, I am the only one that knows the songs and that is all. (Interview with Higdon)

Both Laura Nix and Helen Olsen Chee stressed the fact that they are recognized as carrying on a family tradition. Laura Nix said "They comment about me that 'That is coming from her dad, her brother, all the way down,' so nobody talks against me. When I do a prayer or when I do Blessing Way, I didn't learn it just a while ago, I learned it a long time ago, it has come down the family" (interview with Nix). Because of a similar association, Helen Olsen Chee feels immune to such routine questioning. As she explains, "Sometimes they will say 'Who did she learn from?' or 'Who did you learn from?' They ask you that question a lot of times, but not me. People know that it went down through the family and that I learned from my grandfather and my mother. So people don't challenge me" (interview with Chee).

Confident in her role, Jean Mariano simply stated, "I don't know, they might be talking about me out of my sight. But I never heard anything like that. Nobody has ever come to me face-to-face to ask 'How did you learn?' and all that. Nobody talks against me to my face. I know whom I learned from. That is it" (interview with Mariano). Pearly Yazzie also denied knowledge of any criticism, but coyly pointed out that circumstances might be different if the need for qualified practitioners was less in her area. As she put it, "I was never talked against. No one ever spoke against me about my singing. From here, around me, nobody says anything against me. I have not heard anything said against me. Right here where we are, there are no medicine men. Back where I grew up near Big Mountain they had some medicine men, maybe there they would have said something. But here there is no one. That is why I have been doing it around here. People around here really need me, so nobody says anything against me" (interview with Yazzie).

Concurring with Pearly Yazzie on the shortage of practitioners, Betty Begay noted, "It is scarce these days to find people who know the ceremonies" (interview with Begay). Therefore, rather than challenges, she reports, "Nobody says anything against me, they encourage me and praise me. No one ever speaks against me" (interview with Begay). Instead they say "It is good that you learned all of these things from your husband" (interview with Begay).

Similarly, Laura Nix said "Nobody talked against me. I am only praised about being a practitioner" (interview with Nix). Elizabeth Edison noted "A lot of people just praise me for what I am doing. . . . 'That is how you heal people,' that is what they say to me. 'You have all kinds of prayers in you, so you heal people with them,' that is what they tell me" (interview with Edison).

Those who reported having faced challenges attributed them to two factors—jealousy and ignorance. Juanita Mace simply stated, "It is hard. People envy you if you know a ceremony, that is what I have come to find out. That is how I have come to find out, when one becomes a medicine person" (interview with Mace). In her explanation of such criticisms, Gladys Denny reaffirms the importance for public recognition of a woman's career status change while following a mentor: "I was told by others that some are saying that 'She doesn't know how to sing,' and asking 'Whom did she learn from?' They don't know that I am doing this and they don't know that I learned from my husband. They don't know that I have been helping all this time, for many years. I have done all that needs to be done for my husband and that is how I learned from him. And they don't know this, but they can talk about me if they want because I know. I didn't want to learn! I didn't want to become a singer!" (interview with Denny).

As mentors predicted, ultimately in most situations where challenges arise, such as in the following example provided by Eunice Manson, critics are brought around through the success of a woman's ceremonies.

> **MS** I'm wondering what kind of challenges you've faced as a female practitioner?
>
> **EM** Yes, yes, there were challenges. However, never in my presence. Never to my face. It was hearsay, you know, elsewhere. And eventually someone would come over and tell me. For instance, there was a time when a relative of mine came over and told me that there was this one individual that was claiming that I did not know these songs and prayers, that I just stole from somebody and I was not performing them in an orderly fashion and in an effective fashion. I just let it be. And, as a matter of fact, almost a year later, that same person that was accusing me of that, his wife came to me for help. Their daughter had an awful dream. . . . To be sure that whatever awfulness may be waiting in the future does not occur, a certain ceremony is performed. So, his wife and the daughter came over and said, "My daughter had this dream and we're asking you to perform a ceremony." And, and I said to them, . . . "Where's the father? I thought he knew everything! Isn't he the same man that was accusing me of not knowing these things?" And the mother admitted to me that yes, he said those things, but she knew that he himself did not learn these things properly and for that reason she wasn't going to him with the problem that their daughter was having, she was coming to me. Only when she admitted that he was wrong did I agree to perform the ceremony. He witnessed the ceremony, you know, he stayed in his place and I wasn't afraid to perform the ceremony. I performed the appropriate ceremony and he witnessed it. He said no more after that. (Interview with Manson)

Challenges aside, as with apprenticeship and initiation, rules governing what one can or cannot do while experiencing certain bodily functions or discharging certain bodily fluids must be navigated when practicing. Thus, sexual and reproductive concerns influence the lives of ceremonial practitioners on a day-to-day basis.

PREGNANCY

> I was not told that I could not learn or practice while I was pregnant. Other five-day singing, that is different, they say no, but with the Blessing Way it is all right. (Interview with Yazzie)

Without identifying the ceremony in question, Reichard claims that a female practitioner may sing while pregnant as long as she recites a prayer beforehand to protect her child (1950:174). The women with whom I consulted had various opinions about whether or not a woman can perform ceremonies while pregnant.

According to Jean Mariano and Pearly Yazzie, women can freely perform the Blessing Way ceremony while pregnant. But regarding the Hóchxǫ́ǫ́'jí, Madalin Chavez said, "I didn't do it while I was pregnant. Because while I was pregnant, or when the baby wasn't talking, I wouldn't do it. I am careful with that. After I stopped having my children, I became a regular Hóchxǫ́ǫ́ji singer" (interview with Chavez). Sarah John reported "With my last one, only the last one, I went ahead and did the [Water Way] ceremony when I was pregnant with him," but went on to add, "not everything." As she explains, "If I was making a ǫołáad [herbs such as rabbit brush and cedar wrapped in a bundle with feathers on the end] I could not do it all, I would leave one part untied, so that it is not tied all the way. . . . So that you won't have trouble having the baby. When you tie everything, it ties up the cord around the child's neck" (interview with John).

AADI'

AS When you are performing a sing for a woman, if she gets her aadi' what will you do?

MC I just go out. You just take your paraphernalia out and you don't perform like drypainting or other things. When you are about to go over there, sometimes they say, "My grandma came." And, you just stop and don't go over there. When you get there you ask her, "When are you expecting your grandma?" They will tell you. It all has to do with the moon, half moon, full moon, in between there. (Interview with Chavez)

AS When your patient gets her aadi', what will you do?

MJW You just stop the whole thing. You just stop the whole thing. All the other ceremonies—the five- and nine-day ceremonies—are like that. They all must be stopped if the patient begins to menstruate. (Interview with Whitney)

AS If you are performing and if your patient gets her aadi', what do you do about it?

JM You stop. You stop and then you go home until after she is over with it and washed up and everything, then you can go back and do it again. (Interview with Mariano)

The consensus among the Hózhǫ́ǫ́jí singers with whom I consulted is that should a patient's aadi' commence in the midst of a ceremony, the ceremony must be stopped and rescheduled after her menstrual period is over and she has cleansed herself (interviews with Chee, Higdon, Mariano, Nix, Whitney, Yazzie). According to practitioners of other ceremonies, this also holds true for Hóchxǫ́ǫ́'jí (Evil Way), Tóee (Water Way), and Na'at'oii biką' (Male Shooting Way). Grace Emerson reports that she could not perform the blackening portion of Hóchxǫ́ǫ́'jí on a patient with her aadi'. As she explains, "Some of them, when they come to see me, they tell me right off, 'I am like this. I am on my aadi'. Can you still perform for me?' And I tell them, 'No. You just go on home and wait until it is over and then wash up. After that, come back and I can do the sing for you'" (interview with Emerson). Sarah Ruth John reported that in such a situation, "You use chííh dík'ǫ́ǫ́zh. You stop the ceremony. And then watch, and when your patient's period is over you can plan the ceremony again" (interview with John). In the case of Na'at'oii biką', the ceremony must be stopped and started over after the woman is done with her aadi' (interview with Denny). Betty Begay emphasized that with this ceremony, "You have to start from the beginning again. Not where you stopped, you have to do the entire ceremony all over again" (interview with Begay).

In contrast, Gaye Shorthair reports that if a patient gets her aadi' while a Night Way is being performed over her the ceremony must also be stopped, but it can be started over from wherever the practitioner left off once the patient is done with her aadi'. As she explains, "If you know how far you went, you can start over from there" (interview with Shorthair).

A primary concern of practitioners is to protect their voices and their paraphernalia from the effect of aadi'. Protection is attained by means of avoidance or through the use of chííh dík'ǫ́ǫ́zh. As Elizabeth Edison points out, "I am protective of my paraphernalia and must keep things like that away from it. I really take care of my bundle. I am protective of myself and protective of my children and my patients, so I won't do a ceremony when anybody is on her period. And, when I had aadi' myself when I was younger I would stop, also. Now I am free of that. I don't want to do a prayer or sing or anything when somebody is on her period. I always ask questions about it before we begin" (interview with Edison).

Grace Emerson notes that chííh dík'ǫ́ǫ́zh serves as a general prophylactic against errant menstruating women.

> The medicine men usually watch the cycle of the moon. Navajo women tend to have their periods between the quarter and the full moon and not during the rest of the month. During these times of the month, the singers suspect that women who come into their ceremonies might be on their aadi', so they use the chííh dík'ǫ́ǫ́zh. They take it themselves, and blow it on their paraphernalia. That is

how it is used. When a person is really sick, they put some in the patient's mouth and then they blow it on the patient so that no harm could be done by women on their aadi' being in the ceremony. That is also how the chííh dík'óózh is used. . . . Medicine men must carry chííh dík'óózh with themselves all the time, for their own protection. They carry it in a pouch with their other paraphernalia. . . . When a patient is sick, when other people come around and they are on their periods, it can make them real sick and they will not sit still, and they will perspire and their heart rates go way up. That is where the chííh dík'óózh is used for the patient and the medicine man and his paraphernalia. (Interview with Emerson)

Another central concern is protection of the voice (interviews with Ashley, 1991; Begay; Bekis, 1992, 1993, 1998a; Chee; Dahozy; Agnes B. Dennison; Denny; Deswood; Dooley, 1998; Etcitty; Higdon; John; Mace; Manson; Nix; Walters, 1995a; Whitney; Yazzie). As the spiritual aspect of Navajo persons, voice shares its constitution with Holy People and jish, therefore, like these entities, it is hypersensitive to the dangerous elements of aadi'. Singers must be assiduously cognizant of their voices' susceptibility and, as Betty Begay remarks, wary of all women entering a ceremony. "When you are singing it bothers your voice, you lose your voice. If a woman on her aadi' comes into the ceremony, that is when the singers lose their voices. If this happens, then they usually say amongst themselves, 'I wonder if someone is on her aadi'? I am losing my voice.' The singer takes out the chííh dík'óózh and takes it four times, blows it on himself and he blows it on his paraphernalia. That is how it is used" (interview with Begay).

Despite these concerns, women shared information about several exceptions to the strict prohibition against direct contact between aadi' and ceremonials. Sarah John reports, "If my patient has an aadi' at other than her regular time, then that means that whatever was ailing her came out with the aadi' " (interview with John). Since this flow of blood demonstrates the Water Way's effectiveness in purging the illness from her body, the ceremony can be continued.

Nettie Nez, Laura Nix, and Gaye Shorthair indicated that a protection prayer can be done for a patient while on her aadi'. Nettie Nez notes that the procedure can be done because the arrowhead used in this ceremony "sits" between the aadi' and the patient for protection. As she explains, "Protection prayer, you can do it with aadi'. Because each person present has an arrowhead in front of him or herself as protection. That is between you and the aadi'. That is how you do it" (interview with Nez). According to Laura Nix, chííh dík'óózh is also used on such an occasion. She said, "If you are doing just a prayer, you can use chííh dík'óózh and go on with it. If you are just doing a small protection prayer, just put some chííh dík'óózh in her mouth with an arrowhead and then use it yourself and blow it on your paraphernalia" (interview with Nix). Affirming these accounts, Gaye Shorthair adds, "If you are doing a small ceremony, like a protection prayer, if your patient gets her period, that is when chííh dík'ǫǫzh is used. You put it in her mouth with an arrowhead four times, then you take some yourself and then you blow some on your paraphernalia. That is how it is used. Even a man, if his wife is on her period. For a small prayer, you can go ahead and finish. If the patient gets her period during the night you can use chííh dík'ǫǫzh and finish the prayer in the morning and then leave" (interview with Shorthair).

According to Laura Nix and Helen Olsen Chee, menstruating women can attend Azá'á'nęęł, small ceremonies that are performed for diagnostic purposes (if benefit is noted, a full ceremony is subsequently arranged). In such cases, as described in the following accounts, the use of chííh dík'ǫǫzh plays a vital part in the process.

> If there is a small ceremony going on, there is a medicine for it, it is called chííh dík'ǫǫzh. . . . For just a small ceremony, you put chííh dík'ǫǫzh in the patient's mouth with an arrowhead. Four times, then you take it yourself too. Then you blow it on your patient and the paraphernalia. If it is a real Blessing Way, you don't carry on, you stop. Then you tell them, "I will return later on after you are finished with your period." The use of chííh dík'ǫǫzh is for just a small portion of the sing, like a protection prayer, that is where you use that. (Interview with Nix)

> If someone with her aadi' comes in to the small portions of Yé'ii Bicheii that they do and the small portions of Lightning Way or Flint Way, she can use the chííh dík'ǫǫzh. . . . Just tell the medicine person that you are on your period but that you want to go in and he will tell you that you have to use the chííh dík'ǫǫzh and you have to bless everyone that is in there and all the paraphernalia, you have to bless all of it, and then you can go in there. . . . Just the Blessing Way, you cannot go in when you are on your period. Any other ceremony, you can go in or help with the food if you use chííh dík'ǫǫzh. With Yé'ii Bicheii, you cannot dance with the Yé'ii Bicheii dance group while on your monthly. (Interview with Chee)

Nettie Nez reports that for the Enemy Way Blessing Way, use of chííh dík'ǫǫzh allows the ceremony to be continued if a female patient's aadi' begins unexpectedly. The ceremony must be stopped, however, if the patient's aadi' begins after a certain point in the Enemy Way Blessing Way ceremony.

> AS When you are performing a ceremony, if your patient gets her aadi', what will you do?

NN You have medicine for it.

AS Hmm.

NN Just give them the medicine.

AS What kind of medicine?

NN Chííh dík'óózh. If it is a regular Blessing Way, then you must stop.

AS How about yours?

NN That is Naayée'ee hózhǫǫjí (Enemy Way Blessing Way). It is pointing in the direction of Monster Slayer. The real Blessing Way is different. It is different because in the real Blessing Way you mention jewelry and all the good things in your songs. If I am doing the Blessing Way, the real Blessing Way, then I have to stop if a patient gets her aadi' and wait until she is clear of it. If I am performing Naayee'ee hózhǫǫjí and this happens then I have the patient use chííh dík'óózh. . . . After I wash my patient, and put cornmeal on her to dry her, and after that she has her period. Then, I call it off. Even Naayee'ee hózhǫǫjí. It is not good. (Interview with Nez)

SEXUAL CONTINENCE

My singing is this way and all of the singing is this way. After you come back from performing, you do not sleep with your husband. Even the one I am doing (the Blessing Way), it is the same. If I perform, all the people who are there that take tádídíín, they cannot go home and crawl into bed with their husband or wife. When I come back from performing, I cannot crawl into bed with my own husband. If you crawl into bed with your husband, either side—you or your patient—if you crawled into bed with your husband or had sexual relations, nothing could help—there is no cure! If you are a medicine person you cannot sleep in the cornfield or where the water runs in a gully or wash, you cannot sleep there either, to do so would cause the same thing. (Interview with Whitney)

Over and beyond restrictions against mixing tádídíín with sex, strict continence rules exist to prevent the mixing of sexuality with ceremonial healing in general. Most women agreed that a practitioner must not engage in any sexual activity during a ceremony or for two (interview with Yazzie), three (interview with Chavez), or four days (interviews with Begay, Chee, Edison, Emerson, John, Mariano, Nix, Yazzie) after the close of the ceremony. As Madalin Chavez explains,

A man was given to me, I told the man, "I am going to perform a ceremony tonight and you are not supposed to bother me for four days. If you want to follow me it is OK, if you want to, but you don't have to," I told him that. That is like that, that is how you do. That is how I was told. My dad told his son-in-law, taught him that. He told him, "You are not to sleep together or have any sexual relations while my daughter is performing." I was told the same thing too. When I am cold, I just lay against him. That is it. As soon as I started, I was told, "No-no" . . . After four days, I will wash up and then I could crawl into bed with my husband. But, before I do anything, somebody always comes and I am on my way again to do another performance. So, we never do anything. (Interview with Chavez)

As pointed out by Helen Olsen Chee in the following account, such restrictions on sexual contact can cause marital strain:

That is why I am single, some men can't wait for four days. Even if you are a medicine man or woman you have to keep yourself holy for four days. If you do have sexual relations before four days, you are causing a big problem on your patient. We call it *náos't'qá'* [to cause to become undone], that means if I did a sing last night and then I went home and had sexual relations with my man, then I caused náos't'ąá' on the patient. It is the same for the patient. You tell your patient when you are leaving in the morning, "You leave your man alone for four days. No relations, don't share a bed, don't kiss, don't mess around for four days. After you wash up you can have your sexual relations again" . . . If you are not doing anything (in the capacity of singer), you can have your relationship. But, I am not. I am single. (Interview with Chee)

Given the value placed on children and the fact that she began performing the Blessing Way ceremony at the youthful age of twenty, I was surprised to learn from Juanita Mace, the only childless woman with whom I consulted, what stringent rules regarding sexual activity were conveyed to her by her father at the time of her initiation. With the help of Amelda Sandoval Shay, we had the following conversation on the matter:

MS How about sexual activity? What were the rules about having sexual relations with her husband in regard to while she was performing?

AS When you are conducting a ceremony, could a man come to you?

JM No.

AS You cannot do that, right? So, when can a man come to you?

JM You cannot be bothered with a man as a practitioner. . . . The men are told that they have to sleep alone. That is what he [referring to her husband] was told. That is why there is a bed for him over there and my bed is here [indicating the placement of beds in their home].

AS So that is removed from you, right?

JM Yes, that is completely removed from you.

AS I assumed it was resumed, like after four days. Some say that they can function as a couple after a certain number of days.

JM No, that is not right. Once you become a medicine woman you don't have any sexual activity after that, as long as you live. You have to distance yourself from that. You cannot bother men again. In exchange they cannot bother you. (Interview with Mace)

As noted by Helen Olsen Chee and amplified by several others, breach of sexual continence rules can have dire consequences on all parties involved in a ceremony. For instance, Madalin Chavez points out that her mentor taught her that such behavior would cause items of her own very powerful paraphernalia to work against her: "I have *k'eet'áán yáłti' bik̨a'ii dóó k'eet'áán yáłti' bi'aad'ii* [male and female talking prayer sticks bundled together]. They are what I use when I am performing a Blessing Way. That is why I cannot have sexual relations when I am finished singing. If I did, it would make me go crazy. The person that prepared these for me said that if I were to violate this rule, 'They will work against you and not help your patients,' that is what I was told. Those k'eet'áán are in my pouch bag, I have them in there" (interview with Chavez).

Echoing Mary Ben Jones Whitney's comment that there is no cure for such a breach and Helen Olsen Chee's comments on náos't'ą́á', Elizabeth Edison stresses the negative effect on a singer's patients that would result from violation of these taboos.

AS When you were young, when you were practicing, did you ever do a sexual relationship? How about that?

EE No. I never did that. You are careful with your patient and if you have sexual relations you will be causing problems with your patient. That is one thing that you are told when you are learning, you must wait four days after you come home. It has to be four days. So you have to be careful. . . . I never did anything like that when I came home. You have to wait. I just don't run around when I am doing a singing, I just stay with my bundle. I don't run around on it. I have to fix my bundle right [put everything back in order] and then I have to go home. You keep yourself holy while perform-ing and after you go home, you cannot wash up until four days after that. (Interview with Edison)

Over and beyond nullifying the potential beneficial influences of the ceremony, such violations can affect one in a multitude of ways. After she was widowed, Mae Ann Bekis recalls her uncle warning her "Be careful not to marry your voice away!" (interview with Bekis, 1998b) meaning that if she were to indulge in inappropriate sexual conduct, her voice would lose its ability to call the Holy People to a cere-mony whenever their assistance is needed. As Grace Emerson explains, there is no time limit on when these potential ill effects will become manifest, for they can strike at any point later in life.

GE It will bother you, not right now, after several years. That is what they say, they take care of themselves. They know to avoid sleeping together. You have to be careful with the patient, if you have relations the patient will not heal properly. So it is both sides, the singer and the patients. If a lady is a medicine person it is the same way for her, she is not supposed to be sleeping with her husband. You can't bother the man.

AS How will it affect you?

GE It can cause paralysis or make your body twist or your mouth crooked, that is the way it bothers you. That is not right away, it is later years. Even your eyes, even your sight. Your sight can get crooked so that you cannot see correctly. Or it can blind you. It can make it so that you cannot move, it can cripple you, your legs or your hands. That is the way it bothers you and there is no cure for it, so that is why they said no. . . . When someone is doing the ceremony, she handles corn pollen and medicine paraphernalia like the mountain earth bundle and all different kinds of medicines that are put on patients and the dust from these blows onto the practi-tioner. That is why it is very important that when she comes home she cleanses herself. If you don't have a sweat bath, you can take a shower. Before taking a shower, you must rinse your hair in a bowl—to collect all of the tádídíín that you have put on your head during corn pollen blessing in the ceremony. This water must be poured gently on the ground close to the hooghan. It is given back to Mother Earth. Then, you can take a very hot shower. After that, you can have sexual relations. (Interview with Emerson)

Moreover, as explained by Helen Olsen Chee and Elizabeth Edison, to remain above reproach in the community, women practitioners make a practice of limiting their involvement with certain activities, especially some of those associated with Enemy Way ceremonies. Because of the sexual attraction that accompanies partner interactions in the social dancing portions of this ceremony, women practitioners must follow strict mores. As Helen Chee Olsen explains, "When the social dancing of an Enemy Way is going on, I cannot pull out a man to dance with me. When there is a Round Dance I can join in, because you do not choose a partner. But I cannot pull out a partner" (interview with Chee). Also, because Enemy Way ceremonies are notorious for the sexual indiscretions and drunken revelry that commonly accompany them (Aberle 1982 [1966]:212; Levy and Kunitz 1974:75–77; Schwarz 2001b:152–180; Zion 1991:142), women carefully walk the line between their duty to assist with food preparation, or to provide food products, livestock, and other necessities to relatives hosting the ceremony (Jacobson 1964; Lamphere 1977) and socially appropriate behavior for practitioners. Elizabeth Edison noted,

Some ladies are doing healing but they go out and run around and do things they are not supposed to do, but I am not doing these things because I care for my paraphernalia. If there is an Enemy Way going on, I go there, take food and then come back right away. I never hang around there. All I do is help them and then come back, all I am thinking about is my ceremonies. I am busy, so I just take food over there and come right back. . . . Drinking and all of those things, I do not do that because my voice is so important for me. That is why people say that they are really proud of me as a singer. (Interview with Edison)

Furthermore, Helen Olsen Chee pointed out, "On the last night, members of the staff-receiver's family go as a group to sing outside the hooghan and meet the patient's family. I cannot go with them even though I am a medicine woman. The rest you can do, help with the cooking, bringing food and all of that, get candy when they throw it out, and all of that I can do" (interview with Chee). Over and beyond these restrictions, certain ceremonial procedures are believed by some to be off-limits to women practitioners.

WHAT WOMEN CANNOT DO IN CEREMONIES

AS Were you ever told that there was something that you could not do while performing a ceremony because you are a woman?

GE No. He never told me that. I do all of this [the blackening portion of the Hóchx$\phi\phi'$jí] and no one ever told me not to do this or that. (Interview with Emerson)

A lady can do Hóchx$\phi\phi'$jí, a lady can do all the ceremonies, but Enemy Way. (Interview with Edison)

AS When you started your learning, did your husband ever tell you, "This is what a lady cannot do." Did he ever tell you about anything that only a man can do?

BB No. He never did tell me about anything that only a man can do. He just told me how to do the drypaintings and other things [for the Na'at'oii bik$\mathe{a}$'] and said "Do it right." And even the songs. (Interview with Begay)

The women with whom I consulted shared a wide range of views on exactly what, if anything, a woman cannot do in the ceremonial realm. When a woman from Sanostee, New Mexico, expressed her wish to learn the Fire Dance from an uncle, her father told her "You can't, because that's different, that's only for men. . . . It's not for you because you're a female" (interview with anonymous woman, 2000). Yet, Louella Deswood noted only two restrictions given to her by her grandfather while learning the Fire Dance. As she explained, "I was told that in the nine-night [Fire Dance] ceremony, I cannot be a corn spreader. They call it *ak'áánaaniił'íí*. And then I cannot do the shock treatment, the shock treatment within that ceremony. I have to, I have to designate a couple male people to do those things for me while I just go ahead and give them the instructions on how to do them" (interview with Deswood). She does not see these restrictions as hindrances, however, because as she continued, "But then I would be the chanter and so, the chanter usually does not do those things anyway" (interview with Deswood).

Opinions vary even among those performing the same ceremony. Some such as Mary Ben Jones Whitney pointed out that there are no restrictions on Blessing Way, "Not for Blessing Way. Only the Enemy Way, the Night Way, and others, only that side has parts that women cannot do" (interview with Whitney). Indeed, Gaye Shorthair noted that as a woman she was told not to do one part of the Night Way ceremony. As she explains, "The first group that dances in Yé'ii Bicheii, I was told that 'You don't do that as a woman.' Fred Stevens told me this. There is a song that is sung for the dancers when they are dressing up" (interview with Shorthair).

For nearly every example a woman provided about a specific practice that she was taught not to do, another woman practitioner of the same ceremony offered a counterexample on the same point. For instance, Madalin Chavez provided a detailed account of what her paternal uncles told her she could not do:

> They did the Small Wind Way and Moon Eclipse and Sun Eclipse. They used to do this, but my father told me "Never paint a patient in a Wind Way or any other painting that you are going to do. Just stay away from those things because they are sharp and you are not supposed to do that." My father said "The painting is not for you because it is all with the Enemy Way." I do the moon and sun eclipse ceremony, just a small portion after you give medicine to your patient, which is called "corn pollen." My father performed that ceremony. . . . My dad and my uncle painted the patients. But my dad told me not to do it. "Don't paint a patient, because you will be just putting that paint on yourself and it will not be effective to make the patient heal," he said. And, if I did it for a man, it would just reflect back on me. That is why I just do the moon and sun eclipse, just a small portion. "Just make the white face and the yellow face because that is tádídíín," that is what my daddy told me. (Interview with Chavez)

In variance to Madalin Chavez, Mae Ann Bekis noted that she has done this exact type of body painting for her uncle. As she explains, "He gives me corn pollen when I finish the painting, and I have to go around with corn pollen on every mark that I have made. That is for my protection. I am initiated with that [meaning that she has had this ceremony performed for her and that an abalone shell was made for her to wear on her hair tie to designate this fact]. When I do the painting, I must be sure to wear the hair tie with the beads on it so that the Holy People will recognize that when I do the painting for the Small Wind Way" (personal communication with Bekis, 2001g).

Gladys Denny maintained that there are no limitations on what a woman can do in the Lightning Way. She said, "I was told that there are no restrictions, so I do everything" (interview with Denny). In contrast, Madalin Chavez noted that she was directed not to do the "Lightning Way drypaintings. There is a male and female moon and sun. These are no-nos. Only the men can make these images. A man can do that. . . . These are pertaining to Female Lightning Way and Male Lightning Way" (interview with Chavez). Furthermore, she pointed out, "If a tree was struck by lightning and someone was hurt, only a man can go over there and do the offering, prayers, and the singing. Through hand-trembling you assist, you just do the hand-trembling and tell them what is happening" (interview with Chavez).

When asked if she had been told that as a woman she could not perform any part of the Blessing Way, Laura Nix replied, "No, nobody told me that. I questioned that myself too, but it is made for us, so I learned and I am doing it." They told me that, "If you are a woman, if you learn how to do these things, if you do it right, there is nothing against it, you can do it." I was told, "It is good that you are doing this. You can do it for women or men or children" (interview with Nix). Yet Jean Mariano took the opposite position:

> I was told, "When you are performing ceremonies you are not to talk about all the things that you learned and what you are doing or the story of your songs. When you are performing, you cannot talk about your singing." Some people do that, but I was told not to do that. . . . Some women, they go and say "This is the way I was taught to do," and "This is the way I was told the story," sometimes they talk about that but I cannot. That is it. (Interview with Mariano)

Resonating with what Madalin Chavez's father said regarding avoiding "sharp" elements in ceremonial contexts, Jean Mariano recalls her uncle offering the following explanation: "If it is a man, he can talk about his singing all he wants because the man has a bow and arrows. As for you, all you have is a stirring stick. That is your weapon. You don't have any sharp object for protection," that is what my uncle told me. That is why when I am performing singing I don't talk about all these things—the songs, the stories, and all" (interview with Mariano). In opposition to what Jean Mariano was taught, Mae Ann Bekis reports that she was told it is acceptable for her to discuss the stories that accompany Blessing Way songs and practices (personal communication with Bekis, 2001b).

Contrary to other Blessing Way singers who reported having no restrictions (interviews with Nix, Whitney), however, she went on to indicate two things that she was told not to do. She was directed not to perform Blessing Way in certain circumstances, "like for servicemen, I can't do that" (interview with Bekis, 1998a). As she clarifies, "Not unless, if, I was a soldier myself, because I don't know what goes on over there and what people go through over there, like training and all that, I don't know anything about it. And, uh, my uncle says, 'You can't perform for a service person, like coming back and all that,' he said, 'Don't do it'" (interview with Bekis, 1998a). In addition, she reported being told that she could not mention certain beings while performing one of the closing prayers in Blessing Way. As she explicates, "A prayer, too. He does real strong prayers, John Bull does, toward the end, you know. And he told me, he said a lady can't do that part where they say about the *hajíínái* [place of emergence] and where they say about the red coyote, or the red bird, you know, and that, I can't say that, you know, I can't say that in the prayer, within my prayer I can't say that. He said that's just a man, like, like himself, he was wounded in war and, uh, he can perform Enemy Way, but I can't" (interview with Bekis, 1998a). This latter point—that only men can perform Enemy Way—is not at all out of the ordinary, for most women consulted on this matter maintained that the Enemy Way is the single ceremony women are not to perform (interviews with Chee, Edison, Emerson, Nez, Whitney).

Noting that things have not always been this way, Gaye Shorthair offered the following anecdote about a legendary Navajo woman whose story serves to explain why women do not currently perform the Enemy Way.

> Asdzą́ą́ Awoo'íí [Woman With Teeth] did everything. She partici-
> pated in every aspect of the Enemy Way, killing the scalp and all of
> that. Like one time, they were having an Enemy Way dance and
> she was standing on one side with a group of men, the group on the
> other side were singing about women. Then she sang about men
> *every part of their bodies!* [Laughs]. She outdid them! She was the one
> that did everything before us, so that is how we are doing this too
> of what we are not supposed to do. . . . After they came back from
> Fort Sumner [, New Mexico] and they had a war with the Utes, that
> is when it happened. It happened right around Canyon de Chelly
> and I know what she said too, when she took off. She went over the
> hill, the men that she sang about, she sang against, so they made
> fun of her. They said to her, "Go ahead and take off! I hope the Utes
> catch you and that every one of them has sexual relations with
> you!" She was a warrior, and she would challenge the Utes. She
> would ride up the hill to where the Ute soldiers were within her
> view, then she would yell over to them, "Catch me if you can. If you
> catch me I will have sex with each one of you!" Then she would ride
> off. They never caught her. [Laughter] She said, "Nobody is going
> to copy me. If anybody rides the way I am on a horse then a lady
> can perform Enemy Way!" Meaning, dress the staff and all of that.
> She took off and nobody caught her, she outraced the Utes. (Inter-
> view with Shorthair)

In accordance with Gaye Shorthair's account, and a similar one shared by Mae Ann Bekis (interview with Bekis, 1998a), if any of the Ute warriors had caught Asdzą́ą́ Awoo'íí women would perform the Enemy Way. Since she was never caught however, women are not allowed to perform this ceremony.

Mae Ann Bekis was taught women are restricted in regard to two key elements of the Enemy Way—receipt of and singing for the rattlestick, commonly referred to as the staff (interview with Bekis, 1998a). While acknowledging general consensus against women performing either of these duties in the Enemy Way, Elizabeth Edison disagrees with this view. She notes that should the need arise a woman can both receive and sing for an Enemy Way staff.

> **EE** They said, "No, a woman can't receive the staff." But if there is no one to take it, she can receive it but she doesn't use a basket, she uses the grinding stone to receive it on. . . .
>
> **AS** When they bring the staff in, someone has to sing for the staff before they take the yarn off. Can a woman sing for that staff? Can a woman do that?
>
> **EE** Yes. A woman can sing for the staff if there is no man around. That belongs to women. She can sing for it. Some of them say, "No, a woman cannot sing for it." Sometimes they bring the scalp that needs to be shot at, a woman is not supposed to touch that either, that is what they told me, but I have done it. I said, "Then how come I am a practitioner?" [Meaning that she has been trained and initiated so she therefore believes that she can do all the things that women who are not singers cannot do.] When they bring the staff, they have to look for a young virgin girl. I faced one man when he was saying "A woman cannot sing for it." I told him, "Well if a woman cannot sing for the staff, then why use a girl. When you receive a staff someday, will you carry it back to where it came from by yourself?" So I cornered him. (Interview with Edison)

While describing her challenge to this man at an Enemy Way, Elizabeth Edison points out a marked distinction between the participation of virginal girls in Enemy Way ceremonies and the participation of sexually mature women. This parallels the pre-sexual versus sexual distinction key to understanding Navajo views on different types of menstrual blood.

As Agnes Begay Dennison and Alfred E. Dennison explain, concern over a woman's involvement in the Enemy Way centers on her reproductive abilities and her role as a nurturer of life.

> **AED** Now one ceremony, the Enemy Way, it, the way I hear it, it's hard for a female to be doing that.
>
> **MS** What makes it hard for them to do it?

AED Well, she is given the responsibility when, when she is put on the earth, she is given that responsibility of nourishing life and re-, regenerating this whole growth.

MS Right.

ABD It's going to affect her.

AED Why use her, as, to kill?

MS Oh? [to Agnes] Could you explain?

ABD Uh, it's gonna affect everything . . .

MS Uh-huh.

ABD Whatever you have, like if you have a lot of jewelry, or if you have sheep, cows, horses.

MS Mm-hmm.

ABD It's gonna affect that.

MS So performing the Enemy Way would affect all those blessings?

ABD Yeah. That's why—I guess that's why the women don't do that. (Interview with Agnes B. and Alfred E. Dennison)

As pointed out by Alfred E. Dennison, the central focus of an Enemy Way ceremony is slaying of the enemy who has caused a patient's illness. And, as noted by Nettie Nez in the following, the slaying of enemies has traditionally been the responsibility of Navajo men:

NN When there is an Enemy Way going on, that is with Ndáá' [part of the Enemy Way ceremony], when the women bow their heads as the men take the ashes way over there to put it on the enemy, and then they shoot the enemy too. Only there, we cannot sing there. No. And we cannot shoot either.

AS Why can't we shoot?

NN Because we are women, we can't shoot, only men. . . . That is how it is. We know the songs, but we cannot sing and we cannot shoot. Only the man shoots. The ladies cannot shoot. (Interview with Nez)

According to Grace Emerson, women cannot shoot because "We aren't given a bow and arrows. Only the men were given the bow and arrows, not the women" (interview with Emerson). This was exactly the rationale offered by Jean Mariano's uncle for differences in what men and women can do ceremonially (interview with

Mariano) and it echoes the caution offered by Madalin Chavez's father regarding the need for women to avoid "sharp" elements in ceremonial contexts (interview with Chavez).

In attempting to explain why it is a man who must shoot the enemy, Nettie Nez offers a clue about a fundamental difference between the makeup of men and women in the Navajo world. She told us, "He is going to do it with lightning, that is what he is going to use. That is how it is. As a woman we don't have that in our hand" (interview with Nez). Madalin Chavez further explains this distinction while remembering what her father said to her regarding the difference between men and women in the Navajo world. As she recalls, he said, "The man, he is put down with lightning. And you, sun ray and rainbow, that is all that you [women] are made of" (interview with Chavez). These distinctions came as no surprise to me because I had previously learned that, while sharing a basic constitution and several important characteristics, individuals who will become Navajo men and women are considered to differ from the point of conception, possess some gender-specific attributes (interviews with Chavez; Nez; Walters, 1992), and are meant to fulfill complementary but contrasting roles.[1]

As previously noted by Agnes Begay Dennison and Alfred E. Dennison, the primary culturally sanctioned role for women is that of nurturer. This means that Navajo women are to be mothers whose most important responsibilities are to foster and sustain the development of children (Schwarz 1997:26–27; 238–239). In marked distinction, the culturally sanctioned role for men is that of protector (Schwarz 1997:159–160, 162, 163). This role distinction is symbolized by the traditional weapons of each gender; that is, the *ádístsiin* (stirring sticks) versus the bow and arrows, respectively. As Mae Ann Bekis notes, "Men can do everything because they have, ah, they have a bow and arrows. That was given to the men, and then, uh, the bow guard. These weapons were given to them to fight the war, and to face the war, and that's what it was given to them for, so that's why they can do all the things, you know. And a woman, she was only given a stirring stick for her weapon, and so she can do just so much, that's her weapon. . . . And so there's a lot of difference right there for man and a woman" (interview with Bekis, 1998a).

By some accounts, because these are the only roles and weapons deemed appropriate for men and women, men must initiate apprentices (interviews with Bekis, 1998a; Nix; Shorthair; Yazzie). Indeed, a man initiated each of the women practitioners with whom I consulted. In marked contrast, one woman maintained that women can initiate (interview with Agnes B. Dennison) and, as she explains in the following account, Laura Nix expressed a desire to do so.

> LN I have eight children but only one, the one that is in the service, but he is the only one that is learning the Blessing Way

from me. He is twenty-four years old and he is not married. He is the only one that is trying to learn, he is trying to put them in order yet. He is the only one. He wants to do it when he gets out and when he gets older. He said that, "In that way, it can go on. If somebody goes into old age, another one can pick it up and keep our tradition alive." So he is the only one. . . .

MS Ask who will initiate him once he is done learning?

SM Who is going to initiate him?

LN I guess myself. I will probably do it myself, I did it for him when he was going into the military and when he comes back I do it for him, so I will probably do that for him too. Sometimes over at war, they guard at night by themselves and all this. He usually prays for himself and a song too. So, you stay behind that. [Meaning that the prayer and the song serve as a form of protection for him when in dangerous situations.]

MS Some people have told me that only, only men can initiate.

SM Some people told her that only a man can initiate. Is that true?

LN Yeah, some people do say that, that the men must do it, but I am the one that is training him and he is learning from me so I would like to initiate him myself. Maybe some say that a woman cannot do it, but I am going to do it. He is my baby also, and I want him to know all I know about my songs so I want to do it myself. I want to give my bundle to him myself, if I ever become blind or anything when I get old. (Interview with Nix)

According to Mae Ann Bekis, men must initiate women practitioners because the initiator provides a shield against every illness-causing element encountered throughout their years of practice, a shield not unlike the protection offered to kin and community by a warrior. Only men have the power to wield such a shield and thus to stand between a patient and the source of his or her illness (interview with Bekis, 1998a). As she explains, it is a man's warrior status that enables him to stand up against danger, be it in the form of illness, lightning, or bear: "Only a man does initiation because he's got the authority, like having a gun, bow and arrows, and he can kill animals and things like that. Whereas a lady can't. She can't kill animals. All she has to do is stay home, and take care of her children and the house. And uh, that's the reason why she can't. . . . See, a man stands up against, like, the bear, the snake. The, the danger. He stands between you and the danger of a snake, uh, lightning, and uh, like bears, or lion" (interview with Bekis, 1998a).

When I explained to Elizabeth Edison with the assistance of Amelda Sandoval

Shay what I had been told about men needing to initiate because only they have the requisite weapons to stand between a patient and an illness-causing element, she replied,

> Whoever said this to you doesn't properly ask questions. We have a bow and arrows (points to a fire poker). Fire poker, that is our weapon. Around the fireplace is our bow. So that is our bow and arrows. That is where our prayers originate. The fire poker is our bow. The greasewood is used as arrows. That is ours. So we have bow and arrows. . . . That is how the story goes. . . . Someday, if a man faced me saying "Women don't have a bow and arrows," I would face him with these words. And, that is it. They will not talk back to me! The bear is in front of us. Tsé Nináhálééh [Monster Bird], that is in front of us too. We are the women. Those stand in front of us, so behind that we have a bow and arrows. We have prayers and songs, we are the healers, just as much as they. Where did they come from? They came from us! They are just the fathers of our children. So that is how it is. (Interview with Edison)

Despite their differing opinions, all women maintain that they must do what their particular mentor taught them. This demonstrates the range of variability amongst traditions carried on by specific practitioners across the reservation and the intense sense of loyalty these women maintain to the practitioners with whom they are most closely associated.

CHAPTER VII

FOLLOWING
THE
CEREMONY

AS What do you really appreciate in knowing your ceremony as a medicine woman?

JM It keeps me moving forward. "Come conduct a ceremony for us, come pray for us, we are not able to move on." That is what I am told, each time when people ask me for my help. I simply go from one ceremony to the next. I seem to be just following the ceremony.

AS What is good about that?

JM When one appreciates it, it creates continuity in one's life like that found in the ceremony. . . . It creates a place for me to live. It provides me good thoughts. My father and my mother told me back then, "That is how you will live." (Interview with Mace)

My primary concern has been to document the life-courses of Navajo women who pursue careers as ceremonial practitioners. Navajo exegeses about how women become singers reveal values commonly associated with Navajo society such as flexibility, pragmatism, and personal willingness to adapt and adjust to change. Since many of the women whose narratives are captured in this book have mothers (interviews with Chee, Nez), grandmothers (interview with Whitney), or great-grandmothers (interviews with Chee, Deswood, Higdon) who were singing ladies, we must conclude that the phenomenon of "women as singers" is not a recent development but rather is part of an enduring convention, further emphasizing the long-term nature of these Navajo social traits. To understand the social variables that Navajo women must navigate to take on this role, it was necessary to follow two strands of thought. The first follows the trajectory in apprenticeship, initiation, and practice from performance, through the performative moment when the ceremony is given to the initiate, to witnessing. The second involves unraveling the puzzle of why menstruation and ceremonial matters cannot be mixed. Welcomed by-products of these pursuits are new perspectives on the use of Navajo oral history and the data necessary to analyze whether or not singer is a gender or a role.

FROM PERFORMANCE TO WITNESSING

The life-courses of Navajo women who strive to become ceremonial practitioners are illuminated through analysis of a shift in emphasis from performance to perfomativity that coincides with shifts in emphases from "doing," to "saying," to "witnessing" at critical stages in the process of a woman becoming a singer. Doing is dominant during the apprenticeship phase, the lengthy process wherein an individual attends ceremonies being performed by a particular singer who subsequently becomes a mentor. Gradually, apprentices do more and more of the acts integral to ceremonial practice. Although a woman is "doing" ceremonial practice during her tenure as an apprentice, she is not formally recognized as a practitioner until her new social role is "called into being" through a deliberate performative speech act in the context of an initiation ceremony, which is overseen by the man under whom she apprenticed.

While the point at which her mentor says, "it is yours" may appear to be the quintessential performative moment in the life-course of a Navajo woman becoming a singer, witnessing plays a crucial role in this process. As witnesses, the Holy People must hear the mentor give the ceremony to the initiate. It is they who must ratify and legitimate this act in order for the singer to be efficacious in her career. For if the Navajo Holy People do not hear this speech act, and feel compelled to thenceforth hear the newly initiated singer's pleas for assistance whenever she calls them through the utterance of songs and prayers in a carefully prescribed manner and order, then she will be impotent to help her patients. Moreover, as Butler found with gender, in the case of Navajo women who become ceremonial practitioners, their roles as singers are not manifest by such a singular speech "act," but rather as the reiterative and citational practices that make up the recognitions and negotiations of day-to-day life.

BLOOD

Following Buckley and Gottlieb's urging for researchers to consider the positive as well as the negative effects of menstrual blood and so-called restrictions (1988:3–50), I was alert to the possibility of finding multiple significances associated with menstrual blood in the Navajo world. Decoding this puzzle took me to the revelations that certain types of blood are dangerous to health and well-being and to the important question of why Navajo people distinguish between two types of menstrual blood—that shed during the first two periods (positive) and that shed during all subsequent periods (dangerous), as well as two kinds of animal blood—that shed while butchering livestock (benign) and that shed while butchering game (dangerous). In exploring the means by which these specific types of blood have come to carry such significance, this analysis demonstrates Navajo understandings of desire as both vital and dangerous as well as how language, bodily substances, bodily ills, and ancestral actions intertwine to communicate and control this ambiguity in the contemporary Navajo world.

Hence, I inquired about rules governing the butchering of domestic and game animals as well as those regarding contact with menstrual blood. I also evaluated key portions of the Navajo oral histories, which offer insights into why certain types of blood are deemed dangerous in the contemporary world.

In response to my questions, the Navajo elders, philosophers, medicine people, and educators with whom I consulted on these matters made implicit or explicit reference to various elements and versions of Navajo oral tradition. While emphasizing the importance of these vivid narratives of life-origin to personal and contemporary concerns, Navajo testimonials reveal that health problems, menstrual blood, butchering by-products, certain types of sexual activity, and chííh dík'ǫǫzh are linked to the sexual impropriety and birth of monsters outlined in these accounts. Consultants indicate that the core connection between sexual improprieties and aberrant reproduction and growth derives from what happened before, during, and after the event commonly referred to as the separation of the sexes. The analogy between desire and game animals or menstrual blood articulated in accounts of these particular episodes links dangerous game blood to dangerous menstrual blood by means of a common association with sexual desire.

The type of sexual desire of most concern to the Navajo with whom I consulted is not for the most part the excessive cravings detailed in these poignant narratives, but the sexual propriety between husbands, wives, fathers, daughters, brothers, and sisters within households and clans. Coupled with this interest, these associations demonstrate Navajo understandings of desire as both vital, that is, created to ensure continuation of Navajo people by means of heterosexual reproduction and family life through long-term relationships between men and women yielding children and well-disciplined pleasure, and dangerous, that is, if allowed to go awry or to excess. Most specifically, if it involves incest or the undisciplined pursuit of pleasure outside the context of sanctioned heterosexual relations.

Because impropriety or excess of any kind are forms of disharmony threatening to the Navajo world's sustained order, boundaries are created to contain and control sexual desire and reproductive powers. The salience of marriageabilty and a young woman's evident sexual maturity is that menstrual blood is not dangerous until after a young woman experiences her third menstrual cycle at which time she is believed to have crossed the boundary from pre-sexual to sexual; that is, she is thought to have entered the cultural category of desiring and desirous. At this point, her blood symbolizes the potential for unsanctioned sexual activity such as that which occurred before, during, and after the separation of the sexes. This type of menstrual blood is a sign marking a difference between health and danger.

As has been demonstrated, the menstrual blood of mature Navajo women signifies the connection between health problems or social disorder and ancestral impropriety—excessive and/or inappropriate sexual activity—drawn metaphorically by Navajo interpreters of oral history and made explicit in relation to the blood and hair of game animals. Its dangerousness stems from the idea that it occasions the need to carefully manage desire because desire can all too easily go to extremes or in inappropriate directions—incest, unsanctioned actions or positions. This association explains why menstrual blood is deemed dangerous when it is shed after the second cycle, *whether or not* a young woman has become sexually active.

ORAL HISTORY

Critical to understanding the link made by Navajo consultants between some kinds of menstrual or game animal blood, lasciviousness, and unsanctioned sexual activities is appreciation for contemporary uses of the Navajo emergence life-origin narratives. According to standard accounts of Navajo origin, the songs, prayers, and stories given to the Earth Surface People form a charter for life, a contract between the Nihookáá Dine'é and the Holy People. This charter gives Navajo people the right to live within the area demarcated by their sacred mountains under the special protection of the Holy People for as long as they follow the guidelines established for the Navajo way of life. Thus, stories such as those about the origins of desire, the separation of the sexes, the birth of monsters, or the establishment of gender roles are not simply quaint artifacts of bygone times. They continue to offer guidance to contemporary Navajo people because they compress historical knowledge and human experience into vivid narratives that can illuminate and educate.

Statements lending these stories ontological status do not, however, stand up to ethnographic scrutiny nor are they always supported by Navajo exegesis, which reveals a variety of personal practices and statements. As has been demonstrated, Navajo consultants do not consistently foreground *all* events relayed in these vivid accounts; rather, Navajo medicine people and other tribal intellectuals selectively highlight specific episodes pertinent to their particular stances. For example, men and women focused on different episodes when responding to specific questions about the role of women in ceremonial matters. Harry Walters's account epitomizes the views of men as they are represented in published versions. These accounts rather consistently hark back to the time before, during, and after the separation of the sexes, especially to statements made immediately following the reunion of men and women. Women also referred directly to the separation and other specific events documented in oral history, but female consultants primarily discussed key events that occurred *after* the subsequent emergence of Navajo ancestors into this world, especially the collection of stories centered on Changing Woman.

While most of the women singers with whom I consulted agree that men were given control over the political and ceremonial realms immediately after the separation of the sexes, they note that after the Navajo ancestors migrated to this world chaos again reigned. Furthermore, they point out that it was Changing Woman who restored order, created the Nihookáá Dine'é, and gave them the songs, prayers, and ceremonies essential to the restoration of order whenever it is disrupted. The allusions to key episodes in the origin story made by Navajo individuals with whom I consulted on the role of women are therefore best seen as firmly located in the contemporary context of narration and heard as efforts to conceptualize alternatives to established and traditionalized norms for gender roles in the ceremonial realm.

GENDER

The Blessing Way is the only one I know and that is all I do. *That is how I am a woman.* Day and night, I do reblemishing or smoking and prayers. (Interview with Whitney)

The women ceremonial practitioners with whom I conferred clearly see themselves as women, as do community members. Apprenticing, being initiated, or practicing as a ceremonial practitioner does not alter a woman's gender. Certainly, if singer were a gender then it would override the individual's previous gender status as a woman. Instead, the fact that certain ceremonial activities are gendered and deemed only suitable for men to conduct and forbidden to women practitioners reveals that singer is a role not a gender. For example, consultants document that women cannot perform the shock treatment or corn spreading in Fire Dance (interview with Deswood), sing as Yé'ii Bicheii dancers dress at a Night Way (interview with Shorthair), make offerings at a lightning-struck tree (interview with Chavez), or perform Blessing Way for servicemen (interview with Bekis, 1998a). By some accounts, men must initiate apprentices (interviews with Bekis, 1998b; Nix; Shorthair; Yazzie). Indeed, although two women disagreed on this point (interviews with Agnes B. Dennison, Nix), a man initiated each of the women practitioners with whom I consulted. Moreover, most women consulted on this matter maintained that the Enemy Way is the single ceremony women are not to perform (interviews with Bekis, 1998a; Chee; Edison; Emerson; Nez; Whitney). This makes cultural sense given that the central focus of an Enemy Way ceremony is ritual slaying of the enemy who has caused a patient's illness and that the sanctioned role for men in the Navajo world is that of protector, including, when the need arises, the killing of enemies (Schwarz 1997:159–160, 162, 163). A bow and arrows, the traditional weapons for men, symbolize this role.

As women, ceremonial practitioners accomplish many things with song. They heal patients through communication with the Holy People, they reinforce traditions and familial ties, and they fulfill the primary culturally sanctioned role for women: nurturer. In this capacity, Navajo women are to be mothers whose most important responsibilities are to foster and sustain the development of children (Schwarz 1997:26–27; 238–239). The role of ceremonial practitioners offers women special opportunities to fulfill their gender-specific obligations of providing spiritual as well as physical sustenance for their families. Like women who were motivated to learn a ceremony in order to fulfill family needs (interviews with Agnes B. Dennison; Dooley, 1998; Whitney), many women stressed fulfillment of family need as a prime impetus to perform. Motivations in these directions were clear when Helen Olsen Chee stated, "I have my kids that I stand up for. That is why I do my singing" (interview with Chee); when Jean Mariano told us, "I am praying all the time. I pray for myself and I pray for my children. That is why I am happy about what I am doing" (interview with Mariano); and when Mary Ben Jones Whitney declared, "Even for my children, I pray. And for my household and my sheep and everything" (interview with Whitney).

When I discussed these matters with Laura Nix, she pointed out that as a woman she feels duty-bound to learn as much as possible for the sake of her family. She expressed these sentiments as follows:

> From my standpoint, a woman is a home. Why are they saying that she is not to do things that she wants to do? Yes, they are saying that, but somebody had to know something for life to continue [after the separation of the sexes in the last underworld] and it was not just the men. If I feel like learning something, I can do that. That is why I learned and am doing what I am doing. I want to stand up for my children, I am going to help them out with it—my prayer and my Blessing Way. I pray every morning. I pray all the time about it. I have been praying about it to the Holy People, to the dawn and to the mountains of the four directions. I have been praying about it. (Interview with Nix)

Echoing Elizabeth Edison's motivation to learn a ceremony (interview with Edison), for many women concern does not focus solely on the welfare of one's own children or family members; rather, as Mary Ben Jones Whitney points out, it extends to all fellow Navajo. As she explains, "I am doing it for my children and I am doing it for my people—the Navajo. I have been all over doing my ceremony, I went to Flagstaff, I went to White Horse, I have been used there as well. Those are the people I am doing it for. They are always coming for me from different places and I help them" (interview with Whitney).

Women such as Juanita Mace see themselves as following the ceremony from place to place, as their fellow Navajo need it (interview with Mace). As Agnes Begay Dennison explains, "I want to help the people. . . . To help this person, that's the only thing that, you know, you want to help this person to get well or so that everything is gonna be put back in place for her and for him, then he goes on with life again" (interview with Dennison). This sentiment was shared by many of the women practitioners with whom I consulted. For example, Jean Mariano stated, "I help ladies, women, children of all ages with the Blessing Way. I go everywhere to do what I am doing" (interview with Mariano). Betty Begay put it simply when she said, "I am happy about doing all of these things for my people" (interview with Begay). Mae Ann Bekis noted, "I was thinking that, when I was learning, I said, 'I better become a medicine lady, you know, and help people.' That's the way I was thinking. And, and I'm doing it, too. I'm helping people" (interview with Bekis, 1998a). Sarah Ruth John expressed the satisfaction she finds in this role: "I am here to help. Anybody that needs me, I can help. That is why I learned. After you learn you can help people and I always wondered how I can help people with healing. Now, this is how I help, with singing, doing the ceremony for them. It helps me too, I enjoy seeing people getting well" (interview with John).

When asked what it is that she finds to be most gratifying about being a practitioner, Mae Ann Bekis said "Having what you do really work and turn people's lives around" (interview with Bekis, 1998a). Likewise, Louella Deswood offered the following reply to this question:

> People have gotten better. People have come back and said, like I have seen the place where people, my patients would be in a wheelchair, and then I have done the ceremony on them and then maybe a couple of weeks later, they would come back, they would be walking. And then they said, "Ever since that ceremony, I had a different outlook." And then, the changes I have made in the young people's lives. Like there is a lot of students that have gone wrong, meaning that they were really on a reckless course, and then where they use, where we use the ceremony as an intervention in that area and then it completely turns them around to where they feel that there is a, where they start feeling that there is a need for them to be careful, and there is a need for them to be living a fully decent life

for themselves. And it has happened. I have treated some severe alcoholics and they made a complete turnaround of their lives. Without going through rehab or anything. (Interview with Deswood)

Over and beyond the gratification that comes from fulfilling the immediate needs of fellow Navajo, women noted that practicing offers them opportunities to emulate and remember those who have passed on and to carry on family tradition. "I really liked when my father was singing, his voice was real nice!" says Irma Wheeler Higdon, pointing out that singing her father's songs brings her personal joy. "I enjoy just hearing the songs that I really love, the mountain song, the hooghan song, and ah, running song, horse song, sheep song, and all of these, I really enjoy to sing with that" (interview with Higdon). While reminiscing about performing the Blessing Way, Pearly Yazzie said "All I was thinking about was the way people sang it back at Big Mountain, the way they used to do, that is what I liked about it. When I performed, it made me remember my relatives back home from whom I learned. That is why the songs are very important to me" (interview with Yazzie). Juanita Mace put it eloquently when she said "It [each of her ceremonies] is a tool for remembrance. It helps me remember my father and my mother. When one starts singing a song, it seems to be one's mother. Each song starting is like your father. The medicine bundle is representative of your father and your mother" (interview with Mace).

In similar fashion to women motivated to take up a ceremony in order to retain ceremonial knowledge within a family or clan (interviews with Chee, Nez, Nix), women practitioners repeatedly expressed satisfaction at being able to carry on for a deceased relative. Sarah Ruth John said "I am pleased that since my father died, I can still use all that he knew and what he taught me. With that, I can stand on this ground" (interview with John). Grace Emerson noted, "I am thankful about it. I am just thankful that I learned this from my husband and can continue his ceremony" (interview with Emerson). Ultimately, they see practicing as a means of carrying on time-honored traditions for the benefit of their people. As Laura Nix explains,

> When you have the Blessing Way in your hand, you think about all the people. . . . Just my son is learning from me. I tell my girls, I told them to learn it too. I tell them that we want to hang on to our tradition. . . . Now, I am thinking that I want someone, I want to teach someone, I want someone to pick it up and learn from me before I get too old or blind. I want someone to learn it. That is what I think. We the Navajo, we have these traditions that we are hanging on to. It has been brought down from generation to generation. These we were brought down with from our great-

grandfathers and we want to keep living that way, and that way if we tell our children these stories, maybe they will straighten up, like some of them are just running around out there. If you tell your children about these things, they will understand. (Interview with Nix)

As the narratives collectively presented in this book clearly indicate, Navajo women who choose to pursue careers as ceremonial practitioners face complex challenges—oral accounts dictating that men are to be the leaders of ceremonial and political matters, rules surrounding menstruation, and strict sexual continence rules. Nevertheless, motivated to fulfill the culturally sanctioned role of nurturer, they navigate the social and personal issues raised by these multiple challenges to aid fellow Navajo in times of need and carry forward time-honored traditions.

NOTES

Chapter I. The Study of Navajo Female Ceremonial Practitioners

1. Agnes Begay Dennison of Round Rock, Arizona, is born to the Tódík'ǫzhí (Salt Water Clan), and born for Kinłichíi'nii (Red House People Clan). Since Navajo people refer to themselves as "born to or of" their mother's clan and "born for" their father's clan, this means the former is her mother's clan and the latter is her father's. She attended Saint Michael's Indian School through the fifth grade. She was married to Kenneth Dennison with whom she had seven children and three grandchildren. He passed away in 1988. She was age sixty-six at the time of our interview. Her son Alfred E. Dennison, a pharmacist and a Blessing Way singer, sat in on part of our interview to contribute to the discussion.

2. Louella Deswood of Goosenest, Arizona, was born in Shiprock, New Mexico. She is born to the Kinłichíi'nii (Red House People Clan), and born for the Tó'aheedlínii (Water Flow Together Clan). After completing an associate of arts degree in secondary education at Fort Lewis College, she worked for DNA Legal Services and the Navajo Nation Social Services Division before beginning her ceremonial apprenticeship. She has never married. She was in her mid-forties at the time of our interview.

3. Members of the Navajo Nation number nearly 300,000 people. Most occupy the twenty-five-thousand-square-mile reservation that spans parts of Arizona, New Mexico, and Utah. The Navajo are one of the southern Athapaskan-speaking groups located at the time of European contact in the area the Navajo consider to be their ancestral homeland; before contact the Navajo had a hunting- and gathering-based subsistence system supplemented by some agriculture (Brugge 1983:489–501). The Navajo population and their area of settlement gradually expanded as new crops, animals, and technological innovations were intermittently added to their subsistence base during the Spanish and American periods. Trading posts began to flourish on the reservation in the late 1800s, and a barter economy developed wherein male lambs and items of Navajo manufacture were traded for food staples and other goods. In the early twentieth century economic hardships caused by droughts and overgrazing, coupled with fluctuations in livestock and wool prices, resulted in a shift toward increased dependence on wage labor and the production of woven goods and silverwork for the off-reservation market. To accommodate developing resource extraction-based industries, a federally designed centralized government—the Navajo Tribal Council—was installed on the Navajo Reservation in the 1920s. Federally mandated stock reductions diminished family herds in the 1930s, resulting in increased dependence on wage labor, on

and off the reservation, as well as increased acceptance of non-Navajo religious beliefs and practices. Increased exposure to the non-Navajo world through military service and employment in war-related industries during the Second World War led to increased usage of government-run health care and educational facilities.

In the face of these various changes, Navajo language and culture have proven to be exceptionally resilient. As a leader in bilingual education and in the development of educational curricula centered on native values (Emerson 1983:659–671), the Navajo Nation has sustained high language retention relative to other Native American groups, and Navajo tenets of philosophy are currently taught at all grade levels including courses at Diné College. While reservation unemployment rates far exceed national norms, thousands of Navajo are employed in the fields of health care, education, government service, and commercial farming, or in resource-based industries such as timber and mining. Navajo who are employed off the reservation or in towns on the reservation return to matrilineal family homes in remote areas as frequently as possible in order to participate in family activities.

4. Alternatively, voice can be used to harm (Kluckhohn 1944; Witherspoon 1977).

5. One notable exception to this rule is that origin stories may be told in a *taachééh* [sweat house], during any season (interview with Billie). Just as a patient is returned back to that point in Navajo history when the events upon which the ceremony being performed for his or her benefit are based, those in a sweat house are transported back to the first taachééh at the rim of the place of emergence. The taachééh is a primordial space, and as such it is immune to the regularities imposed by the cycles of the sun, the moon, and the seasons.

6. Henderson notes, however, that in 1981 it was reported that a woman who was an herbalist and a hand-trembler had received part of a Kaibeto area Blessing Way singer's *jish* [medicine bundle] and was apprenticing to learn the ceremony (1982:166).

7. Amelda Sandoval Shay of Lukachukai, Arizona, is born to Mạ'ii Deeshgiizhnii (Coyote Pass/Jemez Clan), and born for Kinłichíí'nii (Red House People Clan). Descended from ceremonial practitioners, she is a wife, mother, and grandmother with a profound interest in Navajo traditions. An avid crocheter, she generously traveled with me throughout the summers of 1998 and 2000, with sequential handiwork projects in her lap, from community to community as we searched out women practitioners. She facilitated arrangements for interviews and served as translator during them.

Mae Ann Bekis of Tó'tsoh, Arizona, is born to Táchii'nii (Red Running into the Water People Clan), and born for the Ta'neeszahnii (Tangle Clan). Although she only finished primary schooling through the seventh grade, she has earned nearly sixty hours of college credits at Diné College, Fort Lewis College, and Adam State College. She and her husband Jim raised eight children and have numerous grandchildren and great-grandchildren. She was born in 1929.

At the time of our collaboration, Percy Deal was president of the Hard Rock Chapter of Arizona. He has extensive experience working as a translator for Navajo involved in the forced relocation mandated by Public Law 93–531, the Navajo-Hopi Land Settlement Act of 1974. Upon receipt of a letter notifying him of my intent to be in the area to interview Eunice Manson, he kindly contacted me to offer to arrange the time and place of the interview and to serve as translator. I took him up on this generous offer.

In addition, as a generous colleague and friend, Wesley Thomas of Mariano Lake, New Mexico, retranslated passages of several interviews over the years, as noted case by case in the bibliography. At the time of this writing, Dr. Thomas is a faculty member in the anthropology department at Indiana University.

8. Nádleehé literally means "one who is in the process of constant change." This term is used to refer to hermaphrodites or male-bodied persons who live as women.

9. On Navajo views of wind please see James McNeley's *Holy Wind in Navajo Philosophy* (1981).

10. Sunny Dooley of Vanderwagen, New Mexico, is born to the Tódík'ǫzhí (Salt Water Clan), and born for the Tábąąhá (Water's Edge Clan). As a former Miss Navajo, she retains her role as ambassador for the Navajo Nation as a storyteller who shares traditional stories to people on and off the reservation. She has never married. She completed a baccalaureate degree from Brigham Young University in communications. She was in her early forties at the time of our interview.

11. Stimulated to greater or lesser degrees by this pioneering collection, scholars have broken new ground in the study of beliefs about menstruation. For example, Susan Rasmussen explores how concerns about "descent and class interests" are dealt with in the Tuareg world through the idiom of sexual pollution imagery (1991:751–769); Elisa Sobo explores "the relations between the meaning of menstruation and ethnophysiological notions" in Jamaica (1992:101–126); Deborah Kaspin explores Chewa beliefs concerning the correspondence between sexual fluids and their cosmological analogues, rain and fire (1996:561–578); and Patricia Galloway explores the connection between menstrual seclusion practices and matrilineality/matrilocality in the archaeological record left by the native peoples of what is now the southeastern United States (1997:47–62).

12. This woman from Sanostee, Arizona, is born to the 'Áshįįhí (Salt People Clan), and born for the Tł'ááshchí'í (The Red Bottom People Clan). She completed two years of college after graduating from the Sherman Indian School in Riverside, California. She is divorced with two children. She was fifty years old at the time of our interview.

13. Mary Ben Jones Whitney is born to the Bit'ahnii (Under His Cover Clan), and born for the Tsi'naajini (Dark Streak Wood People Clan). Born and raised in a hooghan on Tohatchi Mountain, she never attended school. She has seven daughters. After her first husband Elwood Jones passed away, she married John Whitney, with whom she lived until he passed in the late 1990s. She was sixty-eight years old at the time of our interview.

Chapter II. "It is a Gift . . . from the Holy People"

1. Harry Walters is a husband, father, and grandfather from Cove, Arizona. Professor Walters demonstrates his profound commitment to the preservation of Navajo culture on a daily basis in his role as a faculty member at Diné College in Tsaile, Arizona.

2. Juanita Mace of Torreon, New Mexico, is born to the Ta'neeszahnii (Tangle Clan), and born for the Haltsooí (Meadow Field People). She and her husband John Mace have no children. She was seventy years old at the time of our interview.

3. Karl Luckert finds it useful to divide the Navajo philosophy of the life process into two forms: the hunting (male), the wielding of "death power," and the nurturing (female), the wielding of life power (Luckert in Haile 1981b:18 n. 21). For a discussion of the shift in the delicate balance between these forms of power that corresponded with the shift from dependence on hunting to a greater dependence on agriculture, see Luckert 1975.

4. In at least one version of this portion of the origin story, a man who was struck by lightning as punishment for such aberrant sexual behavior was revived by ceremonial means (Haile 1981a:71–72), but First Man's admonishment indicates that the vast majority of these men were being killed because of their actions.

5. Eunice Manson, a relocatee from Hopi Partitioned Land who currently resides in Rocky Ridge, Arizona, is born to the Chíishii Dine'é (Mescalero Apache Clan), and born for the Tł'ízí lání (Many Goats Clan). Her parents cautioned her: "If you go to school, to a white man's school, it will eventually destroy you. It will change you. It will take away all the wonderful, beautiful things. People that go to, to school to learn these white man ways, many of them come home married to a non-Indian, a non-Navajo, and that's an introduction and a beginning toward destruction of life, of who you really are." At age eighteen she began a Bureau of Indian Affairs educational program for young adults in Oklahoma where she attended for one year, followed by a year of schooling in California. Her husband was George Manson. She has five children and two grandchildren. She was sixty-two years of age at the time of our interview.

6. Pearly Yazzie, a relocatee from Hopi Partitioned Land who currently resides in Rim Range, Arizona, was born above Big Mountain. She is born to Kinyaa'áanii (Towering House Clan), and born for Tábąąhá (Water's Edge Clan). She has no formal education. She had ten children with her husband before he passed. She was eighty-two years of age at the time of our interview.

7. Betty Begay, of Red Valley, Arizona, is born to Mą'ii Deeshgiizhnii (Coyote Pass/ Jemez Clan), and born for Hooghan Lani (Many Hooghan Clan). She has no formal schooling. She has five children from her first husband and four from her second husband. She was in her mid-sixties at the time of our interview.

8. Grace Emerson was born and raised at Smith Lake, New Mexico, where she currently resides. She is born to Táchii'nii (Red Running into the Water People Clan), and born for Kinyaa'áanii (Towering House Clan). She has no formal education. She has nine children by her first husband, four boys and five girls, and no children by her second husband, Billie Emerson. She was seventy-nine years old at the time of our interview.

9. Nettie Nez, of Saltwater, Arizona, is born to Tó'aheedlíinii Naakai Dine'é (Mexican People Water Flow Together Clan), and born for Kinłichíi'nii (Red House People Clan). She has no formal schooling. She and her husband Hastiin Nez had six children, three boys and three girls. Her children have given her numerous grandchildren, great-grandchildren and great-great-grandchildren. She was eighty-two years old at the time of our interview.

10. This woman is born to Mąʼii Deeshgiizhnii (Coyote Pass/Jemez Clan). She was born and raised in Canyon de Chelly. She has no formal education. She gave birth to a total of eleven children by two husbands. She was eighty-four years old at the time of our interview.

11. Laura Nix of Tuba City, Arizona, is born to Bįįh Bitoni Dineʼé (Deer People Clan), and born for Tsé Deeshgiizhnii (Rock Sticking Up Clan). She has no formal education. She and her husband have eight children, four girls and four boys. She was sixty-five years old at the time of our interview.

12. Elizabeth Edison of Bear Spring, Arizona, is born to Kinłichííʼnii (Red House People Clan), and born for Tábąąhá (Water's Edge Clan). She has no formal education. She bore eight children by her first husband and remarried once after his death. She was seventy-four years of age at the time of our interview.

13. Jean Mariano of Circle Water, New Mexico, is Deeshchiiʼnii (Start of the Red Streak People Clan), and born for ʼÁshįįhí (Salt People Clan). She has no formal education. She and her husband Wilson Mariano have seven children, three boys and four girls. She was eighty years old at the time of our interview.

14. Gaye Shorthair of Pinon, Arizona, is born to Taʼneeszahnii (Tangle Clan), and born for Tłʼízí lání (Many Goats Clan). She went to school through the sixth grade. She and her husband Juan have eleven children. She was seventy-two years old at the time of our interview.

15. Like Laura Nix, Mae Ann Bekis (personal communication with Bekis, 2001h) attributes the first Blessing Way to the building of a hooghan at the rim, the place of emergence. Mae Ann Bekis noted that "Blessing Way was the first ceremony, it was built as they started putting the female hooghan together. Later other ceremonies began as the Holy People continued to live; for example, the Lightning Way began when the twins went to their father, and others came about like Plume Way, Mąʼii Way and Hózhǫ́ǫ́jí, and then Enemy Way, all these came about after the Blessing Way" (personal communication with Bekis, 2001h). Sunny Dooley (interview with Dooley, 1998) considers Changing Woman's Kinaaldá to be the first Blessing Way; Elizabeth Edison (interview with Edison) reports that the first Blessing Way occurred when the original twelve mountain earth bundles were completed.

16. Madalin Chavez of Coolidge, New Mexico, is born to the Dziłgłaani Deeshchiiʼnii (Mountain Start of the Red Streak People Clan), and born for the Tó baazhníʼázhí (Two Who Came To the Water Clan). She has no formal education. She has been married twice and has three children from each husband, three daughters and three sons. In addition, she has one great-grandchild and two great-great-grandchildren. She was sixty-eight years old at the time of our interview.

Her account is of particular interest because previously scholars have consistently maintained that no negative consequences resulted from the inappropriate sexual practices indulged in by the men during the separation of the sexes. For example, Gladys Reichard wrote, "The men too practiced perversion, but from their excesses no evil survived" (1950:31). John Farella notes that although the men masturbated, "nothing was born of it" (1984:53n). Harry Walters also informed me of negative consequences wrought by the men's actions. As will be discussed at length in a later chapter, he maintains that male use of parts from freshly slain game animals in masturbatory practices rendered the blood and hair from butchered game animals very dangerous to the health and well-being of Navajo people (interview with Walters, 1995a).

17. In addition, monsters such as Big Centipede arose from the blood shed in the slaying of the original monsters (Reichard 1950:390).

18. Irene Kee of Crystal, New Mexico, is a wife, mother, grandmother, and great-grandmother who is an herbalist and diagnostician using the hand-trembling method.

19. There is no consensus in the various accounts of this episode about exactly which clans originated from Changing Woman's flesh, or which clans originated from which parts of her body, but members of the clans believed to have come from her flesh take special pride in their sense of being members of an original clan (Wyman 1970:34). The clans most frequently mentioned as one of the four original clans are Honágháahnii (One-Walks-Around Clan) (Matthews 1994 [1897]:148; Yazzie 1971:74; Austin and Lynch 1983:3), Kinyaa'áanii (Towering House Clan) (Matthews 1994 [1897]:148; Wyman 1970:458; Yazzie 1971:74; Austin and Lynch 1983:3; Aronilth 1985:83), Tódích'íi'nii (Bitter Water Clan) (Matthews 1994 [1897]:148; Wyman 1970:458, 634; Yazzie 1971:74; Austin and Lynch 1983:3; Aronilth 1985:83), Bit'ahnii (Leaf Clan) (Matthews 1994 [1897]:148; Wyman 1970:634), Tó'áhaní (Near The Water Clan), (Wyman 1970:458, 634; Aronilth 1985:83), and Hashtł'ishnii (Mud Clan) (Matthews 1994 [1897]:148; Wyman 1970:458, 634; Yazzie 1971:74; Austin and Lynch 1983:3; Aronilth 1985:83).

20. Her continual maturation, death, and rebirth are mirrored in the changing seasons of the earth: birth is mirrored by spring, youth by summer, maturity by fall, and old age and death by winter. As the inner being of the earth, Changing Woman is considered the mother of all who dwell on the earth's surface.

21. Gladys Denny is born to Tódík'ǫzhí (Salt Water Clan), and born for Ta'neeszahnii (Tangle Clan). She has no formal education. She and her husband William Denny have two sons and six daughters. She was sixty-seven years of age at the time of our interview.

22. In marked contrast, the men interviewed by Sandner unanimously claimed that no "mystic gifts" are prerequisite to becoming a practitioner (1979:29).

23. Sarah Ruth John of "Between Black Butte and the Salt Water," near Indian Wells, Arizona, is born to the Tódích'íi'nii (Bitter Water Clan), and born for the Honágháahnii (One-Walks-Around Clan). She has no formal education. She has four children by her first husband and one by her second. She was fifty-six years of age at the time of our interview.

Chapter III. "The Ceremony Itself Got a Hold of Me"

1. Helen Olsen Chee of Oak Springs, Arizona, is born to the Deeshchii'nii (Start of the Red Streak People Clan), and born for the Ta'neeszahnii (Tangle Clan). She has no formal education. She has been married once and has nine children, five boys and four girls. She was sixty-one years old at the time of our interview.

2. Ramona Etcitty of Round Rock, Arizona, was born and raised in Scattering Rock Canyon. She is born to Tó baazhní'ázhí (Two Who Came To the Water Clan), and born for the Ma'ii Deeshgiizhnii (Coyote Pass/Jemez Clan). She completed a high school education and one year at Haskell Institute. She had six children by her husband before being widowed and a seventh child by another man. She was fifty-two years of age at the time of our interview.

3. Hastiin Tł'ah began following an uncle to learn the Hail Chant well before the age of ten, at which time he was proficient in the ceremony (Newcomb 1964:84–85). Frank Mitchell first began learning about the Blessing Way at the age of twenty-four, but did not seriously begin to apprentice until the age of thirty-eight (Mitchell 1978:358, 361). While each of the two women in Ch'iao's study began apprenticing at twelve years of age, the age at which the interviewed men began apprenticing ranged from eight to forty, with an average age of twenty-four years (1971:25). Henderson's fragmentary information led him to conclude that most men in his study began learning in their late twenties or early thirties (1982:172). Sandner reports men beginning to learn anywhere between their early teens to the age of fifty, with a mean of over twenty-eight years of age (1979:27–28).

4. The one exception was Pearly Yazzie, who reported the use of special incense in the hooghan where apprentices were learning: "There would be a bowl of white cornmeal, and we would toss that into the fire for incense, that purified us and made the house smell good and get smoky inside. White cornmeal. They burned the white cornmeal. It had something to do with allowing the men to sleep with their wives. . . . It is the same as incense that we burn. They probably knew how it works, so they did it" (interview with Yazzie).

5. Irma Higdon of Round Rock, Arizona, is born to Kinyaa'áanii (Towering House Clan), and born for Áshįįhí (Salt People Clan). She completed formal schooling through the eighth grade. She has been married three times and has a total of seven children. She was sixty-eight years of age at the time of our interview.

6. See Kluckhohn, Hill, and Kluckhohn 1971:357–359 for an illustration of this drumstick.

7. Madalin Chavez's account of her mentor's use of corn kernels to aid in the retention of songs correlates with an account recorded by Clyde Kluckhohn. A singer only referred to as Jake gave the following description of how his mentor made sure that he would not forget the Flint Way songs: "Some people can learn the songs, some can't. Finally my maternal uncle took a dry ear of corn, and every time he sings one song he takes off a kernel and puts it in a cup. Then he got an unmarried girl who was related to me to grind the kernels up into mush. He put this in a medicine basket and let it cool. Then he sung and while he was singing he put some of that mush in my mouth. He did this four times while he sang a special song. Then he made me eat the rest of the mush as fast as I could with all five fingers. After that I didn't have much more trouble" (as quoted in Kluckhohn 1962:102–103).

8. For a man's account of the use of turquoise (or a plant emetic) to ensure a strong voice, see David McAllester 1954:73.

9. Two other men in Ch'iao's study reported wanting to learn a ceremony after witnessing it being performed and a third reported being told that it was necessary to fathering healthy children (1971:21).

10. For further information on the necessity for such fees see Aberle 1967, Ch'iao 1971:34–35, Chisholm 1975:89–91, Faris 1990:101, and Frisbie 1987:89–92.

Chapter IV. Blood—Dangerous and Otherwise

1. Several women mentioned that having had medically necessary hysterectomies allowed them greater freedom to apprentice or practice (interview with Begay; Bekis, 1998a; Chee; Denny).

2. In contrast to what other consultants told me, when I mentioned to Louella Deswood of the Lukachukai Mountains of Arizona that many women had told me that they could not attend or perform ceremonies while menstruating, she told me:

> LD For a woman practicing that was generally the case. But, I was given a different kind of herbs. I was given a different kind of herbs to, to, to keep you from, to keep me from, to keep me from maybe feeling really self-conscious about it. And it took me a long time to fully accept that self-conscious bit. It took me quite a while because sometimes within a ceremony I would not like to, I would not like to handle my paraphernalia if I was at that time of the month.... OK, now, an example. If there was an emergency. You have a patient coming over and you are on your monthly, and this guy is near death and they bring this patient over. Would I just turn around and say No, I am on my monthly? That is the question right there, so my grandfather said, "If you did that that would be totally, that would be totally ignorant of you if you decided to do it that way. And tell the person that you are on your monthly, that you will not do the ceremony because of that! Because that is the facts of life. And your role, your number one goal is to put being a practitioner and doctor first before your own, before your own life cycles, whatever that is. That is the main thing. You have to overcome more, more obstacles within your own self in order to achieve what you want," he said....
>
> MS Was this like a onetime thing? That he treated you with these herbs so that from then on it wouldn't matter if you were menstruating or not?
>
> LD A onetime thing. It was a onetime thing, and ...
>
> MS He did a certain ceremony ...
>
> LD And it is not for everybody. It is just a onetime thing.
>
> MS So that when you had your monthlies after that they wouldn't impair your performing?
>
> LD Yeah.... I had to overcome THAT in order to, in order to get to where I am. (Interview with Deswood)

3. Opinions vary about whether or not this rule applies to male singers. The widow of a singer of the Female Lightning Way, Evil Way, Flint Way, Small Wind Way, and Blessing Way, noted that although women cannot perform while on aadi' a husband can perform while his wife is on aadi'. She told me, "My husband used to do singing when I

was menstruating" (interview with anonymous woman, 1998). This point was reinforced by Gaye Shorthair, the wife of a Night Way singer, who reported that when she was on her aadi' "He just went by himself" (interview with Shorthair). In contrast, Pearly Yazzie said that her husband would not perform his Blessing Way when she was on her aadi' because "That is forbidden. He just didn't do it, because the patient needs to be healed" (interview with Yazzie).

4. As has been well documented in the anthropological literature, 'agiziitsoh, "arthritis," especially *arthritis deformans* in males, results from improper contact with a menstruating woman or menstrual blood (Bailey 1950:19; Wyman and Bailey 1943:6; Wyman and Harris 1941:59). Leland Wyman and Flora Bailey point out that contact with menstrual blood causes "crippling, 'humpback'—*arthritis deformans* (if swallowed) or a sprain (if stepped on)" and that "intercourse with a menstruating woman causes impotence and later paralysis" (Wyman and Bailey 1943:6). The connection between arthritis and menstruation is reinforced by the fact that the Navajo word for arthritis medicine, *chooyin azéé,* incorporates one of the terms used to refer to menstruation, *chooyin* (Franciscan Fathers 1910:109; Wyman and Harris 1941:59). Also, according to the Franciscan Fathers the word chooyin can be used to refer to rheumatism as well as menstruation and a person with a hunchback or a stiff back is called a chooyini (1910:109).

5. While readily acknowledging themselves as situated subjects who were in positions to have access to certain bodies of knowledge while not having access to others, the Navajo people with whom I consulted consistently referred to the "natural order"— the Navajo philosophical system which consists of the paradigms established by the Navajo Holy People during their construction of the Navajo universe—as a cohesive whole. Hence, all totalizing statements found in the text of this book such as "in the Navajo world" are simply meant to refer to this philosophical system in the manner employed by the Navajo consultants with whom I conferred.

6. Moreover, general theories of menstrual symbolism may be skewed by mistaken assumptions of menstrual frequency and regularity based on our own Euro-American experiences. As Barbara Harrell (1981) has pointed out, the frequency and regularity of menstruation in contemporary industrial societies may have influenced our interpretations of menstrual symbolism in different types of societies. At the time that many of the researchers who studied Navajo beliefs about menstruation were in the field, Navajo women spent most of their reproductive lives either pregnant or nursing children and menstrual periods were a less frequent occurrence in their lives than they are today. For example, consultants told Flora Bailey that following childbirth, menstrual flow might come every two months instead of every month and that women often had only one menstrual period between children (Bailey 1950:12).

7. According to the literature, a menstruating woman should stay at home (Wyman and Bailey 1943:6), not see drypaintings (Wright 1982b:56; Wyman and Bailey 1943:6), avoid livestock and children (Bailey 1950:10; Wright 1982b:56; Wyman and Bailey 1943:6), stay away from the fields (Wright 1982b:56) or the crops will dry up and die (Bailey 1950:10; Wyman and Bailey 1943:6), not fetch water (Wyman and Bailey 1943:6), not use the sweat bath (Bailey 1950:10; Wyman and Bailey 1943:6),

not urinate where others may have contact with her urine (Wright 1982b:57; Wyman and Bailey 1943:6), or attend ceremonials (Bailey 1950:9; Wright 1982b:56; Wyman and Bailey 1943:6). Many of these proscriptions were reiterated when I inquired what if any restrictions were routinely placed on women while they were menstruating. I was told that menstruating women cannot go into a sweat house (interviews with Ashley, 1991; Kee), a cornfield (interview with Charley), or to ceremonies (interviews with Ashley, 1991; Charley; Dooley, 1992a; Jones; Kee, 1992b; Knoki-Wilson); and that they are not to butcher (interviews with Charley; Dooley, 1992a), weave baskets (interviews with Charley; Dooley, 1992a), ride horses (interview with Charley), or sleep with their husbands or children (personal communication with Billie, 1991; interviews with Dooley, 1992a; Kee, 1992a; Knoki-Wilson).

While in the Navajo case the rules delimiting contact with menstrual blood do seem to leave certain types of power in the hands of men and women past their childbearing years, they cannot be said to be especially meant to oppress women because the husband of a menstruating woman must also restrict his activities. Most specifically, he cannot attend (interviews with Ashley, 1991; Dooley, 1992a; Kee, 1992b) or perform (interviews with Bekis, 1998a; Manson) ceremonies, nor can he have sexual relations with his wife (personal communication with Billie, 1991; interviews with Dooley, 1992a; Kee, 1992a; Knoki-Wilson). Sexually continent men of all ages are immune from these restrictions.

8. In counterpoint to this view, Anne Wright posits that menstrual blood is considered problematic in the Navajo world because it signals that a woman *does not have children;* that is, it "signals momentary infertility," which is socially devalued, and "that social pressure is applied against menstruating women through the operations of menstrual taboos" that limit their daily activities (Wright 1982a:388).

9. Oscar Tso of White Valley, Arizona, is an educator and an educational administrator who, at the time of this writing, teaches at the Pinyon Elementary School in Pinon, Arizona.

10. Mae Charley is a mother and grandmother from north of Rock Point, Arizona, who teaches basket making at the Rock Point Community School.

11. In fact, the second ceremony frequently is not performed when the girl's family lives far from the reservation or when inclement weather, limited family resources, or personal preference prohibit it.

12. Ursula Knoki-Wilson is a supervisory nurse-midwife at the Fort Defiance Indian Hospital in Fort Defiance, Arizona. She is a leading authority on traditional Navajo teachings on prenatal health and childbirth whose publications focus on traditional Native American birthing practices (Wilson 1980) and multicultural health care (Wilson 1983).

13. According to Betty Begay, chííh díkʼǫ́ǫ́zh can be used to allow a husband to perform while his wife is menstruating. She noted that in such cases, "I put chííh díkʼǫ́ǫ́zh on him. Chííh díkʼǫ́ǫ́zh, that is what I put on him. And he takes it four times, and I take it also, and from there on I can go in and out and he can perform" (interview with Begay).

14. For further information on frenzy disorders and their relationship to incest, I direct the reader to Levy, Neutra, and Parker 1987.

15. David Harrison of Wheatfields, Arizona, is a member of the family that sponsored the initial years of my research.

16. This statement correlates with the findings of Thomas Csordas, who in consultation with "four bicultural" Navajo ceremonial practitioners learned that cancer and other diseases originated in the "sexual abuses" such as "incest, homosexuality, and transexuality" committed by inhabitants of the underworlds (1989:461, 463–464). Csordas points out that this origin links cancer to venereal diseases (Csordas 1989:464).

17. Steven Billie of Wheatfields, Arizona, is a member of the family that sponsored my research. Steven and his brother David are recognized across the reservation for their accomplishments in the Shoe Game.

18. Alternately, men used freshly slain female mountain sheep, lions, or antelope to relieve their sexual longings during the separation (O'Bryan 1956:8).

19. Betty Begay pointed out that formal initiation is not necessary for those such as herself who perform the truncated forms of larger ceremonies for diagnostic purposes. She performs the Azá'á'nęęł version of the Na'at'oii bikạ' (Male Shooting Way). Such shortened versions are done on a patient to test the effect of the ceremony; if improvement is noted, then the patient's family proceeds with confidence in planning the larger ceremony, if not, they have spared themselves the trouble and expense (interview with Begay).

Chapter V. "It's Yours Now"

1. See Sandner 1979:28–29 for a man's account of this experience.

2. A long-standing debate focuses on whether or not jish are owned by clans. I direct the reader to Aberle 1961; Chisholm 1975; Frisbie 1987; Haile 1954; Kluckhohn 1939; Reichard 1928:30–35.

3. In her study of jish, Charlotte Frisbie found that preference was to pass bundles on to knowledgeable heirs, or if such a person was not available, to matrikin (1987:145–147).

4. Similarly, Eunice Manson recalls her uncle telling her that if she wanted to pass on her ceremony, "I should, but it would have to be among my own clan that I would pass this ceremony on. And it could be a male or a female, whoever would have to be desirous enough to where that person would be willing to do like I did, say that they are interested in it and then after that, follow me around and begin to learn these songs" (interview with Manson).

5. Seasonal restrictions govern when a mountain earth bundle can be reopened for renewal. Opinions vary regarding the best time of year to renew mountain earth bundles. According to Frisbie, the mountain earth bundles should be renewed on an annual basis in late April or early May (1987:70). According to Frank Mitchell, the ideal time for renewal of a mountain earth bundle is late June to early July or the first of September (1978:207).

6. The sketches shown to us by Grace Emerson called to mind drawings believed to have been used by Frank Mitchell as mnemonic devices (Mitchell 1978:340, n. 7).

Chapter VI. Communicating with the Holy People

1. The sex of a child is determined by the type of fluid the sperm contacts in the mother's womb. Combining sperm with tó ał'tahnáschíín results in a male child, and combining it with tó biyáázh results in a female child (interview with Walters, 1992). Differences in development further distinguish males from females (Schwarz 1997:67–92). On the other hand, all Navajo are believed to possess both male and female aspects or qualities. This pairing is demonstrated in the actual composition of the human body. As Wilson Aronilth explains, "We are divided right in half from the tip of our head down to our feet. One side of our body is male and the other side is female" (1985:147, see also Schwarz 1997:94–101). The left-hand side of every Navajo is considered *naayéé' k'ehjigo,* "on the side of protection," that is, the warrior side of the person, while the right-hand side is *hózhǫ́ǫ́jigo,* "on the side of tranquility, harmony, and order," that is, the female or "peaceful" side of the person (interview with Walters, 1992). Wilson Aronilth is a Navajo elder from Naschitti, New Mexico, who has taught a variety of courses at Diné College since 1969, ranging from silversmithing to Navajo philosophy.

GLOSSARY

aadi'. euphemism for menstruation

Aah ha'iishnííł. extraction rite to remove objects from a patient's body

'abaní'. unwounded buckskin

'acho'. penis

ádístsiin. stirring sticks

'agiziitsoh. arthritis

ak'áánaaniił'íí. ceremonial corn spreading

Áłtsé Asdzą́ą́. First Woman

Áłtsé Hastiin. First Man

Anaa' jí ndáá'. Enemy Way ceremony

anáályééł. protective paraphernalia

'ana'í. enemy

Asdzą́ą́ Awoo'íí. Woman With Teeth

Asdzą́ą Hataałii. Singing Woman or Women

Asdzą́ą́ Nádleehé. Changing Woman

'Áshįįhí. Salt People Clan

'Ats'osee. Plume Way

Azá'á'nęęł. shortened ceremonies performed for diagnostic purposes

Azéé'nast'ąąn. rite to instill singing ability of bird in an initiate

bich'íítoo'. amniotic fluid

Bįįh Bitoni Dine'é. Deer People Clan

Bit'ahnii. Leaf Clan or Under His Cover Clan

cheii. mother's father

chííh. red ochre

chííh dík'ǫ́ǫ́zh. antidote for chooyin

Chííshii Dine'é. Mescalero Apache Clan

Ch'óol'íį́. Gobernador Knob

chooyin. blood shed after second menstrual cycle

chooyin azéé. arthritis medicine

chooyini. a hunch-backed or a stiff-backed person

dá'ák'eh. corn field

Deeshchii'nii. Start of the Red Streak People Clan

Dibé badaadelkaa. ceremony done for protection of livestock

Dibé Nitsaa. La Plata Peak

dił. blood

Dịnááł'yaa.' mountain tobacco smoking rite

diné bahane.' story of the Navajo or Navajo oral history

Diné binítch'ijí. Small Wind Way

Diyin Dine'é. Holy People

Dook'o'oosłííd. San Francisco Peak

Dziłgłaani Deeshchii'nii. Mountain Start of the Red Streak People Clan

dził nát'oh. mountain tobacco

dziłleezh. mountain earth bundle

Dziłná'oodiłii. Huerfano Peak

Ha'a'gaa.' extraction rite to remove objects from the ground

Hááhóyátééh. restoration prayer

Hashtl'ishnii. the Mud Clan

Haltsooí. Meadow Field People

Hajíínáí. the place of emergence

hataałii. ceremonial practitioner

Hóchxǫ́ǫ́'jí. Evil Way

Honágháahnii. One-Walks-Around Clan

hooghan. traditional Navajo home

hooghan ba'áád. female hooghan

hooghan bikạ'. male hooghan

Hooghan Lani. Many Hooghan Clan

Hózhǫ́ǫ́jí. Blessing Way

hózhǫ́ǫ́jigo. on the side of tranquility, harmony, and order

Iizhniidááh. Fire Dance

jish. medicine bundle(s)

jóósh. vagina

k'eet'áán. prayer stick

k'eet'áán yáłti' bikạ'ii dóó k'eet'áán yáłti' bi'aad'ii. male and female talking prayer-sticks bundled together

Kinaaldá. puberty ceremony

kinaaldá. pubescent Navajo

kinaaldstá. blood shed during first and second menstruation

Kinłichíí'nii. Red House People Clan

Kinyaa'áanii. Towering House Clan

ł'azéé. medicine from the earth

Mạ'ii Deeshgiizhnii. Coyote Pass/Jemez Clan

Náá'ha'nįį'. offering of hard goods

Na'at'oii biką'. Male Shooting Way

Na'at'oliijí. Shooting Way

Na'at'oyee. Shooting or Lightning Way

Naayée'ee hózhǫ́ǫ́jí. Enemy Way Blessing Way

Naayéé'jí. Protection Way ceremony

naayéé' k'ehjigo. on the side of protection

nádleehé. male-bodied woman

nahałáii. practitioner

nálí. father's father

náos't'ąá'. to undo a ceremony

niłch'í. wind or inner form

Níłch'ijí. Big Wind Way

Nihookáá Dine'é. Earth Surface People

nt'łiz. hard goods (precious stones)

Nt'łiz ni'nił. an offering of hard goods

ókeed sodizin. a requested prayer

ǫołáad. herbal wrapped bundle

Sinbiłiiyaą'. rite to secure songs in an initiate

sis łichí'í. sash belt

Sisnaajiní. Blanca Peak

taachééh. sweat house

Tábąąhá. Water's Edge Clan

Táchii'nii. Red Running into the Water People Clan

Tádídíín. corn pollen

Ta'neeszahnii. Tangle Clan

Tł'ááshchí'í. The Red Bottom People Clan

Tł'ízí lání. Many Goats Clan

Tó'áhaní. The Near The Water Clan

Tó'aheedlínii. The Water Flow Together Clan

Tó'aheedlíinii Naakai Dine'é. Mexican People Water Flow Together Clan

tó ał'tahnáschíín. all different kinds of water come together

Tó baazhní'ázhí. Two Who Came To the Water Clan

tó biyáázh. child of water

Tódích'ii'nii. Bitter Water Clan

Tódík'ǫzhí. Salt Water Clan

Tóee. Water Way

Tótsohnii. Big Water Clan

Tsé Deeshgiizhnii. Rock Sticking Up Clan

Tsé Nináhálééh. Monster Bird

tsibąąs. colored hoops used in Hóchxǫ́ǫ́'jí
Tsi'naajini. Dark Streak Wood People Clan
Tsoodził. Mount Taylor
Yé'ii Bicheii. Grandfathers of the Holy People
Yé'ii Tsoh. Big Monster

REFERENCES CITED

Interviews and Personal Communications

Anonymous woman

    1998   Interviewed by author, Canyon Del Muerto, Arizona, 28 July, translated by her grandson and Mae Ann Bekis.

Anonymous woman

    2000   Interviewed by author, Sanostee, New Mexico, 26 June.

Ashley, Flora

    1991   Interviewed by author, Tsaile, Arizona, 29 July.

Ashley, Hanson

    1993   Interviewed by author, Shonto, Arizona, 27 August.

Begay, Betty

    2000   Interviewed by author, Red Valley, Arizona, 27 June, translated by Amelda Sandoval Shay and Mae Ann Bekis.

Bekis, Mae Ann

    1992   Interviewed by author, Tó'tsoh, Arizona, 5 August.

    1993   Interviewed by author, Tó'tsoh, Arizona, 28 July.

    1995   Interviewed by author, Tó'tsoh, Arizona, 22 March.

    1998a   Interviewed by author, Tó'tsoh, Arizona, 16 July.

    1998b   Interviewed by author, Tó'tsoh, Arizona, 28 July.

    2001   Interviewed by author, Syracuse, New York, 26 June.

    2001a   Personal conversation with author, Syracuse, New York, 7 June.

    2001b   Personal conversation with author, Syracuse, New York, 12 June.

    2001c   Personal conversation with author, Syracuse, New York, 13 June.

    2001d   Personal conversation with author, Syracuse, New York, 15 June.

    2001e   Personal conversation with author, Syracuse, New York, 18 June.

    2001f   Personal conversation with author, Syracuse, New York, 21 June.

    2001g   Personal conversation with author, Syracuse, New York, 22 June.

    2001h   Personal conversation with author, Syracuse, New York, 25 June.

Billie, Sadie

    1991   Personal communication with author, Tsaile, Arizona, 10 July.

    1992   Personal conversation with author, White Valley, Arizona, 20 July.

Billie, Steven

    1992   Interviewed by author, Wheatfields Lake, Arizona, 18 August.

Charley, Mae

1992   Interviewed by author, north of Rock Point, Arizona, 15 July, translated by Jean Jones and Wesley Thomas.

Chavez, Madalin

2000   Interviewed by author, Coolidge, New Mexico, 29 June, translated by Amelda Sandoval Shay and Mae Ann Bekis.

Chee, Helen Olsen

1998   Interviewed by author, near Many Farms, Arizona, 20 July, translated by Amelda Sandoval Shay and Mae Ann Bekis.

Dennison, Agnes Begay

1998   Interviewed by author, Round Rock, Arizona, 27 July.

Dennison, Alfred E.

1998   Interviewed by author, Round Rock, Arizona, 27 July.

Denny, Gladys

2000   Interviewed by author, Polacca, Arizona, 17 July, translated by Amelda Sandoval Shay and Mae Ann Bekis.

Deswood, Louella

1998   Interviewed by author, Goosenest, in the Lukachukai Mountains, Arizona, 12 July.

Dooley, Sunny

1992a Interviewed by author, Gallup, New Mexico, 21 August.

1992b Interviewed by author, Gallup, New Mexico, 30 August.

1998   Interviewed by author, Gallup, New Mexico, 30 July.

Edison, Elizabeth

2000   Interviewed by author, Bear Spring, Arizona, 17 July, translated by Amelda Sandoval Shay and Mae Ann Bekis.

Emerson, Grace

2000   Interviewed by author, Smith Lake, New Mexico, 27 June, translated by Amelda Sandoval Shay and Mae Ann Bekis.

Etcitty, Ramona

1998   Interviewed by author, Round Rock, Arizona, 22 July.

Harrison, David

1992   Interviewed by author, Wheatfields Lake, Arizona, 18 August.

Higdon, Irma Wheeler

1998   Interviewed by author, near Round Rock, Arizona, 15 July.

John, Sarah Ruth

1998   Interviewed by author, near Indian Wells, Arizona, 22 July, translated by Amelda Sandoval Shay and Mae Ann Bekis.

Jones, Jean

1992   Interviewed by author, Rock Point, Arizona, 15 July.

Kee, Irene

1992a Interviewed by author, Crystal, New Mexico, 3 August, translated by Lillie Tsosie and Wesley Thomas.

1992b   Interviewed by author, Crystal, New Mexico, 4 August, translated by Lillie Tsosie and Wesley Thomas.

Knoki-Wilson, Ursula

1992   Interviewed by author, Chinle, Arizona, 10 August.

Lynch, Regina

1991   Interviewed by author, Tsaile, Arizona, July 16.

Mace, Juanita

1998   Interviewed by author, Torreon, New Mexico, 23 July, translated by Amelda Sandoval Shay and Wesley Thomas.

Manson, Eunice

1998   Interviewed by author, Rocky Ridge, Arizona, 14 July, translated by Percy Deal.

Mariano, Jean

2000   Interviewed by author, Mariano Lake, New Mexico, 29 June, translated by Amelda Sandoval Shay and Mae Ann Bekis.

Nez, Nettie

2000   Interviewed by author at Saltwater, Arizona, 10 July, translated by Amelda Sandoval Shay and Mae Ann Bekis.

Nix, Laura

2000   Interviewed by author, Tuba City, Arizona, 10 July, translated by Sherry Nix and Mae Ann Bekis.

Roessel, Ruth

1991   Interviewed by author, Round Rock, Arizona, 26 July.

Shay, Amelda Sandoval

1998   Personal communication with author, 23 July.

Shorthair, Gaye

2000   Interviewed by author, Pinon, Arizona, 11 July, with Juan Shorthair; translated by Amelda Sandoval Shay and Mae Ann Bekis.

Tso, Nakai

1991   Interviewed by author, Tsaile, Arizona, 10 July, translated by Sadie Billie and Wesley Thomas.

1992   Interviewed by author, Tsaile, Arizona, 8 August, translated by Sadie Billie and Wesley Thomas.

Tso, Oscar

1992a   Interviewed by author, White Valley, Arizona, 18 July

1992b   Interviewed by author, Many Farms, Arizona, 9 August.

Tsosie, Lillie

1992   Interviewed by author, Crystal, New Mexico, 3 August.

Walters, Harry

1992   Interviewed by author, Tsaile, Arizona, 18 August.

1993   Interviewed by author, Tsaile, Arizona, 10 August.

1995a   Interviewed by author, Tsaile, Arizona, 20 March.

1995b   Interviewed by author, Tsaile, Arizona, 24 March.

Whitney, Mary Ben Jones

    2000   Interviewed by author, Tohatchi, New Mexico, 26 June, translated by Amelda Sandoval Shay and Mae Ann Bekis.

Yazzie, Pearly

    1998   Interviewed by author, Rim Range near Newlands, Arizona, 30 July, translated by Nancy Yazzie and Mae Bekis.

Articles and Books

Aberle, David

    1961   Navaho. *In* Matrilineal Kinship, David Schneider and Kathleen Gough, eds. Berkeley: University of California Press.

    1967   The Navaho Singer's 'Fee': Payment or Prestation? *In* Studies in Southwestern Ethnolinguistics. Dell H. Hymes and William E. Bittle, eds. Studies in General Anthropology 3:15–32. The Hague: Mouton and Co.

    1982   The Future of Navajo Religion. *In* Navajo Religion and Culture: Selected Views, pp. 219–231. Papers in Honor of Leland C. Wyman, David Brugge and Charlotte Frisbie, eds. Santa Fe: Museum of New Mexico Press.

    1982   The Peyote Religion among the Navaho. Norman, Okla.: University of Okla-
    [1966] homa Press.

Aronilth, Wilson

    1985   Foundations of Navajo Culture. Unpublished manuscript on file at Navajo Community College Library, Tsaile, Ariz.

Austin, John Langshaw

    1962   How to Do Things with Words. Cambridge, Mass.: Harvard University Press.

Austin, Martha, and Regina Lynch

    1983   Saad Ahaah Sinil Dual Language: A Navajo-English Dictionary. Rough Rock, Ariz.: Rough Rock Demonstration School.

Bailey, Flora

    1950   Some Sex Beliefs and Practices in a Navaho Community. Reports of the Ramah Project. Papers of the Peabody Museum of American Archaeology an Ethnology 40(2). Cambridge, Mass.: Peabody Museum.

Baldinger, Jo Ann

    1992   Navajo Poet Tapahonso Holds Home in Her Heart. New Mexico Magazine, vol. 70 (8):31–35.

Bourdieu, Pierre

    1977   Outline of a Theory of Practice. Cambridge: Cambridge University Press.

    1990   The Logic of Practice. Stanford: Stanford University Press.

Brettell, Caroline, and Carolyn Sargent

    1997   Gender in Cross-Cultural Perspective. Upper Saddle River, N.J.: Prentice Hall.

Brugge, David

    1983   Navajo Prehistory and History to 1850. *In* Handbook of North American Indians, vol. 10: Southwest, pp. 489–501. Alfonso Ortiz, ed. Washington, D.C.: Smithsonian Institution Press.

Buckley, Thomas, and Alma Gottlieb

1988 A Critical Appraisal of Theories of Menstrual Symbolism. *In* Blood Magic: The Anthropology of Menstruation, pp. 3–50. Thomas Buckley and Alma Gottlieb, eds. Berkeley: University of California Press.

Butler, Judith

1988 Performative Acts and Gender Constitution. Theatre Journal 40(4):519–531.

1995 Burning Acts, Injurious Speech. *In* Performativity and Performance, pp. 197–227. Andrew Parker and Eve Kosofsky Sedgwick, eds. New York: Routledge.

Bynum, Caroline, Stevan Harrell, and Paula Richman

1986 Gender and Religion. Boston: Beacon Press.

Ch'iao, Chien

1971 Continuation of Tradition in Navajo Society. Taipei, Republic of China: Institute of Ethnology Academia Sinica Monograph Series B, no. 3.

Chisholm, James

1975 The Social Organization of Ceremonial Practitioners at Navajo Mountain, Utah. Plateau 47(3):82–104.

Csordas, Thomas

1989 The Sore That Does Not Heal: Cause and Concept in the Navajo Experience of Cancer. Journal of Anthropological Research 45(4):457–485.

de Certeau, Michel

1984 The Practice of Everyday Life. Berkeley: University of California Press.

di Leonardo, Micaela

1991 Gender at the Crossroads of Knowledge. Berkeley: University of California Press.

Douglas, Mary

1966 Purity and Danger: An Analysis of Concepts of Pollution and Taboo. London: Routledge and Kegan Paul.

1972 Self-Evidence. The Henry Meyers Lecture. Proceedings of the Royal Anthropological Institute for 1972:27–43.

Durkheim, Emile

1897 La Prohibition de l'inceste et ses origines. L'Année Sociologique 1:1–70.

Dyk, Walter

1951 Notes and Illustrations of Navaho Sex Behavior. *In* Psychoanalysis and Culture, pp. 108–119. George Wilbur and Warner Muensterberger, eds. New York: International Universities Press.

1966 Son of Old Man Hat. Lincoln: University of Nebraska Press.
[1938]

Emerson, Gloria

1983 Navajo Education. *In* Handbook of North American Indians, vol. 10: Southwest, pp. 659–671. Alfonso Ortiz, ed. Washington, D.C.: Smithsonian Institution Press.

Falk, Nancy, and Rita Gross

    2000   Unspoken Worlds: Women's Religious Lives in Non-Western Cultures. New
    [1980] York: Wadsworth Publishing Co.

Farella, John

    1984   The Main Stalk: A Synthesis of Navajo Philosophy. Tucson: University of Ari-
    zona Press.

Faris, James

    1990   The Nightway. Albuquerque: University of New Mexico Press.

Fishler, Stanley

    1953   In the Beginning: A Navaho Creation Myth. Anthropological Papers, 13. Salt
    Lake City: University of Utah.

Franciscan Fathers

    1910   An Ethnological Dictionary of the Navajo Language. St. Michaels, Ariz.: Saint
    Michaels Press.

Frisbie, Charlotte

    1987   Navajo Medicine Bundles or Jish. Albuquerque: University of New Mexico
    Press.

    1989   Gender and Navajo Music: Unanswered Questions. Women in North Ameri-
    can Indian Music: Six Essays. Richard Keeling, ed. Society for Ethnomusicol-
    ogy Special Series 6:22–38.

    1993   Kinaaldá: A Study of the Navaho Girl's Puberty Ceremony. Salt Lake City:
    [1967] University of Utah Press.

Frisbie, Charlotte, and Eddie Tso

    1993   The Navajo Ceremonial Practitioners Registry. Journal of the Southwest
    35(1):53–92.

Galloway, Patricia

    1997   Where Have All the Menstrual Huts Gone? In Women in Prehistory: North
    America and Mesoamerica, pp. 47–62. Cheryl Claassen and Rosemary
    Joyce, eds. Philadelphia: University of Pennsylvania Press.

Goddard, Pliny

    1933   Navajo Texts. Anthropological Papers of the American Museum of Natural
    History 34(1):1–180. New York: American Museum of Natural History.

Gould, Timothy

    1995   The Unhappy Performative. In Performativity and Performance, pp. 19–44.
    Andrew Parker and Eve Kosofsky Sedgwick, eds. New York: Routledge.

Griffen, Joyce, ed.

    1992   Lucky the Navajo Singer. Albuquerque: University of New Mexico Press.

Haile, Berard

    1938   Origin Legends of the Navajo Enemyway. Yale University Publications in An-
    thropology, 17. New Haven, Conn.: Yale University Press.

    1954   Property Concepts of the Navajo Indians. The Catholic University of America
    Anthropological Series 17.

    1981a   Upward Moving and Emergence Way. Lincoln: University of Nebraska Press.

1981b   Women versus Men: A Conflict of Navajo Emergence. American Tribal Religions, vol. 6. Lincoln: University of Nebraska Press.

Harrell, Barbara
1981   Lactation and Menstruation in Cultural Perspective. American Anthropologist 83(4):796–823.

Henderson, Eric
1982   Kaibeto Plateau Ceremonialists, 1860–1980. *In* Navajo Religion and Culture Selected Views, pp. 164–175. David Brugge and Charlotte Frisbie, eds. Santa Fe: Museum of New Mexico Press.

Hill, W. W.
1936   Navaho Warfare. Yale University Publications in Anthropology, 5. New Haven, Conn.: Yale University Press.

Jacobs, Sue-Ellen, Wesley Thomas, and Sabine Lang
1997   Introduction. *In* Two-Spirit People, pp. 1–18. Sue-Ellen Jacobs, Wesley Thomas, and Sabine Lang, eds. Urbana: University of Illinois Press.

Jacobson, Doranne
1964   Navajo Enemy Way Exchanges. El Palacio 71:7–19.

Kaspin, Deborah
1996   A Chewa Cosmology of the Body. American Ethnologist 23(3):561–578.

Keith, Anne
1964   The Navajo Girl's Puberty Ceremony: Function and Meaning for the Adolescent. El Palacio 71(1):27–36.

Klein, Laura, and Lillian Ackerman
1995   Introduction. *In* Women and Power in Native North America, pp. 3–16. Laura Klein and Lillian Ackerman, eds. Norman: University of Oklahoma Press.

Kluckhohn, Clyde
1938   Navaho Women's Knowledge of Their Song Ceremonials. El Palacio 45:87–92.
1939   Some Personal and Social Aspects of Navajo Ceremonial Patterns. Harvard Theological Review 32:67–82.
1944   Navajo Witchcraft. Boston: Beacon Press.
1962   Culture and Behavior. Richard Kluckhohn, ed. New York: The Free Press of Glencoe.

Kluckhohn, Clyde, W. W. Hill, and Lucy Wales Kluckhohn
1971   Navaho material culture. Cambridge, Mass.: Belknap Press of Harvard University Press.

Kluckhohn, Clyde, and Dorothea Leighton
1974   The Navajo. Cambridge, Mass.: Harvard University Press.
[1946]

Kluckhohn, Clyde, and Leland Wyman
1940   An Introduction to Navaho Chant Practice. Memoirs of the American Anthropological Association, 53.

Ladd, John
1957   The Structure of a Moral Code. Cambridge, Mass.: Harvard University Press.

Lamphere, Louise
   1977   To Run After Them: Cultural and Social Bases of Cooperation in a Navajo Community. Tucson: University of Arizona Press.
Lancaster, Roger, and Micaela di Leonardo
   1997   The Gender/Sexuality Reader. New York: Routledge.
Leighton, Alexander, and Dorothea Leighton
   1944   The Navaho Door. Cambridge, Mass.: Harvard University Press.
Leighton, Dorothea, and Clyde Kluckhohn
   1947   Children of the People. Cambridge, Mass.: Harvard University Press.
Levy, Jerrold
   1998   In the Beginning: The Navajo Genesis. Berkeley: University of California Press.
Levy, Jerrold, and Stephen Kunitz
   1974   Indian Drinking: Navajo Practices and Anglo-American Theories. New York: John Wiley & Sons.
Levy, Jerrold, Raymond Neutra, and Dennis Parker
   1987   Hand Trembling, Frenzy Witchcraft, and Moth Madness: A Study of Navajo Seizure Disorders. Tucson: University of Arizona Press.
Luckert, Karl
   1975   The Navajo Hunter Tradition. Tucson: University of Arizona Press.
Matthews, Washington
   1902   The Night Chant, A Navaho Ceremony. Publications of the Hyde Southwestern Expedition. Memoirs of the American Museum of Natural History, Whole Series Volume 6 (Anthropology Series Volume 5). New York.
   1994   Navaho Legends. Memoirs of the American Folklore Society 5. New York: [1897] Houghton Mifflin Co.
McAllester, David
   1954   Enemy Way Music: A Study of Social and Esthetic Values as Seen in Navaho Music. Papers of the Peabody Museum of Archaeology and Ethnology, Harvard University 41 (3).
McClain, Carol
   1989   Women as Healers. New Brunswick: Rutgers University Press.
McNeley, James
   1981   Holy Wind in Navajo Philosophy. Tucson: University of Arizona Press.
Meigs, Anna
   1990   Review of Blood Magic: The Anthropology of Menstruation and Images of Bleeding: Menstruation as Ideology, by Louise Lander. Signs 16(1):180–183.
Mindeleff, Cosmos
   1898   Navaho Houses. Seventeenth Annual Report of the Bureau of Ethnology for 1895–96. Washington, D.C.: Government Printing Office.
Mitchell, Frank
   1978   Navajo Blessingway Singer: The Autobiography of Frank Mitchell, 1881–1967. Charlotte Frisbie and David McAllester, eds. Tucson: University of Arizona Press.

Morgan, William

1936 Human-Wolves among the Navaho. Yale University Publications in Anthropology, 11. New Haven, Conn.: Yale University Press.

Morris, Rosalind

1995 All Made Up. Annual Review of Anthropology 24:567–92.

Nabokov, Peter, and Robert Easton

1989 Native American Architecture. New York: Oxford University Press.

Newcomb, Franc

1964 Hosteen Klah: Navaho Medicine Man and Sand Painter. Norman: University of Oklahoma Press.

Newcomb, Franc, and Gladys Reichard

1937 Sandpaintings of the Navajo Shooting Chant. New York: J. J. Augustin. Republished 1975. Dover Publications.

O'Bryan, Aileen

1956 The Diné: Origin Myths of the Navaho Indians. Bureau of American Ethnology Bulletin 163. Washington, D.C.: Government Printing Office.

Ortner, Sherry

1984 Theory in Anthropology since the Sixties. Comparative Studies in Society and History 26(1):1–26.

Ortner, Sherry, and Harriet Whitehead

1981 Sexual Meanings. Cambridge: Cambridge University Press.

Parker, Andrew, Eve Kosofsky Sedgwick

1995 Introduction: Performativity and Performance. In Performativity and Performance, pp. 1–18. Andrew Parker and Eve Kosofsky Sedgwick, eds. New York: Routledge.

Perrone, Bobette, H. Henrietta Stockel, and Victoria Krueger

1989 Medicine Women, Curanderas, and Women Doctors. Norman: University of Oklahoma Press.

Pinxten, Rik, and Claire Farrer

1990 On Learning a Comparative View. Cultural Dynamics 3(3):233–51.

Rasmussen, Susan

1991 Lack of Prayer: Ritual Restrictions, Social Experience, and the Anthropology of Menstruation among The Tuareg. American Ethnologist 18(4):751–769.

Reichard, Gladys

1928 Social Life of the Navajo Indians: With Some Attention to Minor Ceremonies. New York: Columbia University Press.

1950 Navaho Religion. New York: Pantheon.

Roessel, Ruth

1981 Women in Navajo Society. Navajo Resource Center. Rough Rock, Ariz.: Rough Rock Demonstration School.

1991 Fieldwork interview tape, 26 July.

Sahlins, Marshal

1976 Culture and Practical Reason. Chicago: University of Chicago Press.

Sandner, Donald

1979 Navaho Symbols of Healing. New York: Harcourt Brace Jovanovich.

Schwarz, Maureen Trudelle

1997 Molded in the Image of Changing Woman: Navajo Views on the Human Body and Personhood. Tucson: University of Arizona Press.

2001a Allusions to Ancestral Impropriety: Understandings of Arthritis and Rheumatism in the Contemporary Navajo World. American Ethnologist 28(3):650–678.

2001b Navajo Lifeways. Norman: University of Oklahoma Press.

Sered, Susan

1992 Women as Ritual Experts: The Religious Lives of Elderly Jewish Women in Jerusalem. New York: Oxford University Press.

Shepardson, Mary

1995 The Gender Status of Navajo Women. In Women and Power in Native North America, pp. 159–176. Laura Klein and Lillian Ackerman, eds. Norman: University of Oklahoma Press.

Sobo, Elisa

1992 "Unclean Deed": Menstrual Taboos and Binding "Ties" in Rural Jamaica. In Anthropological Approaches to the Study of Ethnomedicine, pp. 101–126. Mark Nichter, ed. Philadelphia: Gordon and Breach.

Stephen, Alexander

1930 Navajo Origin Legend. Journal of American Folklore 43(167):88–104.

Stephens, William

1962 The Oedipus Complex: Cross-Cultural Evidence. New York: Free Press.

Weideger, Paula

1977 Menstruation and Menopause: The Physiology and Psychology, the Myth and the Reality. New York: Delta.

West, Candace, and Donald Zimmerman

1987 Doing Gender. Gender Sociology 1(2):125–52.

Wheelwright, Mary

1942 Navajo Creation Myth: The Story of the Emergence, by Hasteen Klah. Navajo Religion Series 1. Santa Fe, N.M.: Museum of Navaho Ceremonial Art (Wheelwright Museum of the American Indian).

Williamson, Ray A.

1984 Living the Sky: The Cosmos of the American Indian. Norman: University of Oklahoma Press.

Wilson, Ursula

1980 Traditional Child-Bearing Practices among Indians. In Life Cycle of the American Indian Family, pp. 13–26. Janice Kekahbah and Rosemary Wood, eds. Norman: American Indian and Alaska Native Nurses Association Publishing Co.

1983 Nursing Care of American Indian Patients. In Ethnic Nursing Care: A Multicultural Approach, pp. 272–295. Modesto Orque et al., eds. St Louis: C. V. Mosby Co.

Witherspoon, Gary

1977   Language and Art in the Navajo Universe. Ann Arbor: University of Michigan Press.

1987   Navajo Weaving: Art in Its Cultural Context. Flagstaff: Museum of Northern Arizona.

Wright, Anne

1982a   Attitudes toward Childbearing and Menstruation among the Navajo. *In* Anthropology of Human Birth, pp. 377–394. Margarita Kay, ed. Philadelphia: F. A. Davis Co.

1982b   An Ethnography of the Navajo Reproductive Cycle. American Indian Quarterly 6(1&2):52–70.

Wyman, Leland

1965   The Red Antway of the Navajo. Navajo Religion Series 5. Santa Fe, N.M.: Museum of Navaho Ceremonial Art (Wheelwright Museum of the American Indian).

1970   Blessingway. Tucson: University of Arizona Press.

Wyman, Leland, and Flora Bailey

1943   Navaho Girl's Puberty Rite. New Mexico Anthropologist 15(1):3–12.

Wyman, Leland, and Stuart Harris

1941   Navajo Indian Medical Ethnobotany. University of New Mexico Bulletin, 366. Albuquerque: University of New Mexico Press.

Yazzie, Ethelou

1971   Navajo History. Vol. 1. Navajo Curriculum Center. Chinle, Ariz.: Rough Rock Demonstration School.

Young, Frank, and Albert Bacdayan

1965   Menstrual Taboos and Social Rigidity. Ethnology 4:225–240.

Zion, James

1991   The Use of Navajo Custom in Dealing with Rape. Law and Anthropology 6:131–167.

Zolbrod, Paul

1984   Diné Bahane': The Navajo Creation Story. Albuquerque: University of New Mexico Press.

INDEX

ABOUT THE AUTHOR

Maureen Trudelle Schwarz is an associate professor of anthropology at Syracuse University. Dr. Schwarz has conducted research on the Navajo reservation since 1991. She is a recipient of an Andrew W. Mellon Postdoctoral Fellowship (Wesleyan University 1998–1999) and the Daniel Patrick Moynihan Award for outstanding teaching, research, and service (Maxwell School of Citizenship and Public Affairs 2001–2002). Dr. Schwarz has published essays in *American Ethnologist, Ethnohistory, American Anthropologist,* and *Visual Anthropology.* This is her third book on the Navajo. The first focused on Navajo views of the body and personhood, and the second focused on the explanatory powers that Navajo oral history offers to people coping with contemporary problems.